British Science Fiction

Recent Titles in
Bibliographies and Indexes in World Literature

Literature for Young People on War and Peace: An Annotated Bibliography
Harry Eiss, compiler

A Descriptive Bibliography of *Lady Chatterly's Lover* with Essays Toward a Publishing History of the Novel
Jay A. Gertzman

The Shakespeare Folio Handbook and Census
Harold M. Otness, compiler

Anglo-Irish Literature: A Bibliography of Dissertations, 1873-1989
William T. O'Malley, compiler

Vanguardism in Latin American Literature: An Annotated Bibliographical Guide
Merlin H. Forster and K. David Jackson, compilers

Donald Davie: A Checklist of His Writings, 1946-1988
Stuart Wright, compiler

Recent Studies in Myths and Literature, 1970-1990: An Annotated Bibliography
Bernard Accardi, David J. Charlson, Frank A. Doden, Richard F. Hardin, Sung Ryol Kim, Sonya J. Lancaster, and Michael H. Shaw, compilers

Robinson Crusoe: A Bibliographical Checklist of English Language Editions (1719-1979)
Robert W. Lovett, assisted by Charles C. Lovett

The Soviet Union in Literature for Children and Young Adults: An Annotated Bibliography of English-Language Books
Frances F. Povsic, compiler

The Indian Subcontinent in Literature for Children and Young Adults: An Annotated Bibliography of English-Language Books
Meena Khorana, compiler

Contemporary Spanish American Poets: A Bibliography of Primary and Secondary Sources
Jacobo Sefamí, compiler

British Science Fiction

A CHRONOLOGY, 1478–1990

NICHOLAS RUDDICK

Bibliographies and Indexes in World Literature,
Number 35

GREENWOOD PRESS
New York • Westport, Connecticut • London

Library of Congress Cataloging-in-Publication Data

Ruddick, Nicholas.
  British science fiction : a chronology, 1478-1990 / Nicholas Ruddick.
    p.   cm.—(Bibliographies and indexes in world literature,
  ISSN 0742-6801 ; no. 35)
  Includes bibliographical references and indexes.
  ISBN 0-313-28002-9 (alk. paper)
  1. Science fiction, English—Chronology. 2. Science fiction,
English—Bibliography. 3. Fantastic fiction, English—Chronology.
4. Fantastic fiction, English—Bibliography. I. Title.
II. Series.
PR830.S35R84   1992
016.823'08762—dc20   92-6409

British Library Cataloguing in Publication Data is available.

Copyright © 1992 by Nicholas Ruddick

All rights reserved. No portion of this book may be
reproduced, by any process or technique, without the
express written consent of the publisher.

Library of Congress Catalog Card Number: 92-6409
ISBN: 0-313-28002-9
ISSN: 0742-6801

First published in 1992

Greenwood Press, 88 Post Road West, Westport, CT 06881
An imprint of Greenwood Publishing Group, Inc.

Printed in the United States of America

The paper used in this book complies with the
Permanent Paper Standard issued by the National
Information Standards Organization (Z39.48-1984).

10 9 8 7 6 5 4 3 2 1

To Christopher Johan

Contents

Preface	ix
Acknowledgments	xi
Introduction	xiii
Summary and Guide	xvii
Abbreviations	xxiii
1. The Descent of Scientific Romance: 1478-1894	1
2. The Wellsian Synthesis: 1895-1936	25
3. British Science Fiction: 1937-1961	71
4. New Wave S(peculative) F(iction): 1962-1978	107
5. The British Fantastic: 1979-1990	145
Author Index	167
Title Index	189
FTV Index	237
Works Consulted	247

Preface

This chronology traces British science fiction year by year from 1478, the birth of the author of *Utopia*, to the present, with a cut-off date of 31 December, 1990. A maximum of four main sections will be found under any given year, each with a three-letter abbreviated heading.

Under BIO will be found biographical information about authors of British science fiction, ordered according to dates of birth or death.

Under FIC will be found information about British science fiction published that year, ordered alphabetically according to author.

Under FTV will be found information about British science fiction on film, radio and television, including titles, writers, producers and directors. (These entries do not begin until 1913).

Under GEN will be found, arranged according to eight sub-categories, a variety of general information about anthologies, criticism, comics, non-fiction works, fandom, authors' first appearances in print, periodicals and awards.

A fuller discussion of what is here taken to constitute British science fiction will be found in the introduction. A summary and guide, specifying the kind of information to be found in each section and describing how to interpret it, follows the introduction.

My interest in British science fiction is primarily literary, and this bias affects my criteria of inclusion. I consider the novel or story collection to be usually of more significance than the single story published in a magazine, so the FIC section consists chiefly of books rather than single stories. However, I have included a number of such stories that I feel are important enough to merit inclusion in their own right.

The completeness of the listing of an author's oeuvre here is, I confess, a matter of personal taste, though not (I hope) a taste that is uninformed or particularly controversial. For example, it is my view that H. G. Wells is the most important figure in British science fiction, so the listing of his contributions to the field, direct and indirect, are fairly complete--though I have excluded a large part of his oeuvre that does not strike me as having much to do with the topic at hand.

The listings for such major figures as Brian Aldiss, J. G. Ballard, John Brunner, Arthur C. Clarke and Michael Moorcock are far more complete than they are for lesser figures, even though certain works included by these authors may be quite insignificant in literary terms. Mainstream works by these authors are included only if they are relevant to the field of British science fiction. The historical context of publication is important. (Please see the introduction for a clarification.)

The careers of highly prolific authors of texts of minimal literary significance--hacks, to put it bluntly--are summarized rather than traced book by book. The same is true of authors of works, such as thrillers with a futuristic gloss, that are marginally science-fictional. Certain major works of generic fantasy or of juvenile science fiction, from Lewis Carroll to Terry Pratchett, are included, sometimes parenthetically.

Having not yet completed the lifetime needed to read all the works contained herein, not to mention the other lifetime needed to adjudicate the works jostling for inclusion, I have naturally been dependent on secondary sources for information about many of the titles included here. I have not seen hard copies of some of the titles. Of these unseen texts, I have tried to include only those whose existence seems to be verified independently in as many trustworthy secondary sources as possible. However, as most secondary sources are not truly independent, I fear I am probably perpetuating several errors. I apologize for these, as well as the omissions (both inadvertent and deliberate), and the inconsistencies (usually inadvertent), that I hope will not completely ruin the exercise for most readers. I would of course be very grateful to receive corrections and suggestions for a future revision of this book.

Acknowledgments

This book began as a short supplementary chronology to my book *Ultimate Island: On the Nature of British Science Fiction*. However, it became clear to me that any work which sought to focus on British science fiction as a historical field--more precisely, a discourse--rather than as a theoretical genre, needed first to establish clearly its own historical parameters. This chronology, swollen to many times its original size, is the result, and may be viewed as a companion volume to *Ultimate Island*.

I am grateful to many people, directly and indirectly. Marshall Tymn gave me important early encouragement. Dr. C. W. Blachford, Dean, and Janet Campbell, Research Administrator, of the Faculty of Graduate Studies and Research at the University of Regina, supported me in practical terms with the loan of a word processor and software. A grant from the University of Regina President's Fund allowed me to visit the Science Fiction Foundation Library at the Polytechnic of East London, where Joyce Day was, as always, an invaluable help. I'm also very grateful to Pat Green and the late Ted Chapman (whose death I was saddened to hear of as I completed this project) of the SF Foundation for their kindness and hospitality.

Professor D. de Vlieger, Dean, Faculty of Arts, University of Regina, came to the rescue when I requested a six-month sabbatical at very short notice. Marion Lake and her staff at Interlibrary Loan at the University of Regina Library were outstanding in their ability to track down my many abstruse requests, and Allison Dixon at the University of Winnipeg Library provided a much-needed item. I am very grateful to Marilyn Brownstein of Greenwood Press, whose enthusiasm for this project at the prospectus stage allayed my anxieties about its executability.

Finally, this work is deeply indebted to many earlier researchers in the field: especially to the critical, biographical and bibliographical endeavors of Mike Ashley, Neil Barron, E. F. Bleiler, I. F. Clarke, John Clute, Donald B. Day, George Locke, Peter Nicholls, David Pringle, R. Reginald, Brian Stableford, Darko Suvin, Donald H. Tuck, and Marshall B. Tymn.

Introduction

The purpose of this book is to provide a chronological outline of British science fiction that will be of use to the literary historian as well as to the historically-minded sociologist of literature. It will also, it is hoped, be of interest to the general reader of science fiction, science fantasy, utopian and dystopian fiction and even so-called mainstream fiction. It does not aspire to the kinds of completion implied by the tag 'checklist.' It does, however, try to find a place for most of the important biographical and publishing events in the field of British science fiction literature and fandom, as well as for the highlights of British science fiction in other media.

All compilers of literary chronologies, bibliographies, checklists and the like soon come to realize that in the matter of selection their best attempts to be objective and merely stick to the facts are doomed to be defeated. Every choice is, in the end, contaminated with subjectivity or, to put it another way, ideological. It is best to confront this issue from the beginning. The aim of this introduction, then, is to deal briefly with the criteria behind the choice of what goes into this chronology, what gets left out and why.

I have treated science fiction as a field, not as a theoretical genre or subgenre. The idea of a genre, with its biological associations, suggests a group of texts that have a close family resemblance based on shared internal characteristics. A field, on the other hand, implies a much looser association of different elements by contiguity. If a genre is like the human race, in which the individual members resemble each other as a result of their common genetic material, then a field--which might contain such diverse elements as a farmer, a cow, a barn, grass and rocks--is constituted by external agency, and defined by whatever the perceiving eye interprets its boundary to be.

There have been many worthy attempts to define science fiction as a genre. I have chosen to approach it as a field for pragmatic reasons. The most successful reference work about science fiction to date, *The Encyclopedia of Science Fiction* (1979) edited by Peter Nicholls, owes its success not only to its accuracy but also to its comprehensive coverage of whatever the average science fiction reader is likely to be interested in. It makes no claims that Plato was a science fiction writer or that John Russell Fearn was an important literary figure or that FTL travel is scientifically respectable, but it recognizes that readers of science fiction will want some information, preferably intelligently written, on these subjects. This chronology approaches the phrase 'science fiction' in a similar spirit.

British science fiction, however, instantly introduces a new set of problems. Nicholls's *Encyclopedia* has no entry on this subject, preferring to view Anglo-American science fiction as a unity (though it does have separate entries for Canada and Australia). This, it seems to me, reveals a certain ideological innocence, but this is not the place to take up that issue. I would refer the reader instead to this chronology's companion volume, *Ultimate Island: On the Nature of British Science Fiction*, for a fuller discussion of that and related issues.

What I have tried to do here is trace the historical development of what (according to the field theory) might be reasonably subsumed under the heading of British science fiction, from the birth of the author of *Utopia* to the present day. In particular, I trace matters relating to the biography and works of writers who (regardless of where they were born) either live(d) and write/wrote, or publish(ed) first, chiefly in Britain. (Even such a broad net fails to catch a big fish like Arthur C. Clarke. Moreover, the idea of what constitutes a British science fiction film is extremely problematic. So it must suffice here to emphasize the inclusiveness of the British epithet.) A more detailed summary of the kinds of information included in this chronology, with annotated examples, follows the introduction.

Although a chronology might seem far from a subject thesis, the sorts of compromise with the material that a compiler makes while in the process of selection lead almost inevitably to the drawing of certain general conclusions. I have already implied that I think that British science fiction has a measure of autonomy and is not merely to be included in an Anglo-American science fiction field. Moreover, in a chronology, to decide on an answer to the obvious question, namely, where one should begin, is already to start the process of imposing a pattern on history. I do not claim to have solved the problem of the origin of science fiction, British or otherwise, a problem that has produced some of the field's most interesting critical debate. Instead, I propose that More's *Utopia* (1516) offers a useful starting-point if British science fiction is viewed as a field rather than as a genre. That does not exclude the possibility of choosing a different starting point--say, Mary Shelley's *Frankenstein* (1818)--but this would, in turn, give the resulting field a different shape and its chronology a different configuration.

The first general observation I would offer about the present configuration is that though there is a measure of continuity in the field of British science fiction from More to the present day--a continuity which itself offers strong support to this particular field theory--there are also discontinuities large enough to warrant labeling five major divisions in the field. There are, however, few clear historical watersheds that make such divisions self-evident and beyond argument.

Furthermore, though the measure of continuity is sufficient to warrant that the field, at least from our contemporary perspective, be properly referred to as British science fiction, it is not meaningful to refer to the decontextualized divisions (with one exception) by that phrase, unless it is further qualified. Put simply, though More's *Utopia* is part of the proposed field of British science fiction, this does not necessarily make it meaningful to speak of More's *Utopia* as a work of British science fiction.

For the purposes of this chronology, the five major divisions of the field of British science fiction are:

1. The Descent of Scientific Romance (1478-1894)
2. The Wellsian Synthesis (1895-1936)
3. British Science Fiction (1937-1961)
4. New Wave S(peculative) F(iction) (1962-1978)
5. The British Fantastic (1979-1990)

The five periods seem, it must be confessed, singularly disproportionate in terms of numbers of years covered. In practice, however, this disproportion disappears, and there is a rough symmetry to the arrangement of the five periods in this chronology. This fact alone seems to me to be a kind of justification of the present arrangement.

Though there is evidence for an early British provenance of the term 'science fiction,' there is in the end little doubt that the phrase itself came into popular usage as a result of activities in the field of American popular magazine publishing from the 1920s on. The importance of Hugo Gernsback and, later, John W. Campbell, in establishing modern science fiction cannot be overestimated.

Actually, the eclectic Gernsback created the *field* by bringing together for the benefit of a particular readership works as different in historical origin, intention and literary merit as those filling the pages of the early *Amazing Stories*. Subsequently, Campbell created the *genre* by establishing certain common criteria for accepting fiction in *Astounding* and bringing together a group of young writers who could produce work that met those criteria.

If Americans had the leading role in the foundation of science fiction, then it would appear to be about as meaningful to speak of 'British science fiction' as it is to speak of 'British Coca-Cola.' Strictly, 'British science fiction' ought to be restricted to science fiction produced in Britain by British authors in the wake of Gernsback and according to American criteria. Indeed, that is the rationale for the naming of chapter 3 of this chronology, for during the period it covers American-style science fiction was becoming dominant in Britain. There is little point in dwelling on the British characteristics of this material (some of which is still being produced), for it mimics, sometimes perfectly, American models.

Yet there is also a tradition of writing in Britain of much earlier origin than the 1920s, if it can be said to have an 'origin' at all, which it is useful to place in the category of 'British science fiction' only if one is conscious of the paradox in that phrase. It is a tradition constituted retrospectively from a late twentieth-century perspective by any literary historian who follows to some degree the eclectic Gernsbackian path. The tradition includes a number of works of very different kind, produced under different historical circumstances, but all aimed at a less specific readership than American pulp science fiction. These works are often, but not always, more artistically ambitious and of higher literary merit than the average typical product of Gernsbackian or even Campbellian science fiction. Such aesthetic comparisons are probably inappropriate, however, given that the works could hardly be said to be competing on the same ground.

Traced to the present, the configuration I have described contains some quite significant implications. One of them is that there has been an inability in Britain--far more widespread and pronounced than in America--to reconcile the idea of an indigenous science fiction with the idea of literary value. That is to say, there has been for some years now a drift away from the idea of 'science fiction' (even in its New Wave incarnation as SF or speculative fiction) by 'serious' writers, readers and critics who formerly tolerated the phrase. Yet this is not to suggest that there is in Britain a significant body of work of literary merit which is being ignored because it is published as science fiction. Instead, the good work is being published, but not as science fiction even though formerly it might have been categorized thus. Work by younger British writers published as science fiction today is usually (but not always) heavily dependent on the American science fiction tradition.

This situation does not strike me as evidence of crisis, though it does have implications for the idea of 'British science fiction.' I would predict that, if present trends continue (perhaps a rather naive assumption for a science fiction critic), science fiction will simply die out in Britain except as a term used for a specific formulaic fiction--a fate similar to that of the term 'romance' in both Britain and America. Yet if this process also leads to the recuperation of H. G. Wells as one of the major literary figures of the twentieth century, to the recognition that all serious fiction should confront in some way the dominant scientific ideology, and to the promotion of the fantastic mode in fiction to a rank of importance equal to that of the realistic, then it will not be necessary to mourn the death of British science fiction.

Summary and Guide

What follows is a description of the major categories of information included in this chronology, together with sample annotated entries.

A. THE CHRONOLOGY

1. <u>Biographical Information</u> [BIO]

   1.1. The **date and place of birth** of most writers whose work is included in the chronology; their **date of death** if applicable. The birth entry indicates their **usual professional name in bold**, with their birthname (if different) and title (if any) in parentheses.

   Example (under 1896)

   b. **Lance**(lot de Giberne) **Sieveking**, 19 Mar., Harrow, Middlesex.
   b. **R**(obert) **C**(harles) **Sherriff**, 6 Jun., Kingston-on-Thames, Surrey.
   b. **Katherine** (Penelope) **Burdekin** (also wrote as **'Murray Constantine'**), 23 Jul., Spondon, Derbyshire.
   b. **John** (Edward) **Gloag**, 10 Aug., London.
   b. **Charman Edwards** (?F. A. Edwards), London.
   *
   d. William Morris, 3 Oct.
   d. George Du Maurier, 6 Oct.

   <u>Notes</u>

   1.1.1. Writers appear in chronological order according to date of birth or death; those whose dates are unknown appear in alphabetical order after the chronological entries.
   1.1.2. Single quotation marks indicate true pseudonym; these are maintained in subsequent references. Pseudonyms based on the author's birthname (e.g. those used by John Wyndham Parkes Lucas Beynon Harris) do not receive quotation marks.

1.1.3. If in England, place of birth includes town and (when appropriate) county, the latter as it was at the writer's birth; birth-locations in other parts of the U.K. (e.g. Scotland) and world are specified.

2. Information About Works of Science Fiction [FIC]

2.1. Works are listed alphabetically by author under the **year of first publication**. Entry information includes the **author's name, title**, and **first publisher**, whether British or American, of significant **novels, poetic** and **dramatic works, short story** and **omnibus collections**; and of less significant ones when the author is important in the field by virtue of an oeuvre. Significant **later** or **transatlantic reprints** and **retitlings** are also noted in the first entry. **All the fantastic fiction of H. G. Wells** is included in order to emphasize the unique importance of his work in the field. **Certain works of short fiction by other hands** are also included, under the year of their first appearance, when the writer is eminent but not traditionally associated with science fiction. A few significant **works of (generic) fantasy** and/or **juvenile sf** are also included, often between {brackets} thus.

Example (under 1909)

Forster, E. M. "The Machine Stops." *Oxford & Cambridge Review* (Michaelmas) [rep. in *The Eternal Moment* (Sidgwick & J 1928)].

Examples (under 1974)

Brunner, John. *Total Eclipse* (Doubleday; Weidenfeld & N 1975).
---. *The Web of Everywhere* (Bantam; NEL 1977).
Carter, Angela. *Fireworks: Nine Profane Pieces* [SS] (Quartet).
Compton, D. G. *The Continuous Katherine Mortenhoe* (Gollancz) [US *The Unsleeping Eye*] [F 1980 as *La Mort en Direct*, trans. *Deathwatch*].

Example (under 1956)

Creasey, John. *The Flood* (Hodder & S).
---. **Several other sf thrillers, through 1973.**

Example (under 1937)

{Tolkien. J. R. R. *The Hobbit; or, There and Back Again* (Allen & U).}

Notes

2.1.1. Book and periodical titles are italicized.

Summary and Guide xix

2.1.2. Publication information appears parenthetically.
2.1.3. Some well-known publishers' names appear in common abbreviated forms: see Abbreviations for clarification.
2.1.4. American publishers are italicized (e.g. *Bantam* above); if a work was published in both the U.K. and the U.S.A. in the same year, then for the purposes of this chronology its first publisher is assumed to be British.
2.1.5. Titles of short story collections which include *and Other Stories* or similar formulae are abbreviated; subtitles are included when significant.
2.1.6. Abbreviations in the entry indicate literary genre if work is not a novel (e.g. [SS]= volume of short stories in Carter entry above).
2.1.7. Posthumous publication is indicated by [P] after the author's name.
2.1.8. Certain entries, under year of first sf novel publication and cross-referenced in **bold type**, summarize careers of extremely prolific authors of formulaic sf (e.g. John Russell Fearn, E. C. Tubb) or of authors of formulaic 'marginal' sf (see Creasey entry above).
2.1.9. Works filmed or televised include date and retitling (if any) after entry: see Compton entry above. FIC/FTV cross-references are indicated by an asterisk: see Note 3.1.2 below.

3. Information about Films, Radio and T.V. Series [FTV]

   3.1. Entries are listed alphabetically by **title**, under the headings [F] for film, [R] for radio series, [TV] for television series, and [TVF] made-for-T.V.-film. The information may include **variant title(s)**, the names of the **director** or **producer**, the **production company**, the screen/teleplay **writer(s)**, the **length of the series run**, and the **literary source** or later **novelization**.

   Examples (under 1961)

   [F] *The Damned* (US *These Are the Damned*). Dir. Joseph Losey. Hammer/Columbia. Wr. Evan Jones, from novel *The Children of Light* (1960) by H. L. Lawrence.

   [TV] *A for Andromeda*. Prod. Michael Hayes & Norman Jones. BBC miniseries, 7x50 minutes. Wr. & *nov. 1962 Fred Hoyle & John Elliot.

   Notes

   3.1.1. Important non-British films based on works of British science fiction are noted in the FIC entry only: see Note 2.1.9. above.
   3.1.2. Cross-references to FIC entries are indicated by an asterisk, as in *The Children of Light* above.

4. Other General Information [GEN]

   4.1. **Anthologies** significant because of their editorial introductions or contents.

   Example (under 1967)

   [A] Moorcock, Michael, ed. *Best SF Stories from New Worlds 1* (Panther).
   ---. **7 more vols., through 1974.**

   4.2. **Volumes of criticism and/or scholarship** significant because of their focus on the whole field or an aspect of the field of British science fiction.

   Example (under 1961)

   [C] Bergonzi, Bernard. *The Early H. G. Wells: A Study of the Scientific Romances* (Manchester UP).

   4.3. Selected notable science fiction **comics**; entries may include **creator, artist** and **first publication.**

   Example (under 1954)

   [CX] "Jeff Hawke." Cr. Eric Souster & Sydney Jordan. *(Junior) Daily Express*, 15 Feb., through 1974.

   4.4. **Volumes of essays** and **certain other nonfiction works** significant because of their authorship or influence on the field.

   Example (under 1927)

   [E] Dunne, J. W. *An Experiment with Time* (A. C. Black).

   4.5. **Milestones in British fandom,** including **important fanzines.**

   Example (under 1958)

   [FAN] BSFA founded, Eastercon, 4-7 Apr., Kettering.
   [FAN] *Vector* [organ of BSFA], 1st. ed. E. C. Tubb, Summer, through present.
   [FAN] *Science Fiction Adventures*, ed. E. J. Carnell, Mar., through May 1963 (32 issues).

   4.6. **The first professional science fiction publication or sale of selected writers** who emerged in the age of the science fiction magazines (note: certain well-known American sf magazines are abbreviated and underlined: e.g. *AMZ* for *Amazing Stories*); in the case of H. G. Wells, a chronological listing of his appearances in Hugo Gernsback's *AMZ* from 1926 to 1929.

Example (under 1956)

[FP] Ballard, J. G. "Prima Belladonna." *Science Fantasy* (Dec.).
---. "Escapement." *New Worlds* (Dec.).

4.7. **Publishing milestones**, especially **first publication of (semi-) professional magazines** in the field; entries may include **first editor, date of first and last issues** and **number of issues.**

Example (under 1950)

[PUB] *Science Fantasy*, 1st. ed. Walter Gillings, Summer, through Feb. 1966 (81 issues).

4.8. **Works of British science fiction winning major Anglo-American sf awards;** entries may include **title** and **author** of work, **name** and **category** of award.

Example (under 1974)

[W] *Rendezvous with Rama* (Arthur C. Clarke): 21st. Hugo novel, US; 9th. Nebula novel, US; John W. Campbell Memorial novel (joint); BSFA novel.

B. THE INDEXES

1. Author Index

The author index lists more than 800 authors' names and pseudonyms alphabetically, with their dates of birth and death if known (which refer to biographical entries in the chronology), and the other years in which references to them appear. Entries are fully cross-referenced and include, when appropriate, the subsection of GEN in which the entry may be found (e.g. in Ashley, Mike entry below, 1977[A] refers to an anthology edited by him in the GEN section for 1977).

Example

'Ashley, Fred,' see Atkins, Francis Henry: 1840, 1905
Ashley, Mike (*1948-*): 1974[C/A], 1977[A]
Ashton, Francis (*1904-*): 1946, 1948, 1952
Ashton, Stephen: 1951 under Ashton, Francis

2. Title Index

The (short) title index lists alphabetically the more than 2,400 titles (and their variants) of books, stories, periodicals and organizations included in the chronology, including (when appropriate) the author's or editor's name and the year under which the work is listed in the chronology. If the work was not actually published in the year under which it appears in the chronology, then the year given is italicized in this index. If the work was first published under a different name from the one under which it appears in the chronology, then the name is italicized in this index.

Example

"Beyond Time's Aegis" (*Stableford*): 1965[FP]
Beyond Tomorrow (Carlton): 1975
Beyond: 1964[FAN]
Big Death, The (Maine): *1962*
Big Step (Passes): 1977
Billenium (Ballard): 1962
Billion Year Spree (Aldiss): 1973[C], 1974[W]

3. FTV Index

This index includes the more than 300 references in the FTV category, including titles, variants, producers, directors and writers.

Example

Anderson, Michael: 1955[F]
Anderson, Sylvia: 1969[F], 1969[TV], 1975[TV]
Andromeda Breakthrough: 1962[TV]
Animal Farm: 1954[F]

4. Works Consulted

This list contains full bibliographical references of the chief works consulted in compiling the chronology. A headnote summarizes other reference sources used.

Abbreviations

<u>General</u>

Note: months of the year are abbreviated to their first three letters throughout

?	indicates unknown/unverified element
...	indicates omitted material
{ }	{brackets work of generic fantasy or juvenile sf}
*	divides births from deaths in <u>BIO</u>; indicates cross-reference elsewhere

[A]	Anthology
abr.	abridged (as/in)
Anon.	Anonymous
<u>ASF</u>	*Astounding Stories/Analog Science Fiction* (US)
<u>AMZ</u>	*Amazing Stories* (US)
b.	birth (of)
<u>BIO</u>	Biographical Information
<u>BSFA</u>	British Science Fiction Association
ca.	*circa*
[C]	(Volume of) Criticism or Scholarship
cont.	(entry) continues
Cr.	Created by
[CX]	Comic Strip
d. ,	death (of)
[D]	Dramatic Work
Dir.	Directed by
[E]	(Volume of) Essays
ed(s).	edition/edited (by)
enl.	enlarged (in)
[F]	Film
[FAN]	Fandom Milestone
<u>FIC</u>	Information about Science Fiction Works
<u>FSF</u>	*The Magazine of Fantasy and Science Fiction* (US)
<u>FTV</u>	Information about Film, Radio and Television
fl.	*floruit*
[FP]	First Significant Magazine Publication
<u>GEN</u>	General Information

Abbreviations

```
i.e.      that is (full name follows)
mins.     minutes
Nov.      Novelized by/in
[O]       Omnibus Collection
[P]       Posthumous publication
PP        Privately Published
Prod.     Produced by
pub.      published (in)
[PUB]     Publishing Milestone
[R]       Radio Series
rep.      reprinted (in)
rev.      revised (in)
[SP]      Screenplay
[SS]      (Volume of) Short Stories
trans.    translated (by/as)
[TV]      Television Series
[TVF]     Made-for-T.V.-Film
UK        (Published/Released in the) UK (as)
US        (Published/Released in the) USA (as)
vol(s).   volume(s)
[V]       (Volume of) Verse
[W]       Award Winner
Wr.       (Screen- or teleplay) written by
```

Publishers

```
Allen & U(nwin)
Allison & B(usby)
Chapman & H(all)
Chatto & W(indus)
David & C(harles)
Eyre & S(pottiswoode)
H(amish) Hamilton
Hodder & S(toughton)
Houghton M(ifflin)
N(ew) A(merican) L(ibrary)
N(ew) E(nglish) L(ibrary)
Rapp & W(hiting)
Secker & W(arburg)
Sidgwick & J(ackson)
Simon & S(chuster)
Weidenfeld & N(icolson)
```

British Science Fiction

1
The Descent of Scientific Romance: 1478-1894

This period spans the more than 400 years between the birth of Thomas More and the eve of the publication of the first masterpiece of scientific romance, H. G. Wells's *Time Machine* (1895). In it will be found the names of many of the great names of English literature: Bacon, Marlowe, Shakespeare, Milton, Defoe, Swift, Dr. Johnson and so on. They are included not because they were science-fiction writers, nor even because they wrote works which might be considered science fiction in any meaningful sense. Their inclusion is to indicate how certain works by these writers--often but not always major works--became highly significant in the development of British scientific romance, particularly through the work of H. G. Wells.

The key works in the period are several world-books of English literature whose influence on the development of the Wellsian scientific romance was unquestionably important: More's *Utopia* (1516), Marlowe's *Dr. Faustus* (1604), Shakespeare's *Tempest* (1623), Milton's *Paradise Lost* (1667), Defoe's *Robinson Crusoe* (1719), Swift's *Gulliver's Travels* (1726), Mary Shelley's *Frankenstein* (1818), and perhaps the greatest of all, in its influence if not in its aesthetic achievement, Darwin's *Origin of Species* (1859). These works represent the various strains synthesized by Wells in his great early scientific romances: utopia, the Faustian or Promethean theme, the fantastic voyage, the island as metaphor, the Enlightenment satire, the Gothic, and evolutionary biology.

Paradise Lost, the great English epic, and *The Origin of Species*, a work of science not fiction, may seem out of place here. Viewed from our late twentieth-century perspective, however, they may be read as two competing versions of the greatest myth of all, that of origin. At the historical moment when the latter comes to prevail over the former, emerges the Wellsian scientific romance.

1478

BIO

b. (Sir; also Saint) **Thomas More**, 7 Feb., London.

1516

FIC

More, Thomas. *Utopia* (in Latin as *Libullus Vere Aureus Nec Minus Salutaris Quam Festivus De Optimo Reip. Statu Deque Nova Insula Utopia*) (Louvain, Belgium: Thierry Martin) [trans. Ralph Robynson as *A Fruteful and Pleasaunt Worke of the Beste State of a Publyque Weale, and of the New Yle Called Vtopia* (A. Vele 1551)].

1535

BIO

d. Thomas More, 5 Jul.

1561

BIO

b. **Francis Bacon** (1st. Baron Verulam and Viscount St. Albans), 22 Jan., London.

1562

BIO

b. **Francis Godwin** (Bishop of Llandaff and later of Hereford), Hannington, Northamptonshire.

1564

BIO

b. **Christopher Marlowe**, *ca.* 26 Feb., Canterbury, Kent.
b. **William Shakespeare**, 22 or 23 Apr., Stratford-on-Avon, Warwickshire.

1593

BIO

d. Christopher Marlowe, 1 Jun.

1604

FIC

Marlowe, Christopher [P]. *Dr. Faustus* [D] (as *The Tragicall History of D. Faustus* (T. Bushell) [1st. performed 1588].

1608

BIO

b. **John Milton**, 9 Dec., London.

1612

BIO

b. **Samuel Butler**, ?8 Feb., Strensham, Worcestershire.

1614

BIO

b. **John Wilkins** (Bishop of Chester), Fawsley, Northamptonshire.

1616

BIO

d. William Shakespeare, 23 Apr.

1623

FIC

Shakespeare, William [P]. *The Tempest* [D] (E. Blount & I. Jaggard) [written *ca.* 1611].

1626

BIO

d. Francis Bacon, 9 Apr.

1627

FIC

Bacon, Francis [P]. *New Atlantis. A Worke Unfinished.* [written before 1617]. In *Sylva Sylvarum: or, A Natural History* (W. Rawley).

1633

BIO

d. Francis Godwin, Apr.

1638

FIC

Godwin, Francis (as 'Domenico Gonsales'). *The Man in the Moone; or, A Discourse of a Voyage Thither, by Domenico Gonsales, the Speedy Messenger* (J. Kirton & T. Warren).

GEN

[E] Wilkins, John. *The Discovery of a World in the Moone. Or, A Discourse Tending To Prove That 'Tis Probable There May Be Another Habitable World in that Planet* (M. Sparke & E. Forrest) [enl. J. Maynard 1640].

1648

GEN [E] Wilkins, John. *Mathematicall Magick. Or, The Wonders That May Be Performed by Mechanicall Geometry* (S. Gellibrand).

1660 or 1661

BIO b. **Daniel Defoe**, London.

1667

BIO b. **Jonathan Swift** (Dean of St Patrick's, Dublin), 30 Nov., Dublin, Ireland.

FIC Milton, John. *Paradise Lost* [V] (P. Parker et al.).

1672

BIO d. John Wilkins, 19 Nov.

1674

BIO d. John Milton, 8 Nov.

1680

BIO d. Samuel Butler, 25 Sep.

?1693

BIO b. (Mrs.) **Eliza Haywood** (née Fowler), ?London.

1697

BIO b. **Robert Paltock**, London.

1703

FIC Russen, David [fl. 1702-05, Hythe, Kent]. *Iter Lunare: Or, a Voyage to the Moon. Containing Some Considerations on the Nature of That Planet: The Possibility of Getting Thither, with Other Pleasant Conceits about the Inhabitants, Their Manners, and Customs* (J. Nutt).

1705

FIC Defoe, Daniel (as Anon.). *The Consolidator; or, Memoirs of Sundry Transactions from the World in the Moon. Translated from the Lunar Language* (B. Bragg).

1709

BIO b. (Dr.) **Samuel Johnson**, 18 Sep., Lichfield, Staffordshire.

1717

BIO b. **Horace Walpole** (4th. Earl of Orford), 24 Sep., London.

1719

FIC Defoe, Daniel. *Robinson Crusoe* (as *The Life and Strange Surprizing Adventures of Robinson Crusoe of York, Mariner*) (W. Taylor).

1722

FIC Defoe, Daniel (as 'H. F.'). *A Journal of the Plague Year* (E. Nutt).

1726

FIC Swift, Jonathan. *Gulliver's Travels* (as *Travels into Several Remote Nations of the World...By Lemuel Gulliver*) (B. Motte).

1727

FIC 'Brunt, Captain Samuel.' *A Voyage to Cacklogallinia: With a Description of the Religion, Policy, Customs and Manners of That Country* (J. Watson).

1728

FIC 'McDermot, Murtagh.' *A Trip to the Moon...Containing Some Observations and Reflections, Made by Him During His Stay in That Planet, Upon the Manners of Its Inhabitants* (Roberts).

1731

BIO

b. **Erasmus Darwin**, 12 Dec., Elston Hall, Nottinghamshire.

*

d. Daniel Defoe, 26 Apr.

1736

FIC

Haywood, Eliza. *The Adventures of Eovaai, Princess of Ijaveo: A Pre-Adamitical History. Interspersed with a Great Number of Remarkable Occurrences...Written Originally in the Language of Nature...* (S. Baker) [rep. *The Unfortunate Princess* (?1741)].

1745

BIO

d. Jonathan Swift, 19 Oct.

1751

FIC

'Morris, Ralph.' *A Narrative of the Life and Astonishing Adventures of John Daniel, a Smith at Royston in Hertfordshire. Taken from His Own Mouth by Mr...* (M. Cooper).

Paltock, Robert. *The Life and Adventures of Peter Wilkins: A Cornish Man...* (Robinson & Dodsley).

1755

FIC

Anon. *A Voyage to the World in the Centre of the Earth: Giving an Account of the Manners, Customs, Laws, Government and Religion of the Inhabitants...* (S. Crowder & H. Woodgate).

1756

BIO

d. Eliza Haywood, 25 Feb.

1759

FIC

Butler, Samuel [P]. "The Elephant in the Moon" [V]. In *The Genuine Remains in Verse and Prose of Mr. Butler* (Tonson).

Johnson, Samuel. *Rasselas* (as *The Prince of Abissinia: A Tale in Two Volumes*) (Dodsley & Johnston).

1763

FIC   Anon. *The Reign of George VI, 1900-1925* (W. Nicoll).

1764

FIC   Walpole, Horace (as 'Onuphrio Muralto'). *The Castle of Otranto* (as *Otranto, A Story*) (T. Lownds).

1767

BIO   d. Robert Paltock, 20 Mar.

1775

BIO   b. **Matthew Gregory Lewis**, 9 Jul., London.

1780

BIO   b. (Rev.) **George Croly**, 17 Aug., Dublin, Ireland.

1782

BIO   b. **Charles R**(obert) **Maturin**, Dublin, Ireland.

1784

BIO   d. Samuel Johnson, 13 Dec.

1788

BIO   b. **Thomas Erskine**, Linlathen, Forfar, Scotland.

1791

FIC   Darwin, Erasmus. *The Botanic Garden; A Poem, in Two Parts. Part I. Containing the Economy of Vegetation. Part II. The Loves of the Plants* [V] (J. Johnson).

1794

GEN   [E] Darwin, Erasmus. *Zoonomia; or the Laws of Organic Life* (J. Johnson).

1795

FIC
Lewis, Matthew Gregory. *The Monk* (as *Ambrosio, or The Monk*).

1797

BIO
b. **Mary Wollstonecraft Shelley** (née Godwin), 30 Aug., London.

*

d. Horace Walpole, 2 Mar.

1802

BIO
d. Erasmus Darwin, 18 Apr.

1803

BIO
b. **Richard Henry Horne**, 1 Jan., London.
b. **Edward** (George Earle Lytton) **Bulwer-Lytton** (1st. Baron Lytton of Knebworth), 25 May, London.

FIC
Darwin, Erasmus [P]. *The Temple of Nature; or, the Origin of Society* [V] (J. Johnson).

1807

BIO
b. **Jane Loudon** (née Webb), Ritwell House, Warwickshire.

1809

BIO
b. **Charles** (Robert) **Darwin**, 12 Feb., Shrewsbury, Shropshire.

1815

BIO
b. **Anthony Trollope**, 24 Apr., London.

1817

FIC
Erskine, Thomas (as Anon.). *Armata: A Fragment* (Murray) [in two parts].

1818

BIO

d. Matthew Gregory Lewis, 14 May.

FIC

Shelley, Mary Wollstonecraft (as Anon.). *Frankenstein; or, The Modern Prometheus* (Lackington, Hughes, Harding, Mavor & Jones) [rev. 1831] [F 1931, *TVF 1973, etc].

1820

BIO

b. **Alfred Bate Richards**, 17 Feb., Baskerville House, Worcestershire.

FIC

Maturin, Charles R. (as 'The Author of *Bertram*'). *Melmoth, the Wanderer* (Constable).

1824

BIO

b. **George MacDonald**, 10 Dec., Huntly, Aberdeen, Scotland.
b. **Edward Maitland**, Ipswich, Suffolk.

*

d. Charles R. Maturin, 30 Oct.

1826

BIO

b. (Rev.) **James William Barlow**, 21 Oct., ?Dublin, Ireland.

FIC

Shelley, Mary Wollstonecraft. *The Last Man* (H. Colburn).

1827

FIC

Loudon, Jane (as Anon.). *The Mummy!: A Tale of the Twenty-Second Century* (H. Colburn).

1828

BIO

b. **Mrs.** (Margaret Oliphant) **Oliphant**, 4 Apr., Wallyford, near Musselburgh, Midlothian, Scotland.

FIC

Croly, George. *Salathiel: A Story of the Past, the Present and the Future* (H. Colburn).

1829

BIO

b. **William** (Ford Robinson) **Stanley**, 2 Feb., Buntingford, Hertfordshire.

1830

BIO

b. **James Payn**, 28 Feb., Cheltenham, Gloucestershire.
b. (Lieutenant-Colonel) (Sir) **George T**(omkyns) **Chesney**, 30 Apr., Tiverton, Devon.

1831

BIO

b. **Philip H**(oward) **Colomb**, 29 May, Scotland.

1832

BIO

b. **'Lewis Carroll'** (Charles Lutwidge Dodgson), 27 Jan., Daresbury, Cheshire.

1834

BIO

b. **William** (Bury) **Westall**, 7 Feb., near Blackburn, Lancashire.
b. **George** (Louis Palmella Busson) **Du Maurier**, 6 Mar., Paris, France.
b. **William Morris**, 24 Mar., Walthamstow, Essex.

1835

BIO

b. **Samuel Butler**, 4 Dec., Langar Rectory, Nottinghamshire.

1836

BIO

b. (Sir) **Walter Besant**, 14 Aug., Portsea, Hampshire.
b. **Percy Greg**, Bury, Lancashire.

1839

BIO

b. (Rev.) **Edwin A**(bbott) **Abbott**, 20 Dec., London.

1840

BIO

b. (William) **Gordon Stables**, 21 May, Aberchirder, Banff, Scotland.

1840(cont.)

BIO

b. **Francis Henry Atkins**, (wrote as '**Fenton Ash**,' '**Fred Ashley**,' '**Frank Aubrey**,' etc.), Oxford.

1841

BIO

b. **W**(illiam) **H**(enry) **Hudson**, 4 Aug., Quilmes, near Buenos Aires, Argentina.
b. **Robert** (Williams) **Buchanan**, 18 Aug., Caverswall, Staffordshire.
b. (The Rev.) **W**(ladislaw) **S**(omerville) **Lach-Szyrma**, Devonport, Devon.

1842

FIC

Bray, John Francis. *A Voyage from Utopia* [not pub. till 1957 by Laurence & Wishart].

1844

BIO

b. **Andrew Lang**, 31 Mar., Selkirk, Scotland.

1845

BIO

b. **William Minto**, 16 Oct., Alford, Aberdeen, Scotland.
b. **Henry Curwen**, Workington Hall, Cumberland.

1846

BIO

b. **Frank Challice Constable**, 16 Jun., ?London.
b. '**Luke Netterville**' (Standish James O'Grady), 18 Sep., Castletown Bere, County Cork, Ireland.
?b. **T**(h)**om**(as) **Greer**, County Down, Northern Ireland.

1847

BIO

b. **Bram** (i.e. Abraham) **Stoker**, 24 Nov., Dublin, Ireland.

1848

BIO

b. (Charles) **Grant** (Blairfindie) **Allen**, 24 Feb., Alwington, Ontario, Canada.
b. (John) **Richard Jefferies**, 6 Nov., Coate Farm, Wiltshire.

1849

BIO
- b. **James MacLaren Cobban**, 24 Apr., Aberdeen, Scotland.
- b. **John Munro**.

FIC
Horne, Richard Henry. *The Poor Artist; or, Seven Eye-Sights and One Object* (Van Voorst).

1850

BIO
- b. **Robert Barr**, 16 Sep., Glasgow, Scotland.
- b. **Robert Louis Stevenson**, 13 Nov., Edinburgh, Scotland.

1851

BIO
d. Mary Shelley, 1 Feb.

GEN
[C] Wilson, William. *A Little Earnest Book upon a Great Old Subject* (Darton) [1st. recorded use of term 'science-fiction,' of Horne 1849].

1853

BIO
b. **C**(harles) **Howard Hinton**, London.

1855

BIO
b. **'Marie Corelli'** (Mary Mackay), 1 May, Perth, Scotland.

1856

BIO
- b. (Sir) **W**(illiam) **Laird Clowes**, 1 Feb., London.
- b. **H**(enry) **Rider Haggard**, 22 Jun., Bradenham, Norfolk.
- b. **George Bernard Shaw**, 26 Jul., Dublin, Ireland.
- b. **'F. Anstey'** (Thomas Anstey Guthrie), 8 Aug., London.
- b. **Robert Cromie**, ?Clough, County Down, Northern Ireland.

1857

BIO
- b. **John Davidson**, 11 Apr., Barrhead, Renfrew, Scotland.
- b. (Sir) **Edwin Lester** (?Lynn/Linden) **Arnold**, 14 May, Swanscombe, Kent.
- b. **Lady Florence** (Caroline) **Dixie** (née Douglas), 24 May, London.

1857-1863

1857(cont.)

BIO

b. **George Griffith** (i.e. George Chetwynd Griffith-Jones), 20 Aug., Plymouth, Devon.
b. **Joseph Conrad** (né Josef Teodor Konrad Korzeniowski), 3 Dec., near Berdichev, Polish Ukraine.

1858

BIO

d. Jane Loudon, 13 Jul.

FIC

MacDonald, George. *Phantastes* (Smith, Elder).

1859

BIO

b. **Jerome K**(lapka) **Jerome**, 2 May, Walsall, Staffordshire.
b. (Sir) **Arthur Conan Doyle**, 22 May, Edinburgh, Scotland.
b. **Fergus**(on) **W**(right) **Hume**, 8 Jul.
b. **Fred**(erick) **M**(errick) **White**.

GEN

[E] Darwin, Charles. *On the Origin of Species by Means of Natural Selection, or the Preservation of Favoured Races in the Struggle for Life* (Murray).

1860

BIO

d. George Croly, 24 Nov.

1861

BIO

b. **'Christopher Blayre'** (Edward Heron-Allen), 17 Dec., London.

1862

BIO

b. **Eden Phillpotts**, 4 Nov., Mount Aboo, Rajputana, India.

1863

BIO

b. **'Arthur Machen'** (Arthur Llewellyn Jones), 3 Mar., Caerleon, Monmouthshire.
b. **Louis Tracy**, 18 Mar., Liverpool.
b. (Sir) **Max Pemberton**, 19 Jun., Birmingham.

1863(cont.)

BIO

b. **H**(enry) **B**(rereton) **Marriott Watson**, 20 Dec., Melbourne, Australia.

1864

BIO

b. **William** (Tufnell) **Le Queux**, 2 Jul., London.
b. **Barry** (Eric Odell) **Pain**, 16 Sep., Cambridge.

FIC

'Trueman, Chrysostom.' *The History of a Voyage to the Moon: With an Account of the Adventurers' Subsequent Discoveries* (Lockwood).

1865

BIO

b. **H**(enry) **de Vere Stacpoole**, Apr., Kingstown, County Dublin, Ireland.
b. **C**(harles) **J**(ohn) **Cutliffe** (Wright) **Hyne**, 11 May, Bibury, Gloucestershire.
b. **M**(atthew) **P**(hipps) **Shiel**, 21 Jul., Monserrat, West Indies.
b. (Prof.) **John Mastin**, 15 Oct., Marchamley, Shropshire.
b. (Henry) **Roger** (Ashwell) **Pocock**, 9 Nov., Tenby, Pembroke, Wales.
b. (Joseph) **Rudyard Kipling**, 30 Dec., Bombay, India.

FIC

'Carroll, Lewis.' *Alice's Adventures in Wonderland* (Macmillan).

1866

BIO

b. **Archibald Marshall**, 6 Sep., London.
b. **H**(erbert) **G**(eorge) **Wells**, 21 Sep., Bromley, Kent.
b. **E**(dward) **Phillips Oppenheim**, 22 Oct., London.
b. **Paul Creswick**, Kingston-on-Thames, Surrey.
b. **E**(dward) **Douglas Fawcett**, Hove, Sussex.

1867

BIO

b. **'AE'** (George William Russell), 10 Apr., Lurgan, County Armagh, Northern Ireland.

1868

BIO

b. **Norman Douglas**, 8 Dec., Thüringen, Austria.
b. **T**(homas) **C**(harles) **Bridges**, France.

1868(cont.)

BIO

b. **Harold E**(dward) **Gorst**.

GEN

[PUB] *Pall Mall Budget*, 1st ed. C. Lewis Hind, 3 Oct., through 27 Dec. 1894.

1870

BIO

b. (Major) **C**(harles) **C**(yril) **Turner**, 30 Apr.
b. **J. Storer Clouston**, 23 May, Cumberland.
b. (Robert) **Erskine Childers**, 25 Jun., London.
b. (Joseph) **Hilaire** (Pierre René) **Belloc**, 27 Jul., St. Cloud, France.
b. **Fred**(erick) **T**(homas) **Jane**, 6 Aug., Upottery, Devon.
b. **'Saki'** (Hector Hugh Munro), 18 Dec., Akyab, Burma.
b. **Herbert M**(illingchamp) **Vaughan**, Llangoedmor, Cardigan, Wales.

*

d. Thomas Erskine, 20 Mar.

FIC

Richards, Alfred Bate. *The Invasion of England: A Possible Tale of Future Times* (PP).

1871

BIO

b. (Very Rev. Monsignor) **Robert Hugh Benson**, 18 Nov., Wokingham, Berkshire.
b. George C. Wallis.

FIC

Bulwer-Lytton, Edward. *The Coming Race* (Blackwood).
Chesney, George T. (as Anon.). "The Battle of Dorking: Reminiscences of a Volunteer." *Blackwood's* (May) [rep. Blackwood].
MacDonald, George. *At the Back of the North Wind* (Strahan).

1872

BIO

b. **Bertrand** (Arthur William) **Russell** (3rd. Earl Russell), 18 May, Trelleck, Monmouthshire.
b. **Cicely** (Mary) **Hamilton** (née Hammill), 15 Jun., London.
b. (Andrew James Fraser) **'Hamish' Blair**, 30 Sep., Dingwall, Ross & Cromarty, Scotland.
b. **John Cowper Powys**, 8 Oct., Shirley, Derbyshire.

1872-1876

1872 (cont.)

FIC

Butler, Samuel. *Erewhon; or, Over the Range* (Trübner).
'Carroll, Lewis.' *Through the Looking-Glass, and What Alice Found There* (Macmillan) [released 1871].

1873

BIO

b. **J**(ohn) **D**(avys) **Beresford**, 7 Mar., Castor, Northamptonshire.
b. **Ford Madox Hueffer**, 17 Dec., Merton, Surrey.
b. (George) **Oliver Onions**, Bradford, Yorkshire.

*

d. Edward Bulwer-Lytton, 18 Jan.

FIC

Maitland, Edward. *By and By: An Historical Romance of the Future* (Bentley).

1874

BIO

b. **S**(ydney) **Fowler Wright**, 6 Jan., Birmingham.
b. **G**(ilbert) **K**(eith) **Chesterton**, 29 May, London.

FIC

Blair, Andrew (as Anon.). *Annals of the Twenty-Ninth Century; or, The Autobiography of the Tenth President of the World-Republic* (Tinsley).
Lach-Szyrma, W. S. (as 'W.S.L.S.'). *A Voice from Another World* (J. Parker) [rev. and enl. as by Rev. W. S. Lach-Szyrma, *Aleriel; or, A Voyage to Other Worlds* (Wyman 1883)].

1875

BIO

b. **'Lester Lurgan'** (Mabel Winifred Knowles), Jan., London.
b. (Richard Horatio) **Edgar Wallace**, 1 Apr., London.
b. **J**(ohn) **Henry Harris**, 10 Sep.
b. **Frank Buckland Dilnot**, Hayling, Hampshire.
b. **J**(ohn) **W**(illiam) **Dunne**, Kildare, Ireland.

1876

BIO

b. **'Guy Thorne'** (Cyril Arthur Edward Ranger-Gull), Rushall, England.

*

d. Alfred Bate Richards, 12 Jun.

1877

BIO

b. **Shaw Desmond**, 19 Jan., County Waterford, Ireland.
b. **Ladbroke** (Lionel Day) **Black**, 21 Jul., Burley-in-Wharfedale, Yorkshire.
b. **William Hope Hodgson**, 15 Nov., Blackmore End, Essex.

1878

BIO

b. **David Lindsay**, 3 Mar., London.
b. **E**(dward) **H**(arold) **Visiak**, 20 Jul., London.
b. **Lord** (Edward John Moreton Drax Plunkett) (18th. Baron of) **Dunsany**, 24 Jul., London.
b. **Stacey Blake**, Bradford, Yorkshire.

1879

BIO

b. **E**(dwin) **M**(organ) **Forster**, 1 Jan., London.
b. **Francis Hernaman-Johnson**, Apr., Crosby, Lancashire.

FIC

Chesney, George T. (as Anon.). *The New Ordeal* (Blackwood).
Payn, James. *High Spirits: Being Certain Stories Written in Them* [SS] (Chatto & W).

1880

BIO

b. (Hardinge Goulburn Gifford) (2nd.) **Earl of Halsbury**, 20 Jun.
b. **Alfred Noyes**, 16 Sep., Wolverhampton, Staffordshire.
b. **'J. J. Connington'** (Prof. Alfred Walter Stewart).

FIC

Greg, Percy. *Across the Zodiac: The Story of a Wrecked Record* (Trübner).
Hay, W(illiam) Delisle. *The Doom of the Great City: Being the Narrative of a Survivor, Written A.D. 1942* (Newman).
Oliphant, Mrs. *A Beleaguered City... A Story of the Seen and the Unseen* (Macmillan).

1881

BIO

b. (Elfric Wells) **Chalmers Kearney**, 3 Feb., Geelong, Australia.
b. (Dame) (Emilie) **Rose Macaulay**, 1 Aug., Rugby, Warwickshire.
b. **Noel L**(ambert) **Godber**, Nottingham.
b. **'Frank Morison'** (?A. H. Ross), Birmingham.

1881-1884

1881 (cont.)

FIC

Hay, W. Delisle. *Three Hundred Years Hence; or, A Voice from Posterity* (Newman).

1882

BIO

b. (Adeline) **Virginia Woolf** (née Stephen), 25 Jan., London.
b. **P**(ercy) **Wyndham Lewis**, 18 Nov., off Nova Scotia, Canada.
b. **E**(ric) **R**(ucker) **Eddison**, 24 Nov., Adel, Yorkshire.
b. **'Hugh Addison'** (Harry Collinson Owen).
b. **E**(velyn) **Charles Vivian**, Norfolk.

*

d. Charles Darwin, 19 Apr.
d. Anthony Trollope, 6 Dec.

FIC

Besant, Walter (as Anon.). *The Revolt of Man* (Blackwood).
'Green, Nunsowe.' *A Thousand Years Hence: Being Personal Experiences as Narrated by...* (Sampson Low).
Trollope, Anthony. *The Fixed Period* (Blackwood).

1883

BIO

b. (Sir) (Edward Montague) **Compton Mackenzie**, 17 Jan., West Hartlepool, County Durham.
b. **'Sax Rohmer'** (Arthur Henry Sarsfield Ward), 13 Feb., Birmingham.
b. **J**(oseph) **Jefferson Farjeon**, 4 Jun., London.
b. **A**(lexander) **S**(utherland) **Neill**, 17 Oct., Forfar, Angus, Scotland.
b. **R**(alph) **H**(ale) **Mottram**, 30 Oct., Norwich, Norfolk.
b. **Horace Horsnell**, St. Leonards, Sussex.
b. **Aelfrida Tillyard** (Mrs. Constantine Graham), Cambridge.
b. **T**(revor) **C. Wignall**, Swansea, Glamorgan, Wales.

1884

BIO

b. **Gilbert Frankau**, 21 Apr., London.
b. (John Gilbert) **Bohun Lynch**, 21 May, London.
b. (Herman) **James Elroy Flecker**, 5 Nov., London.
b. (William) **Douglas Newton**, London.
b. (Sir) **J**(ohn) **C**(ollings) **Squire**, Plymouth, Devon.
b. **'Martin Swayne'** (Maurice Nicoll).

1884 (cont.)

BIO

d. Richard Henry Horne, 13 Mar.

FIC

Abbott, Edwin A. (as 'A Square'). *Flatland: A Romance of Many Dimensions* (Seeley).
Allen, Grant. *Strange Stories* [SS] (Chatto & W).

1885

BIO

b. J(ohn) L(eslie) **Palmer**.

*

d. Andrew Blair.

FIC

Greer, Tom. *A Modern Daedalus* (Griffith, Farran, Okeden & Welsh).
Haggard, H. Rider. *King Solomon's Mines* (Cassell).
Jefferies, Richard. *After London; or, Wild England* (Cassell).

1886

BIO

b. (William) **Olaf Stapledon**, 10 May, near Wallasey, Cheshire.
b. **Charles** (Walter Stansby) **Williams**, 20 Sep., London.
b. (Sir) **Harold** (George) **Nicolson**, 21 Nov., Teheran, Persia.
b. **Joseph** (James) **O'Neill**, 18 Dec., Tuan, Galway, Ireland.

FIC

Allen, Grant, with May Cotes. *Kalee's Shrine* (Arrowsmith).
'Corelli, Marie.' *A Romance of Two Worlds* (Bentley).
Haggard, H. Rider. *She: A History of Adventure* (Harper; Longman 1887).
Hinton, C. Howard. *Scientific Romances* [SS] (Swan Sonnenschein).
Lang, Andrew. *In the Wrong Paradise* [SS] (Kegan Paul).
Minto, William. *The Crack of Doom* (Blackwood).
Stevenson, Robert Louis. *The Strange Case of Dr. Jekyll and Mr. Hyde* (Longman) [F 1920, 1931, 1941 etc].
Westall, William. *The Phantom City: A Volcanic Romance* (Cassell).

1887

BIO

b. **Victor MacClure**, 20 Mar., ?Elgin, Moray, Scotland.
b. **Julian** (Sorell) **Huxley**, 22 Jun., London.

1887 (cont.)

BIO

b. **Hope Mirrlees**.
b. **Stephen Southwold** (real name possibly Stephen H. Critten; wrote as **'Neil Bell'** or **'Miles'**), Southwold, Suffolk.

*

d. Richard Jefferies, 14 Aug.

FIC

Allen, Grant. *The Beckoning Hand* [SS] (Chatto & W).
Curwen, Henry. *Zit and Xoe: Their Early Experience* (Blackwood).
Haggard, H. Rider. *Allan Quatermain* (Longman).
Hudson, W. H. *A Crystal Age* (Unwin).
Wells, H. G. "A Tale of the Twentieth Century." *Science Schools Journal* (May).
———. "A Vision of the Past." *Science Schools Journal* (Jun.).
Westall, William. *A Queer Race: The Story of a Strange People* (Cassell).

1888

BIO

b. **Ronald A**(rbuthnott) **Knox**, 17 Feb., Kibworth, Leicestershire.
b. **A**(rchibald) **M**(ontgomery) **Low**, 17 Oct.
b. (Archibald) **Fenner Brockway**, 1 Nov., Calcutta, India.
b. **Lionel Britton**, Redditch, Worcestershire.
b. **Jean Delaire** (Mrs. Muirson Blake), France.
b. (Sir Arthur) **Ronald Fraser**, London.
b. **George Goodchild**, Kingston-on-Thames, Surrey.
b. **Francis D**(urham) **Grierson**, Dublin, Ireland.
b. **Charles Ernest Jacomb**, Godalming, Surrey.
b. **'John Kendall'** (Margaret Maud Brash), Lancaster, Lancashire.
b. **E**(dward) **F**(rank) **Spanner**, Portsmouth, Devon.

FIC

Besant, Walter. *The Inner House* (Arrowsmith).
Payn, James. *The Eavesdropper: An Unparalleled Experience* (Smith, Elder).
Watson, H. B. Marriott. *Marahuna: A Romance* (Longmans, Green).
Wells, H. G. "The Chronic Argonauts." *Science Schools Journal* (Apr.-Jun.).
Westall, William. *Nigel Fortescue; or, The Hunted Man: An Andean Romance* (Ward & Downey) [US *Mr. Fortescue*].

1889

BIO

b. (Sir) **Geoffrey** (Cust) **Faber**, 23 Aug., Malvern, Worcestershire.
b. **H**(enry) **F**(itzgerald) **Heard**, 6 Oct., London.
b. **Hugh Kingsmill** (i.e. Hugh Kingsmill Lunn), 21 Nov., London.
b. **Claude Houghton** (i.e. Claude Houghton Oldfield), Sevenoaks, Kent.
b. **'Michael Maurice'** (Rev. Conrad Arthur Skinner), Dereham, Norfolk.
b. **'Mairi O'Nair'** (Constance Mary Evans), Montréal, Quebec, Canada.
b. **Edmund Snell**, London.

*

d. Percy Greg, 24 Dec.

FIC

Allen, Grant. *The Jaws of Death* (Simpkin Marshall).
Cromie, Robert. *For England's Sake* (Warne).
Doyle, Arthur Conan. *Mysteries and Adventures* [SS] (W. Scott).
Grove, W. *The Wreck of a World* (Digby, Long).
Hyne, C. J. Cutliffe. *Beneath Your Very Boots...Being a Few Striking Episodes from the Life of Anthony Merlwood Haltoun, Esq.* (Digby, Long).
MacColl, Hugh. *Mr. Stranger's Sealed Packet* (Chatto & W).

1890

BIO

b. **'John Trevena'** (Ernest G. Henham), Lower Norwood, Surrey.
b. (William) **Vaughan Wilkins**, London.
b. **S**(amuel) **Andrew Wood**, Ashton-Under-Lyne, Lancashire.

FIC

Allen, Grant. *The Great Taboo* (Chatto & W).
Arnold, Edwin Lester. *The Wonderful Adventures of Phra the Phoenician* (Chatto & W).
Cobban, James MacLaren. *Master of His Fate* (Blackwood).
Cromie, Robert. *A Plunge into Space* (Warne).
Dixie, Lady Florence. *Gloriana; or, The Revolution of 1900* (Henry).
Doyle, Arthur Conan. *The Captain of the Polestar* [SS] (Longman).
Morris, William. *News from Nowhere: An Epoch of Rest, Being Some Chapters from a Utopian Romance* (*Roberts*; Reeves & Turner 1891).

GEN

[PUB] *Pearson's Weekly*, 1st. ed. Peter Kerry, 26 Jul., through 1 Apr. 1939 (2540 issues).

1891

BIO

b. (Margaret) **Storm Jameson** (also wrote as **'William Lamb'**), 8 Jan., Whitby, Yorkshire.
b. **Neil M**(iller) **Gunn**, 8 Nov., Caithness, Scotland.
b. **'Lewis Gibbs'** (J. W. Cove).

FIC

'Anstey, F.' *Tourmalin's Time Cheques: A Farcical Extravaganza* (Simpkin Marshall).
Barlow, James William (as 'Antares Skorpios'). *History of a World of Immortals Without a God* (McGee) [rep. as by JWB. *The Immortals' Great Quest* (Smith, Elder 1909)].
Doyle, Arthur Conan. *The Doings of Raffles Haw* (Lovell; Cassell 1892).
'Folingsby, Kenneth.' *Meda: A Tale of the Future* (Aird & Cogshill).
Haggard, H. Rider. *Eric Brighteyes* (Longman).
Hume, Fergus W. *The Year of Miracle: A Tale of the Year One Thousand Nine Hundred* (Routledge).
Jerome, Jerome K. "The New Utopia." In *Diary of a Pilgrimage* (Simpkin Marshall).
Shelley, Mary Wollstonecraft [P]. *Tales and Stories* [SS] (W. Paterson).
Stables, Gordon. *The Cruise of the Crystal Boat: The Wild, the Weird, the Wonderful* (Hutchinson).

GEN

[E] Wells, H. G. "The Rediscovery of the Unique." *Fortnightly Review* (Jul.).

[PUB] *Strand Magazine*, 1st. ed. Sir George Newnes, Jan., through Mar. 1950.

1892

BIO

b. **J**(ohn) **R**(onald) **R**(euel) **Tolkien**, 3 Jan., Bloemfontein, Orange Free State.
b. **Geoffrey** (Pomeroy) **Dennis**, 20 Jan., Barnstaple, Devon.
b. **David Garnett**, 9 Mar., Brighton, Sussex.
b. **Victoria** (Mary) **Sackville-West**, 9 Mar., Knole, Kent.
b. **J**(ohn) **K**(eith) **Stanford**, 29 Apr., Bromley, Kent.
b. **'Edward Shanks'** (Richard Buxton), 11 Jun., London.
b. **J**(ohn) **B**(urdon) **S**(anderson) **Haldane**, 5 Nov., Oxford.
b. **Monica** (Mary) **Curtis**, London.
b. **Dorothy E**(mily) **Stevenson**, Edinburgh, Scotland.

*

d. Henry Curwen, 22 Feb.

1892(cont.)

FIC

Clowes, W. Laird. *The Captain of the 'Mary Rose': A Tale of To-Morrow* (Tower).
Hyne, C. J. Cutliffe. *The New Eden* (Longmans, Green).
Lach-Szyrma, W. S. *Under Other Conditions* (A. C. Black).
Morgan, Arthur and Charles R. Brown. *The Disintegrator: A Romance of Modern Science* (Digby, Long).
'Seaforth, A. Nelson' (George Sydenham Clarke). *The Last Great Naval War* (Cassell).

GEN

[PUB] *The Idler*, 1st. eds. Jerome K. Jerome & Robert Barr, Feb., through Mar. 1911.

1893

BIO

b. **Capt. W**(illiam) **E**(arle) **Johns**, 5 Feb., Bengeo, Hertfordshire.
b. (Sir) **Herbert** (Edward) **Read**, 4 Dec., Kirkbymoorside, Yorkshire.
b. **Robert** (Maurice Browne) **Nichols**, Shanklin, Isle of Wight.
?b. **Muriel Jaeger**.

*

d. William Minto, 1 Mar.

FIC

Allen, Grant. *Ivan Greet's Masterpiece* [SS] (Chatto & W).
Clowes, W. Laird. *The Great Peril and How It Was Averted* (Black & White).
Colomb, Philip H., et al. *The Great War of 189-: A Forecast* (Heinemann).
Doyle, Arthur Conan. *My Friend the Murderer* [SS] (Lovell).
Fawcett, E. Douglas. *Hartmann the Anarchist; or, The Doom of the Great City* (Arnold).
Hyne, C. J. Cutliffe. *The Recipe for Diamonds* (Heinemann).
Jerome, Jerome K. "Novel Notes." *Idler* (Aug.).
Wells, H. G. "The Advent of the Flying Man." *Pall Mall Gazette* (8 Dec.).

GEN

[E] Wells, H. G. "The Man of the Year Million." *Pall Mall Gazette* (9 Nov.).

[PUB] *Pall Mall Magazine*, 1st ed. Lord Frederick Hamilton, May, through Aug. 1914.

1894

BIO

b. **Aldous** (Leonard) **Huxley**, 26 Jul., Godalming, Surrey.
b. **J**(ohn) **B**(oynton) **Priestley**, 13 Sep., Bradford, Yorkshire.
b. **I**(drisyn) **O**(liver) **Evans**, 11 Nov., Bloemfontein, Orange Free State.
b. **F**(rank) **L**(awrence) **Lucas**, 28 Dec., Hipperholme, Yorkshire.
b. **John** (Gordon) **Hargrave**, Midhurst, Kent.

*

d. Robert Louis Stevenson, 3 Dec.

FIC

Barr, Robert. *The Face & the Mask* [SS] (Hutchinson).
Clowes, W. Laird. *The Double Emperor: A Story of a Vagabond Cunarder* (Arnold).
Doyle, Arthur Conan. *The Great Keinplatz Experiment* [SS] (Rand McNally).
---. *The Parasite* (Constable).
Fawcett, E. Douglas. *Swallowed by an Earthquake* (Arnold).
Griffith, George. *The Angel of the Revolution: A Tale of the Coming Terror* (Tower).
---. *Olga Romanoff; or, The Syren of the Skies* (Tower).
Haggard, H. Rider. *The People of the Mist* (Longman).
Le Queux, William. *The Great War in England in 1897* (Tower).
'Machen, Arthur.' *The Great God Pan* and *The Inmost Light* (J. Lane).
Wells, H. G. "Aepyornis Island." *Pall Mall Budget* (Xmas).
---. "The Diamond Maker." *Pall Mall Budget* [rep. *Pearson's Magazine* Mar. 1905].
---. "The Flowering of the Strange Orchid." *Pall Mall Budget* (2 Aug.).
---. "In the Avu Observatory." *Pall Mall Budget* (9 Aug.).
---. "The Lord of the Dynamos." *Pall Mall Budget* (6 Sep).
---. "The Stolen Bacillus." *Pall Mall Budget* (21 Jun.).

GEN

[E] Wells, H. G. "The Extinction of Man." *Pall Mall Gazette* (25 Sep.).
[E] ---. "From an Observatory." *Saturday Review* (1 Dec.).

2
The Wellsian Synthesis: 1895–1936

This period spans the approximately forty years between the publication of *The Time Machine* in book form (1895) and the eve of the appearance of a native fandom revealing the increasing influence of American science fiction in Britain. It is dominated by the career of H. G. Wells, whose scientific training, literary gifts and extraordinary powers of synthesis enabled him to produce a body of work that engaged, more fully than the realistic mode dominant in serious British literature at that time, contemporary cultural anxieties in the wake of the victory of Darwinism and its enthronement as dominant ideology. Wells's writings generated their own interesting though until recently neglected subgenre, the scientific romance, which persisted as late as the 1950s, according to Brian Stableford in his *Scientific Romance in Britain 1890-1950* (1985).

The key works here are, above all, the great early scientific romances of Wells: *The Time Machine* (1895), *The Island of Dr. Moreau* (1896), *The Invisible Man* (1897), *The War of the Worlds* (1898), and *The First Men in the Moon* (1901). But highly significant, too, is the huge body of Wells's other writings--from "The Star" (1897) to *The Shape of Things to Come* (1933)--that elevated him into an intellectual eminence over the first third of the twentieth century in Britain akin to that of Voltaire over mid-eighteenth-century France.

The urgency of the Wellsian project, namely, to force technological man to confront himself and his unprecedented predicament, was intensified by that great cultural trauma, the First World War, and still more by the political polarization of the 1930s and the increasing sense of inevitability about the next conflict. In general, the important scientific romancers of the time--Stapledon, Fowler Wright, Southwold, Gloag--share the Wellsian anxieties, even if they do not propose similar remedies.

BIO
- b. **Robert** (Ranke) **Graves**, 24 Jul., London.
- b. **'Michael Arlen'** (Dikran Kouyoumdjian), 16 Nov., Roustchouk, Bulgaria.
- b. **William** (Alexander) **Gerhardi**(e), 21 Nov., St. Petersburg, Russia.
- b. **L**(eslie) **P**(oles) **Hartley**, 30 Dec., Whittlesey, Cambridgeshire.
- b. **S**(ydney Muller) **Parkman**, Mumbles, Glamorgan, Wales.

*

d. George T. Chesney, 31 Mar.

FIC

Allen, Grant. *The British Barbarians: A Hill-Top Novel* (Lane).
---. *The Desire of the Eyes* [SS] (Digby, Long).
Arnold, Edwin Lester. *The Story of Ulla* [SS] (Longman).
Constable, Frank Challice (as Anon.). *The Curse of Intellect* (Blackwood).
Cromie, Robert. *The Crack of Doom* (Digby, Long).
Ellis, T. Mullett (fl. 1893-1916). *Zalma* (Tower).
Griffith, George. *The Outlaws of the Air* (Tower).
---. *Valdar the Oft-Born: A Saga of Seven Ages* (Pearson).
Haggard, H. Rider. *Heart of the World* (*Longman*; Longman 1896).
Hinton, C. Howard. *Stella, and An Unfinished Communication: Studies of the Unseen* [SS] (Swan Sonnenschein).
Jane, Fred T. *Blake of the 'Rattlesnake'; or, The Man Who Saved England. A Story of Torpedo Warfare in 189-* (Tower).
Le Queux, William. *Stolen Souls* [SS] (Tower).
MacDonald, George. *Lilith* (Chatto & W).
Mears, A(melia) Garland. *Mercia, the Astronomer Royal* (Simpkin Marshall).
Pemberton, Max. *The Impregnable City* (Cassell).
Wells, H. G. "The Argonauts of the Air." *Phil May's Annual*.
---. "A Moth--Genus Novo." *Pall Mall Gazette* (28 Mar.).
---. "Pollock and the Porroh Man." *New Budget* (23 May).
---. "The Remarkable Case of Davidson's Eyes." *Pall Mall Budget* (28 Mar.).
---. *The Stolen Bacillus, and Other Incidents* [SS] (Methuen).
---. "The Temptation of Harringay." *St. James Gazette* (9 Feb.).
---. "The Time Machine." *New Review* (Jan.-May).
---. *The Time Machine: An Invention* (Heinemann).
---. *The Wonderful Visit* (Dent).

BIO
- b. **Lance** (lot de Giberne) **Sieveking**, 19 Mar., Harrow, Middlesex.
- b. **R**(obert) **C**(harles) **Sherriff**, 6 Jun., Kingston-on-Thames, Surrey.
- b. **Katherine** (Penelope) **Burdekin** (also wrote as **'Murray Constantine'**), 23 Jul., Spondon, Derbyshire.
- b. **John** (Edward) **Gloag**, 10 Aug., London.
- b. **Charman Edwards** (?F. A. Edwards), London.

*

- d. William Morris, 3 Oct.
- d. George Du Maurier, 6 Oct.

FIC

Allen, Grant. *A Bride from the Desert* [SS] (*Fenno*).
Atkins, Francis Henry (as 'Frank Aubrey'). *The Devil-Tree of El Dorado: A Romance of British Guiana* (Hutchinson).
Cromie, Robert. *The Next Crusade* (Hutchinson).
Davidson, John. *The Pilgrimage of Strongsoul* [SS] (Ward & Downey).
Hinton, C. Howard. *Scientific Romances: Second Series* [SS] (Swan Sonnenschein).
Jane, Fred T. *The Incubated Girl* (Tower).
Morris, William. *The Well at the World's End* (Longman).
Pallander, Edwin. *Across the Zodiac: A Story of Adventure* (Digby, Long).
Shiel, M. P. *Shapes in the Fire* [SS] (J. Lane).
Tracy, Louis. *The Final War: A Story of the Great Betrayal* (Pearson).
Wells, H. G. "The Apple." *Idler* (Oct.).
---. "In the Abyss." *Pearson's Magazine* (Aug.).
---. *The Island of Doctor Moreau* (Heinemann) [F 1933, 1977].
---. "The Plattner Story." *New Review* (Apr.).
---. "The Purple Pileus." *Black & White* (Xmas).
---. "The Red Room." *Idler* (Mar.).
---. "The Sea Raiders." *Weekly Sun Literary Supplement* (6 Dec.).
---. "The Story of the Late Mr. Elvesham." *Idler* (May).
---. "Under the Knife." *New Review* (Jan.).

GEN

[E] Wells, H. G. "Intelligence on Mars." *Saturday Review* (4 Apr.).

[PUB] *Pearson's Magazine*, 1st. ed. C. Arthur Pearson, Jan., through Nov. 1939.

BIO
- b. **Dennis** (Yates) **Wheatley**, 8 Jan., London.
- b. **Sid**(ney) **G**(eorge) **Hedges**, 25 Mar., Bicester, Oxfordshire.
- b. **Bernard** (Charles) **Newman**, 8 May, Ibstock, Leicestershire.
- b. **Rodney Quest**, 27 May, Bolton, Lancashire.
- b. **'Doreen Wallace'** (Dora Eileen Agnew Wallace Rash), 18 Jun., Lorton, Cumberland.
- b. **Naomi** (Margaret) **Mitchison** (née Haldane), 1 Nov., Edinburgh, Scotland.
- b. **Anthony Armstrong** (i.e. George Anthony Armstrong Willis), Esquimalt, British Columbia, Canada.
- b. **J**(ames) **M**(organ) **Walsh**, Geelong, Victoria, Australia.
- b. **Barbara** (Frances) **Wootton**, (Baroness Wootton of Abinger), Cambridge.

*

- d. Mrs. Oliphant, 25 Jun.
- d. Edward Maitland, 2 Oct.

FIC

Cromie, Robert. *The King's Oak* [SS] (Newnes).
Gorst, Harold E. *Without Bloodshed: A Probability of the Twentieth Century* (Roxburghe).
Griffith, George. *Briton or Boer? A Tale of the Fight for Africa* (White).
---. *The Romance of Golden Star* (White).
Jane, Fred T. *To Venus in Five Seconds; Being an Account of the Strange Disappearance of Thomas Plummer, Pillmaker* (A. D. Innes).
Le Queux, William. *The Eye of Istar* (White).
---. *A Madonna of the Music Halls; Being the Story of a Secret Sin* (White).
Munro, John. *A Trip to Venus* (Jarrold).
Stoker, Bram. *Dracula* (Constable).
Tracy, Louis (and M. P. Shiel). *An American Emperor: The Story of the Fourth Empire of France* (Pearson).
Wells, H. G. "The Crystal Egg." *New Review* (Vol. 16).
---. *The Invisible Man: A Grotesque Romance* (Pearson) [F 1933 etc].
---. *The Plattner Story, and Others* [SS] (Methuen).
---. "The Star." *Graphic* (Xmas).
---. "A Story of the Days to Come." *Pall Mall Magazine*.
---. "A Story of the Stone Age." *Idler* (May-Sep.).
---. *Thirty Strange Stories* [SS] (Arnold).

BIO
- b. **Hilary** (Aidan) **St. G**(eorge) **Saunders**, 14 Jan., Clifton, Gloucestershire.
- b. **Esmé Wynne-Tyson**, 29 Jun., London.
- b. (Arthur) **Owen Barfield**, 9 Nov., London.
- b. **C**(live) **S**(taples) **Lewis**, 29 Nov., Belfast, Northern Ireland.
- b. **Jeffery Lloyd Castle**, Surbiton, Surrey.

*

- d. 'Lewis Carroll,' 14 Jan.
- d. James Payn, 25 Mar.

FIC

Buchanan, Robert. *The Rev. Annabel Lee: A Tale of Tomorrow* (Pearson).
Du Maurier, George [P]. *The Martian* (Harper).
Gorst, Harold E. *Sketches of the Future* [SS] (MacQueen).
Griffith, George. *The Destined Maid* (White).
———. *The Gold-Finder* (White).
Hyne, C. J. Cutliffe (as 'Weatherby Chesney'). *The Adventures of a Solicitor* [SS] (Bowden).
——— (as 'Weatherby Chesney'). *The Adventures of an Engineer* [SS] (Bowden).
Le Queux, William. *The Great White Queen* (White).
Shiel, M. P. *The Yellow Danger* (Richards).
Tracy, Louis. *The Lost Provinces* (Pearson).
Wells, H. G. "Jimmy Goggles the God." *Graphic* (Dec.).
———. "The Man Who Could Work Miracles." *Illustrated London News* (Jul.).
———. "The Stolen Body." *Strand* (Nov.).
———. *The War of the Worlds* (Heinemann) [F 1953].

BIO

b. **Nevil Shute** (i.e. Nevil Shute Norway), 17 Jan., London.
b. **Eric** (Robert Russell) **Linklater**, 8 Mar., Penarth, Glamorgan, Wales.
b. **'C. S. Forester'** (Cecil Lewis Troughton Smith), 27 Aug., Cairo, Egypt.
b. **Francis H**(enry) **Sibson**, Eaglescliff, County Durham.

*

d. Philip H. Colomb, 13 Oct.
d. Grant Allen, 28 Oct.

FIC

Atkins, Francis Henry (as 'Frank Aubrey'). *A Queen of Atlantis: A Romance of the Caribbean Sea* (Hutchinson).
Griffith, George. *The Great Pirate Syndicate* (White).
---. *Gambles with Destiny* [SS] (White).
Jane, Fred T. *The Violet Flame: A Story of Armageddon and After* (Ward Lock).
Le Queux, William. *England's Peril* (White).
Wells, H. G. *Tales of Space and Time* [SS] (Harper).
---. "A Vision of Judgement." *Butterfly* (Sep.).
---. *When the Sleeper Wakes* (Harper) [rev. *The Sleeper Awakes* (Nelson 1910)].

BIO
- b. **James Hilton**, 9 Sep., Leigh, Lancashire.
- b. **Geoffrey Household**, 30 Nov., Bristol.
- b. **'Alan Griff'** (William Donald Suddaby), Leeds, Yorkshire.

FIC

'Anstey, F.' *The Brass Bottle* (Smith, Elder).
Cole, Robert William. *The Struggle for Empire: A Story of the Year 2236* (Elliot Stock).
Hyne, C. J. Cutliffe. *The Lost Continent* (Hutchinson).
'Netterville, Luke.' *The Queen of the World; or, Under the Tyranny* (Lawrence & Bullen).
White, Fred M. *The White Battalions* (Pearson).

BIO

b. **'Hector Hawton'** (Virginia Curzon), 7 Feb., Plymouth, Devon.
b. J(ames) **Leslie Mitchell**, 13 Feb., near Auchterless, Aberdeen, Scotland.
b. **'Anna Kavan'** (Helen Woods), 10 Apr., Cannes, France.
b. **John Collier**, 3 May, London.
b. J(ohn) D(esmond) **Bernal**, 10 May, Nenagh, County Tipperary, Ireland.
b. **Henry Brinton**, 27 Jul., Wolverhampton, Staffordshire.
b. (John Percy Vyvian) **Dacre Balsdon**, 4 Nov., Bideford, Devon.
b. **Alfred Gordon Bennett**, Warrington, Lancashire.
b. **Ernest** (Carpenter) **Elmore**, Maidstone, Kent.

*

d. Walter Besant, 9 Jun.
d. Robert Buchanan, 10 Jun.

FIC

Arnold, Edwin Lester. *Lepidus the Centurion: A Roman of Today* (Cassell).
Butler, Samuel. *Erewhon Revisited Twenty Years Later* (Richards).
Conrad, Joseph & Ford Madox Hueffer. *The Inheritors: An Extravagant Story* (Heinemann).
Green, A. Lincoln. *The End of an Epoch: Being the Personal Narrative of Adam Godwin, the Survivor* (Blackwood).
Griffith, George. *Captain Ishmael* (Hutchinson).
---. *Denver's Double: A Story of Inverted Identity* (White).
---. *A Honeymoon in Space* (Pearson).
---. *The Justice of Revenge* (White).
Phillpotts, Eden. *Fancy Free* [SS & V] (Methuen).
Shiel, M. P. *The Lord of the Sea* (Richards) [rev. Gollancz 1929].
---. *The Purple Cloud* (Chatto & W) [rev. Gollancz 1929] [F 1958 as *The World, the Flesh and the Devil*].
Tracy, Louis. *The Invaders* (Pearson).
Wallis, George C. *Children of the Sphinx* (Cosmopolitan).
Wells, H. G. "A Dream of Armageddon." *Black & White*.
---. "Filmer." *Graphic*.
---. *The First Men in the Moon* (Newnes) [*F 1964].
---. "Mr. Skelmersdale in Fairyland." *Strand*.
---. "The New Accelerator." *Strand* (Dec.).
Westall, William. *Don or Devil?* (Pearson).

GEN

[E] Wells, H. G. *Anticipations of the Reaction of Mechanical and Scientific Progress Upon Human Life and Thought* (Chapman & H).

BIO

d. Samuel Butler, 18 Jun.

FIC

Cromie, Robert. *A New Messiah* (Digby, Long).
'Kuppord, Skelton' (J. Adams). *A Fortune from the Sky* (Nelson).
Pallander, Edwin. *The Adventures of a Micro-Man* (Digby, Long).
Pemberton, Max. *The House Under the Sea* (Newnes).
Pinkerton, T. A. *No Rates and Taxes: A Romance of Five Worlds* (Arrowsmith).
Wells, H. G. *The Sea Lady: A Tissue of Moonshine* (Methuen).
---. "The Story of the Inexperienced Ghost." *Strand* (Mar.).

GEN

[E] Wells, H. G. *The Discovery of the Future: A Discourse Delivered to the Royal Institution on January 24, 1902* (Unwin).

BIO

b. (David William) **Alun Llewellyn**, 17 Apr., London.
b. **'George Orwell'** (Eric Arthur Blair), 25 Jun., Motihari, India.
b. **John Wyndham** (i.e. John Wyndham Parkes Lucas Beynon Harris), 10 Jul., Knowle, Warwickshire.
b. **'George Sava'** (Alexis Milkomanovich Milkomane), 15 Oct., Baku, Russia.
b. **Evelyn** (Arthur St. John) **Waugh**, 28 Oct., London.
b. **A. L. Morton**.
b. **E**(ileen) **Ar**(buth)**not Robertson** (Lady Turner), Holmwood, Surrey.
b. **T**(heodore) **Stanhope Sprigg**, Castor, Northamptonshire.

*

d. William Westall, 9 Sep.
d. James MacLaren Cobban, 31 Oct.

FIC

Atkins, Francis Henry (as 'Frank Aubrey'). *King of the Dead: A Weird Romance* (MacQueen).
Childers, Erskine. *The Riddle of the Sands: A Record of Secret Service Recently Achieved* (Smith, Elder).
Dixie, Lady Florence. *Isola; or, The Disinherited* [P] (Leadenhall).
Griffith, George. *The Lake of Gold: A Narrative of the Anglo-American Conquest of Europe* (White).
---. *The World Masters* (J. Long).
Stables, Gordon. *An Island Afloat* (Nisbet).
Stanley, William. *The Case of The Fox: Being His Prophecies under Hypnotism of the Period Ending 1950. A Political Utopia* (Truslove & Hanson).
Wells, H. G. "The Land Ironclads." *Strand* (Dec.).
---. "The Magic Shop." *Strand* (Jun.).
---. "The Truth about Pyecraft." *Strand* (Apr.).
---. *Twelve Stories and a Dream* [SS] (Macmillan).
---. "The Valley of Spiders." *Pearson's Magazine* (Mar.).

BIO
b. **Margery Allingham**, 20 May, London.
b. **Francis** (Leslie) **Ashton**.

*

d. Tom Greer.

FIC
Chesterton, G. K. *The Napoleon of Notting Hill* (Lane).
Delaire, Jean. *Around a Distant Star* (J. Long).
Griffith, George. *A Criminal Croesus* (J. Long).
---. *The Stolen Submarine* (White).
Haggard, H. Rider. *Stella Fregelius: A Tale of Three Destinies* (Longman).
Hyne, C. J. Cutliffe. *Atoms of Empire* [SS] (Macmillan).
'Thorne, Guy' *When It Was Dark* (Greening).
Wells, H. G. "The Country of the Blind." *Strand* (Apr.).
---. *The Food of the Gods and How It Came to Earth* (Macmillan) [F 1976].

1905

BIO

b. **Eric Frank Russell**, 6 Jan., Camberley, Surrey.
b. **Festus Pragnell**, 16 Jan.
b. **Rex Warner**, 9 Mar., Birmingham.
b. **Arthur Koestler**, 5 Sep., Budapest, Hungary.
b. **'Jane Lane'** (Elaine Dakers, née Kidner), Ruislip, Middlesex.

*

d. W. Laird Clowes, 14 Aug.
d. George MacDonald, 18 Sep.
d. Lady Florence Dixie, 7 Nov.

FIC

Arnold, Edwin Lester. *Lieut. Gullivar Jones: His Vacation* (Brown, Langham) [US *Gulliver of Mars* 1964].
{Atkins, Francis Henry (as 'Fenton Ash'). *The Radium Seekers; or, The Wonderful Black Nugget* (Pitman).}
{--- (as 'Fred Ashley'). *The Temple of Fire; or, The Mysterious Island* (Pitman).}
Griffith, George. *A Mayfair Magician: A Romance of Criminal Science* (White).
Haggard, H. Rider. *Ayesha: The Return of She* (Ward Lock).
Kipling, Rudyard. "With the Night Mail." *McClure's* (Jul.) [rep. in *Actions and Reactions* 1909].
Mastin, John. *The Stolen Planet: A Scientific Romance* (P. Wellby).
Shiel, M. P. *The Yellow Wave* (Ward Lock).
Wells, H. G. "The Empire of the Ants." *Strand* (Dec.).
---. *A Modern Utopia* (Chapman & H).

BIO
b. **T**(erence) **H**(anbury) **White**, 29 May, Bombay, India.
b. **Angus MacLeod**, 13 Sep., Wester Ross, Scotland.

*

d. George Griffith, 4 Jun.

FIC
Griffith, George. *The Great Weather Syndicate* (White).
---. *The Mummy and Miss Nitocris: A Phantasy of the Fourth Dimension* (Werner Laurie).
Haggard, H. Rider. *Benita: An African Romance* (Cassell) [US *The Spirit of Bambatse*].
Harris, J. Henry. *A Romance in Radium* (Greening).
Hernaman-Johnson, Francis. *The Polyphemes: A Story of Strange Adventures Among Strange Beings* (Ward Lock).
Le Queux, William. *The Invasion of 1910: With a Full Account of the Siege of London* (Eveleigh Nash).
Seymour, Cyril. *Comet Chaos: A Romance of Love, Treasure and Prophecy* (Chatto & W).
Shiel, M. P. *The Last Miracle* (Werner Laurie) [rev. Gollancz 1929].
Stables, Gordon. *The Meteor Flag of England: The Story of a Coming Conflict* (Nisbet).
'Thorne, Guy.' *Made in His Image* (Hutchinson).
--- (as Ranger Gull). *The Soul-Stealer* (White).
Tracy, Louis. *Karl Grier, the Strange Story of a Man with a Sixth Sense* (Hodder & S).
Wells, H. G. "The Door in the Wall." *Daily Chronicle* (14 Jul.).
---. *In the Days of the Comet* (Macmillan).

1907

BIO

b. **Michael Harrison**, 25 Apr., Milton, Kent.
b. **Daphne Du Maurier**, 13 May, London.
b. **Paul Charkin**, 20 Jul., London.
b. **Meir** (Selig) **Gillon**, 11 Aug., Sibiu, Transylvania.
b. **John Marsh** (also wrote as **'John Elton'**), Halifax, Yorkshire.

*

d. Robert Cromie, Apr.
d. C. Howard Hinton.

FIC

Benson, Robert Hugh. *Lord of the World* (Pitman).
Griffith, George [P]. *The World Peril of 1910* (White).
Hinton, C. Howard. *An Episode of Flatland; or, How the Plane Folk Discovered the Third Dimension* (Swan Sonnenschein).
Hodgson, William Hope. *The Boats of the 'Glen Carrig'* (Chapman & H).
Mastin, John. *The Immortal Light* (Cassell).

BIO

b. **H**(enry) **L**(ionel) **Lawrence**, 22 Apr., London.
b. **Paul Tabori**, 8 May, Budapest, Hungary.
b. **Frank Baker**, 22 May, London.
b. **John** (Francis) **Russell Fearn**, 5 Jun., Worsley, Lancashire.
b. **John Creasey**, 17 Sep., Southfields, Surrey.
b. (Brigadier) **Nigel** (Marlin) **Balchin**, 3 Dec., Potterne, Wiltshire.
b. '**Robert Crane**' (Bernard Glemser), London.

FIC

Doyle, Arthur Conan. *Round the Fire Stories* [SS] (Smith, Elder).
Flecker, J. Elroy. *The Last Generation* (New Age).
Griffith, George [P]. *The Sacred Skull* (Everett).
Haggard, H. Rider. *The Yellow God* (Cupples & Leon; Cassell 1909).
Hodgson, William Hope. *The House on the Borderland* (Chapman & H).
'Thorne, Guy.' *The Angel* (Ward Lock).
Wells, H. G. *The War in the Air, and Particularly How Mr. Bert Smallways Fared While It Lasted* (Bell).

BIO

b. **Hugh Sykes Davies**, 17 Aug., Prescot, Lancashire.
b. (Arnold) **Roger Manvell**, 10 Oct., Leicester.
b. **'William Dexter'** (W. T. Pritchard).

*

d. John Davidson, 23 Mar.
d. William Stanley, 14 Aug.

FIC

{Atkins, Frank (as 'Fenton Ash.') *A Trip to Mars* (Chambers).}
Forster, E. M. "The Machine Stops." *Oxford & Cambridge Review* (Michaelmas) [rep. in *The Eternal Moment* (Sidgwick & J 1928)].
Hodgson, William Hope. *The Ghost Pirates* (Paul).
Holt-White, William. *The Man Who Stole the Earth* (T. Fisher Unwin).
Mastin, John. *Through the Sun in an Airship* (C. Griffin).
Shiel, M. P. *The Isle of Lies* (Werner Laurie).
---. *This Knot of Life* (Everett).

BIO

b. **W**(illiam) **Grey Walter**, 19 Feb., Kansas City, Missouri, USA.
b. **Nicholas** (John Turney) **Monsarrat**, 22 Mar., Liverpool.
b. **Kathleen M. Sully**, 14 Apr., London.
b. (Jessie) **Jacquetta Hawkes** (née Hopkins), 5 Aug., Cambridge.
b. **Harold** (Charles Hugh) **Mead**, 25 Sep., Ootacamund, India.
b. **Edward** (Solomon) **Hyams**, 30 Sep., London.
b. (**General Sir**) **John** (Winthrop) **Hackett**, 5 Nov., Perth, Australia.
b. **J**(ohn) **W**(illiam) **Groves**, 6 Nov.
b. **'Sarban'** (John William Wall), 6 Nov.
b. **Roy** (Lethbridge) **Meyers**, 17 Nov., Hounslow, Middlesex.
b. **Bridget Chetwynd**, Dolgellau, Merioneth, Wales.
b. **Kathleen** (Cecilia) **Nott**, London.
b. **Kathleen M. Sully**.

*

d. Gordon Stables, 10 May.

FIC

Beresford, Leslie. *The Second Rising: A Romance of India* (Hurst & Blackett).
Ford, D. M. (as Anon.). *The Raid of Dover: A Romance of the Reign of Woman, A.D.1940* (King, Sell & Olding).
Glendon, George. *The Emperor of the Air* (Methuen).
Haggard, H. Rider. *Queen Sheba's Ring* (Eveleigh Nash).
Horner, Donald W. *By Aeroplane to the Sun* (Century).
Hyne, C. J. Cutliffe. *Empire of the World* (Everett; Newnes 1915 as *Emperor of the World: The Story of an Anglo-German War*).
Le Queux, William. *The Unknown To-Morrow* (White).

1911

BIO

b. **Mervyn** (Laurence) **Peake**, 9 Jul., Kuling, China.
b. **Gerald Kersh**, 6 Aug., Teddington-on-Thames, Middlesex.
b. (Sir) **William** (Gerald) **Golding**, 19 Sep., St. Columb Minor, Cornwall.
b. **'John Lymington'** (John Newton Chance), London.

FIC

Benson, Robert Hugh. *The Dawn of All* (Hutchinson).
Beresford, J. D. *The Hampdenshire Wonder* (Sidgwick & J) [US *The Wonder* 1917].
Doyle, Arthur Conan. *The Last Galley: Impressions and Tales* [SS] (Smith, Elder).
Griffith, George [P]. *The Lord of Labour* (White).
Haggard, H. Rider. *The Mahatma and the Hare: A Dream Story* (Longmans, Green).
Pain, Barry. *An Exchange of Souls* (Eveleigh Nash).
Pocock, Roger. *The Chariot of the Sun* (Chapman & H).
Shiel, M. P. *The Pale Ape and Other Pulses* [SS] (Werner Laurie).
'Trevena, John.' *The Reign of the Saints* (Alston Rivers).
Wells, H. G. *The Country of the Blind* [SS] (Nelson).
---. *The Door in the Wall* [SS] (*Mitchell Kennerley*).
{Wicks, Mark. *To Mars Via the Moon: An Astronomical Story* (Seeley).}

BIO
- b. **B**(ertram) **A**(rthur) **Young**, 20 Jan., London.
- b. **Lawrence** (George) **Durrell**, 27 Feb., Julundur, India.
- b. **E**(dward) **J**(ohn) **Carnell**, 8 Apr., London.
- b. **'Harvey Graham'** (Isaac Harvey Flack), 26 Oct., Radcliffe, Lancashire.
- b. **Paul Capon**, 18 Dec., Kenton Hall, Suffolk.
- b. **Margot Bennett**, Lenzie, Stirling, Scotland.
- b. **Ian Colvin**.
- b. **'John Gawsworth'** (T. I. Fytton-Armstrong), London.
- b. **Walter Gillings**.
- b. **Benson Herbert**.

*

- d. Bram Stoker, 20 Apr.
- d. Andrew Lang, 20 Jul.
- d. Robert Barr, 21 Oct.

FIC

Doyle, Arthur Conan. *The Lost World* (Hodder & S) [F 1925, 1960].
Hodgson, William Hope. *The Night Land* (Eveleigh Nash).
Horner, Donald W. *Their Winged Destiny: Being a Tale of Two Planets* (Simpkin Marshall).
Kennedy, R. A. (as 'Author of Space and Spirit'). *The Triuneverse: A Scientific Romance* (Charles Knight).
Kipling, Rudyard. "As Easy as ABC." *London Magazine* (Apr.) [rep.in *A Diversity of Creatures* 1917].
'Lurgan, Lester,' with Richard Ganthony. *A Message from Mars* (Greening) [*F 1913].
Wallace, Edgar. *Private Selby* (Ward Lock).

BIO
- b. (Bertram) **John Boland**, 12 Feb., Birmingham.
- b. **Catherine Storr** (née Cole), 21 Jul., London.
- b. **Angus** (Frank Johnstone) **Wilson**, 11 Aug., Bexhill, Sussex.
- b. **D**(avid) **S**(tephen) **Martin**, 24 Oct., Gravesend, Kent.
- b. **'John Paget'** (John Kempton Aiken), Oct., Cambridge, Massachusetts, USA.
- b. **Roy Lewis**, 6 Nov., Felixstowe, Suffolk.
- b. **Charles** (MacKinnon) **Barren**, 21 Dec., London.
- b. **Robert** (Ferns) **Waller**, Manchester.

*

d. James William Barlow, 4 Jul.

FIC

Beresford, J. D. *Goslings* (Heinemann) [US *A World of Women*].
Doyle, Arthur Conan. *The Poison Belt* (Hodder & S).
Fleming, Brandon. *Masks* (Everett).
Raphael, John N. *Up Above* (Hutchinson).
'Rohmer, Sax.' *The Mystery of Dr. Fu-Manchu* (Methuen).
---. **Series continued through 1959.**
Shiel, M. P. *The Dragon* (Richards) [rev. *The Yellow Peril* (Gollancz 1929)].
Wallace, Edgar. *The Fourth Plague* (Ward Lock).

FTV

[F] *A Message from Mars*. Dir. J. Wallett Waller. UK Film. Wr. J. W. Waller, from play by Richard Ganthony, *nov. (1912) 'Lester Lurgan.'

BIO
- b. **Frank Edward Arnold**, 3 Jan.
- b. **William F**(rederick) **Temple**, 9 Mar., London.
- b. (Henry) **Chapman Pincher**, 29 Mar., Ambala, India.
- b. **Philip E**(mpson) **High**, 28 Apr., Biggleswade, Bedfordshire.
- b. **Ruthven Todd**, 14 Jun., Edinburgh, Scotland.
- b. **Anthony West**, 4 Aug., Hunstanton, Norfolk.
- b. **Ronald Duncan**, (Bishop of Marsland), 6 Aug., Salisbury, Rhodesia.
- b. **L**(eslie) **P**(urnell) **Davies**, 20 Oct., Crewe, Cheshire.

*

d. Robert Hugh Benson, 19 Oct.

FIC

Gubbins, Herbert. *The Elixir of Life; or, 2905 A.D.* (Drane).
Newton, Douglas. *The North Afire: A Picture of What Might Be* (Methuen).
---. *War!* (Methuen).
'Saki' (as H. H. Munro). *When William Came: A Story of London Under the Hohenzollerns* (J. Lane).
Wells, H. G. *The World Set Free: A Story of Mankind* (Macmillan).

BIO
- b. **Gilbert** (Henry) **Phelps** (Jr.), 23 Jan., Gloucester.
- b. **Leonard** (John) **Daventry**, 7 Mar., London.
- b. **'Dighton Morel'** (Kenneth Lewis Warner), 10 Apr., Gosport, Hampshire.
- b. **'John Kippax'** (John Charles Hynam), 10 Jun., Alwalton, Huntingdonshire.
- b. (Sir) **Fred Hoyle**, 24 Jun., Bingley, Yorks.
- b. **Ernest Hill**, 14 Jul., Stourbridge, Worcestershire.
- b. **Kay Dick**, 29 Jul., London.
- b. **Michael** (Dunlop) **Young**, 9 Aug., Manchester.
- b. **Diana** (Pleasance) **Gillon** (née Case), 1 Sep., London.
- b. **Marghanita Laski**, 24 Oct., London.
- b. **Frank R**(obson) **Crisp**, ?15/30 Nov., Durham.

*

- d. J. Elroy Flecker, 3 Jan.
- d. W. S. Lach-Szyrma.

FIC

Le Queux, William. *The Mystery of the Green Ray* (Hodder & S).
Marshall, Archibald. *Upsidonia* (Paul).
'Thorne, Guy.' *The Secret Sea-Plane* (Hodder & S).
---. (as Ranger Gull). *The Enemies of England* (Werner Laurie).
Wallace, Edgar. *'1925': The Story of a Fatal Peace* (Newnes).

GEN

[C] Beresford, J. D. *H. G. Wells* (Nisbet).

1916

BIO

b. **R**(eginald) **C**(harles) **Churchill**, 9 Feb., Bromley, Kent.
b. **John** (Alfred) **Atkins**, 26 May, Carshalton, Surrey.
b. **Roald Dahl**, 13 Sep., Llandaff, Glamorgan, Wales.
b. **Jerzy Peterkiewicz**, 29 Sep., Fabianki, Poland.
b. **Ronald** (William) **Clark**, 2 Nov., London.
b. **'John Rackham'** (John Thomas Phillifent), 10 Nov., Durham.
b. **Richard Pape**.

*

d. Fred T. Jane, 8 Mar.
d. 'Saki,' 14 Nov.

FIC

Clouston, J. Storer. *Two's Two* (Blackwood).
Le Queux, William. *The Zeppelin Destroyer: Being Some Chapters of Secret History* (Hodder & S).
'Thorne, Guy.' *And It Came to Pass* (Jarrold).
Vaughan, Herbert M. *Meleager* (M. Secker).

BIO

b. **Anthony Burgess** (i.e. John Anthony Burgess Wilson), 25 Feb., Manchester.
b. **'Rex Gordon'** (Stanley Bennett Hough), 25 Feb., Preston, Lancashire.
b. **Jack Trevor Story**, 20 Mar., Bengeo, Hertfordshire.
b. (George) **Robert** (Ackworth) **Conquest**, 15 Jul., Malvern, Worcestershire.
b. **'Richard Savage'** (Ivan Roe), 12 Nov., London.
b. (Sir) **G**(eorge Andrew) **D**(ick-) **Lauder**, 17 Nov., Poona, India.
b. **Arthur C**(harles) **Clarke**, 16 Dec., Minehead, Somerset.

FIC

'Machen, Arthur.' *The Terror: A Fantasy* (Duckworth).
Vaughan, Herbert M. *The Dial of Ahaz* (M. Secker).

1918

BIO
- b. **I**(gnatius) **F**(rederick) **Clarke**, 10 Jul., Wallasey, Cheshire.
- b. **Eric C**(yril) **Williams**, 22 Jul., London.
- b. **'John Rankine'** (Douglas Rankine Mason), 26 Sep., Hawarden, Flint, Wales.
- b. **Roger** (Gilbert) **Lancelyn Green**, 2 Nov., Norwich, Norfolk.
- b. **'Densil Neve Barr'** (Douglas Norton Buttrey), Harrogate, Yorkshire.
- b. **John Elliot**.
- b. **D**(ennis) **F**(eltham) **Jones**.

*

d. William Hope Hodgson, 19 Apr.

FIC

Beresford, J. D. *Nineteen Impressions* [SS] (Sidgwick & J).
Beresford, Leslie (as 'Pan'). *The Kingdom of Content* (Mills & Boon).
'Corelli, Marie.' *The Young Diana: An Experiment of the Future* (Hutchinson).
Doyle, Arthur Conan. *Danger!* [SS] (Murray).
Gregory, Owen. *Meccania, The Super-State* (Methuen).
Haggard, H. Rider. *Love Eternal* (Cassell).
Onions, Oliver. *The New Moon: A Romance in Reconstruction* (Hodder & S).
'Swayne, Martin.' *The Blue Germ* (Hodder & S).

BIO

b. **Cyril Donson**, 26 May, Mexborough, Yorkshire.
b. **Robert Kee**, 5 Oct., Calcutta, India.
b. **E**(dwin) **C**(harles) **Tubb**, 15 Oct., London.
b. **Doris** (May) **Lessing** (née Tayler), 22 Oct., Kermanshah, Persia.
b. **John** (Alfred) **Petty**, Walsall, Staffordshire.

FIC

Doyle, Arthur Conan. *The Black Doctor* [SS] (Newnes).
Haggard, H. Rider. *When the World Shook: Being an Account of the Great Adventure of Bastin, Bickley, and Arbuthnot* (Cassell).
Macaulay, Rose. *What Not: A Prophetic Comedy* (Constable).
'Thorne, Guy' (as C. Ranger Gull). *The Air Pirate* (Hurst & Blackett).
Wallace, Edgar. *The Green Rust* (Ward Lock).
Winsor, G(eorge) MacLeod. *Station X* (Jenkins).

BIO
- b. **'Elleston Trevor'** (Trevor Dudley-Smith), 17 Feb., Bromley, Kent.
- b. **Victor** (George Charles) **Norwood**, 21 Mar., Scunthorpe, Lincolnshire.
- b. **Ronald Hingley**, 26 Apr., Edinburgh, Scotland.
- b. **Richard Adams**, 9 May, Newbury, Berkshire.
- b. **Peter Vansittart**, 27 Aug., Bedford.
- b. **Philip** (Donald) **McCutchan**, 13 Oct., Cambridge.
- b. **Sydney J**(ames) **Bounds**, 4 Nov., Brighton, Sussex.

FIC

Blake, Stacey. *Beyond the Blue* (Books Ltd.).
Le Queux, William. *The Terror of the Air* (Lloyds).
Lindsay, David. *A Voyage to Arcturus* (Methuen).
'Shanks, Edward.' *The People of the Ruins* (Stokes; Collins 1921).

GEN

[E] Wells, H. G. *The Outline of History: Being a Plain History of Life and Mankind.* 2 vols. (Newnes).

1921

BIO

b. (Henry) **Kenneth Bulmer**, 14 Jan., London.
b. **'Charles Eric Maine'** (David McIlwain), 21 Jan., Liverpool.
b. **Michael Cooney**, 28 Apr., Ireland.
b. **'Arthur Sellings'** (Arthur Gordon Ley), 31 May, Tunbridge Wells, Kent.
b. **Francis G**(eorge) **Rayer**, 6 Jun., Longdon, Worcestershire.
b. **Desmond Leslie**, 9 Jun., London.
b. **'Edmund Crispin'** (Robert Bruce Montgomery), 2 Oct., Chesham Bois, Buckinghamshire.
b. **David I**(rvine) **Masson**, 6 Nov., Edinburgh, Scotland.
b. **James Barlow**, 1 Dec., Birmingham.
b. **Peter Phillips**.

*

d. H. B. Marriott Watson, 30 Oct.

FIC

Beresford, J. D. *Revolution: A Story of the Near Future in England* (Collins).
---. *Signs and Wonders* [SS] (Golden Cockerel).
Beresford, Leslie (as 'Pan'). *The Great Image* (Odhams).
'Blayre, Christopher.' *The Purple Sapphire and Other Posthumous Papers Selected from the Unofficial Records of the University of Cosmopoli by...* [SS] (P. Allan) [enl. *The Strange Papers of Dr. Blayre* (P. Allan 1932)].
Haggard, H. Rider. *She and Allan* (Hutchinson).
Shaw, George Bernard. *Back to Methuselah: A Metabiological Pentateuch* [D] (Constable).
'Thorne, Guy' (as C. Ranger Gull). *The City in the Clouds* (Hurst & Blackett).
Wells, H. G. "The Grisly Folk and Their War with Men." *Storyteller Magazine* (Apr.).

1922

BIO
- b. **Peter Leslie**, 5 Feb., Launceston, Cornwall.
- b. **Raymond** (John) **Hitchcock**, 9 Feb., Calcutta, India.
- b. **Mervyn Jones**, 27 Feb., London.
- b. **John** (Frederick) **Burke**, 8 Mar., Rye, Sussex.
- b. (Sir) **Kingsley** (William) **Amis**, 16 Apr., London.
- b. '**John Christopher**' (Christopher Samuel Youd), 16 Apr., Knowsley, Lancashire.
- b. (Thomas) **Nigel Kneale**, 28 Apr., Barrow-in-Furness, Lancashire.
- b. **Robert** (Moyes Carruthers) **Bateman**, 21 Jun., Manchester.
- b. **Douglas Orgill**, 10 Aug., Walsall, Staffordshire.
- b. **D**(onald) **G**(abriel) **Barron**.
- b. **George Hay**.

*

- d. W. H. Hudson, 18 Aug.
- d. Erskine Childers, 24 Nov.

FIC
- Eddison, E. R. *The Worm Ouroboros: A Romance* (Cape).
- Gayton, Bertram. *The Gland Stealers* (H. Jenkins).
- Hamilton, Cicely. *Theodore Savage: A Story of the Past or the Future* (L. Parsons) [rev. *Lest Ye Die* (Cape 1928)].
- Lindsay, David. *The Haunted Woman* (Methuen).
- Scrymsour, Ella. *The Perfect World: A Romance of Strange People and Strange Places* (Eveleigh Nash & Grayson).
- Wallace, Edgar. *Captains of Souls* (Small Maynard; J. Long 1923).

BIO

b. **Arthur Wise**, 12 Jan., York.
b. (Prof.) **Christine Brooke-Rose**, 16 Jan., Geneva, Switzerland.
b. **Patrick Moore**, 4 Mar., Pinner, Middlesex.
b. (Thomas Gordon) **Lindsay Gutteridge**, 20 May, Easington, County Durham.
b. **John F**(enwick) **Blackburn**, 26 Jun., Northumberland.
b. **Lan** (i.e. Lionel Percy) **Wright**, 8 Jul., Watford, Hertfordshire.
b. **Peter Crowcroft**, 25 Nov., Watford, Hertfordshire.

*

d. 'Guy Thorne,' 9 Jan.

FIC

'Addison, Hugh.' *The Battle of London* (Jenkins).
'Blayre, Christopher.' *The Cheetah-Girl* (PP).
Broomhead, Reginald. *A Voice from Mars* (Stockwell).
'Connington, J. J.' *Nordenholt's Million* (Constable).
Graham, P. Anderson. *The Collapse of Homo Sapiens* (Putnam).
Haggard, H. Rider. *Wisdom's Daughter* (Hutchinson).
Hargrave, John. *Harbottle: A Modern Pilgrim's Progress from This World to That Which Is to Come* (Duckworth).
Knox, Ronald A. (as ed.). *Memories of the Future: Being Memoirs of the Years 1915-1972 Written in the Year of Grace 1988 by Opal, Lady Porstock* (Methuen).
Lindsay, David. *Sphinx* (J. Long).
'Maurice, Michael.' *Not in Our Stars* (T. Fisher Unwin).
Odle, E(dwin) V. *The Clockwork Man* (Heinemann).
Turner, C. C. *The Secret of the Desert* (Hurst & Blackett).
Wells, H. G. *Men Like Gods* (Cassell).
Wignall, T. C. & G. D. Knox. *Atoms* (Mills & Boon).

GEN

[E] Haldane, J. B. S. *Daedalus; or, Science and the Future: A Paper Read to the Heretics, Cambridge, on February 4th, 1923* (Trübner).

BIO
- b. **'Ian Cameron'** (Donald Gordon Payne), 3 Jan., London.
- b. **E**(dward) **P**(almer) **Thompson**, 3 Feb., Oxford.
- b. **John** (Griffith) **Bowen**, 5 Nov., Calcutta, India.
- b. **Peter** (Bryan) **George**, Wales.
- b. **'Paul MacTyre'** (R. J. Adam).
- b. **Peter Van Greenaway**.

*

- d. 'Marie Corelli,' 21 Apr.
- d. Joseph Conrad, 3 Aug.

FIC

Beresford, Leslie. *The Venus Girl* (J. Long).
Fraser, Ronald. *The Flying Draper* (T. Fisher Unwin).
Haggard, H. Rider. *Heu-Heu; or, The Monster* (Hutchinson).
'Hussingtree, Martin' (Oliver Baldwin). *Konyetz* (Hodder & S).
Kingsmill, Hugh. *The Dawn's Delay* [SS] (Elkin Mathews).
MacClure, Victor. *Ultimatum* (Harrap) [US *The Ark of the Covenant: A Romance of the Air and of Science*].
Mills, Lady Dorothy. *The Arms of the Sun* (Duckworth).
Sieveking, Lance. *Stampede!* (Cayme).
Tayler, J. Lionel. *The Last of My Race* (J. W. Ruddock).
'Thorne, Guy' [P]. *When the World Reeled* (Ward Lock).
Wells, H. G. *The Dream* (Cape).
---. *The Works of H. G. Wells* (Unwin) [Atlantic Edition in 28 vols.].

BIO

b. **Russell** (Conwell) **Hoban**, 4 Feb., Lansdale, Pennsylvania, USA.
b. '**J. T. McIntosh**' (James Murdoch MacGregor), 14 Feb., Paisley, Renfrew, Scotland.
b. **Brian** (**W**ilson) **Aldiss**, 18 Aug., East Dereham, Norfolk.
b. **Madelaine** (Elizabeth) **Duke**, 21 Aug., Geneva, Switzerland.
b. **Dan Morgan**, 24 Sep., Holbeach, Lincolnshire.
b. **H**(erbert) **J**(ames) **Campbell**, 18 Nov., London.

*

d. H. Rider Haggard, 14 May.
d. P. Anderson Graham, 25 Oct.

FIC

Armstrong, Anthony. *Wine of Death: A Tale of the Lost Long Ago* (Paul).
Faber, Geoffrey. *Elnovia* (Faber & Gwyer).
Hadfield, Robert L. & Frank E. Farncombe. *Ruled by Radio* (Jenkins).
Lynch, Bohun. *Menace from the Moon* (Jarrolds).
Murray, V. T. *The Rule of the Beasts* (Paul).
Oppenheim, E. Phillips. *The Wrath to Come* (Hodder & S).
Sieveking, Lance. *The Ultimate Island: A Strange Adventure* (Routledge).
Vivian, E. Charles. *Star Dust* (Hutchinson).
Wright, S. Fowler. *The Amphibians: A Romance of 500,000 Years Hence* (Merton).

BIO
- b. **John Fowles**, 31 Mar, Leigh-on-Sea, Essex.
- b. **Edmund Cooper**, 30 Apr., Marple, Cheshire.
- b. **'Richard Cowper'** (John Middleton Murry, Jr.), 9 May, Abbotsbury, Dorset.
- b. **Colin** (Symons) **Cooper**, 25 Jul., Berkhamstead, Hertfordshire.
- b. (John) **Christopher** (Glazebrook) **Hodder-Williams**, 25 Aug., London.
- b. **Philip Bedford Robinson**, 10 Dec.

*

d. Edwin A. Abbott, 12 Oct.

FIC

Dent, Guy. *Emperor of the If* (Heinemann).
Desmond, Shaw. *Ragnarok* (Duckworth).
Doyle, Arthur Conan. *The Land of Mist* (Hutchinson).
George, W(alter) L. *Children of the Morning* (Chapman & H).
Halsbury, Earl of. *1944* (Butterworth).
Huxley, Julian. "The Tissue-Culture King." In *The Cornhill* [rep. *AMZ* Aug. 1927].
Jacomb, Charles Ernest. *And a New Earth: A Romance* (Routledge).
Jaeger, Muriel. *The Question Mark* (Hogarth).
Mirrlees, Hope. *Lud-in-the-Mist* (Collins).
Phillpotts, Eden. *The Miniature* (Watts).
Spanner, E. F. *The Broken Trident* (Williams & Norgate).
---. *The Naviators* (Williams & Norgate).
Wallace, Edgar. *The Day of Uniting* (Hodder & S).

GEN

[FP] H. G. Wells in *AMZ*: "The New Accelerator" (Apr.); "The Crystal Egg" (May); "The Star" (Jun.); "The Man Who Could Work Miracles" (Jul.); "The Empire of the Ants" (Aug.); "In the Abyss" (Sep.); *The Island of Dr. Moreau* (Oct.-Nov.); *The First Men in the Moon* (Dec.-Feb. 1927).

BIO

b. **Kenneth Harker**, 2 Apr., Darlington, County Durham.
b. **Alan Seymour**, 6 Jun., Perth, Australia.
b. **Kit** (i.e. Christopher Magnus Howard) **Pedler**, 11 Jun., London.
b. **Paul** (Victor) **Ableman**, 13 Jun., Leeds, Yorkshire.
b. **Clive** (Frederick) **Egleton**, 25 Nov., South Harrow, Middlesex.
b. **Peter** (Malcolm de Brissac) **Dickinson**, 16 Dec., Livingstone, Rhodesia.
b. **Charles** (Frederick William) **Chilton**.

*

d. Jerome K. Jerome, 14 Jun.
d. William Le Queux, 13 Oct.
d. Francis Henry Atkins.

FIC

Burdekin, Katherine. *The Burning Ring* (Thornton Butterworth).
Douglas, Norman. *In the Beginning* (Florence, Italy: PP).
Goodchild, George (as 'Alan Dare'). *The Eye of Abu* (H. Jenkins).
Hadfield, Robert L. & Frank E. Farncombe. *Red Radio* (Jenkins).
Haggard, H. Rider [P]. *Allan and the Ice-Gods* (Hutchinson).
Jaeger, Muriel. *The Man with Six Senses* (Hogarth).
Priestley, J. B. *Adam in Moonshine* (Heinemann).
Turner, C. C. *Unlawful* (Paul).
Wells, H. G. *The Short Stories of H. G. Wells* [SS] (Benn) [rep. *The Complete Short Stories of H. G. Wells* (Benn 1965)].
Wright, S. Fowler. *Deluge* (Fowler Wright) [F 1933].

GEN

[E] Dunne, J. W. *An Experiment with Time* (A. C. Black).
[E] Haldane, J. B. S. *Possible Worlds* (Chatto & W).

[FP] H. G. Wells in *AMZ*: "Under the Knife" (Mar.); "The Remarkable Case of Davidson's Eyes" (Apr.); *The Time Machine* (May); "The Story of the Late Mr. Elvesham" (Jun.); "The Plattner Story" (Jul.); *The War of the Worlds* (Aug.-Sep.); "Aepyornis Island" (Oct.); "A Story of the Stone Age" (Nov.); "The Country of the Blind" (Dec.).

1928

BIO

b. **Alan Sillitoe**, 4 Mar., Nottingham.
b. **James White**, 7 Apr., Belfast, Northern Ireland.
b. **Patrick Tilley**, 4 Jul., Southend, Essex.
b. **'Roger Carlton'** (Donald Sydney Rowland), 23 Sep., Great Yarmouth, Norfolk.
b. **Kyril Bonfiglioli**, Eastbourne, Sussex.
b. **'A. J. Merak'** (John S. Glasby), East Retford, Nottinghamshire.

*

d. Barry Pain, 5 May.
d. 'Luke Netterville,' 18 May.
d. Louis Tracy, 13 Aug.
d. Bohun Lynch, 2 Oct.

FIC

Belloc, Hilaire. *But Soft!--We Are Observed!* (Arrowsmith).
Beresford, J. D. *All or Nothing* (Collins).
Creswick, Paul. *The Turning Wheel* (Heath Cranton).
Elmore, Ernest. *The Steel Grubs* (Selwyn & Blount).
Gerhardi, William. *Jazz and Jasper: The Story of Adams and Eva* (Duckworth) [US *Eva's Apple*].
Grierson, Francis D. *Heart of the Moon* (Alston Rivers).
Lewis, P. Wyndham. *The Childermass* (Chatto & W).
Snell, Edmund. *Kontrol* (Benn).
Wells, H. G. *Mr. Blettsworthy on Rampole Island* (Benn).
Woolf, Virginia. *Orlando: A Biography* (Hogarth).
Wright, S. Fowler. *The Island of Captain Sparrow* (Gollancz).

GEN

[FP] H. G. Wells in *AMZ*: "The Stolen Body" (Jan.); "Pollock and the Porroh Man" (Feb.); "The Flowering of the Strange Orchid" (Mar.); "A Story of the Days to Come" (Apr.-May); *The Invisible Man* (Jun.-Jul.); "The Moth" (Aug.).
[FP] Wallis, George C. (as B. & G. C. Wallis). "The World at Bay." *AMZ* (Nov./Dec.).

BIO

b. (Frank Charles) **Robert Wells**, 31 Jan., London.
b. **Len** (i.e. Leonard Cyril) **Deighton**, 18 Feb., London.
b. **Bernard Bergonzi**, 13 Apr., London.
b. **'David Craig'** (Allan James Tucker), 15 Aug., Cardiff, Wales.
b. **'Philip James'** (James Cawthorn), 21 Dec.
b. **Brian Earnshaw**, 26 Dec., Wrexham, Denbigh, Wales.
b. **K. D. Franklin**, Yorkshire.
b. **Colin Kapp**.

*

d. 'Seamark.'

FIC

Beresford, J. D. *The Meeting Place* [SS] (Faber).
---. *Real People* (Collins).
Burdekin, Katherine. *The Rebel Passion* (Thornton Butterworth).
Doyle, Arthur Conan. *The Maracot Deep* [SS] (Murray).
Guest, Ernest. *At the End of the World* (Elkin Mathews & Marrot).
Hyne, C. J. Cutliffe. *Abbs, His Story Through Many Ages* (Hutchinson).
Kingsmill, Hugh. *The Return of William Shakespeare* (Duckworth).
Phillpotts, Eden. *The Apes* (Faber).
Robertson, E. Arnot. *Three Came Unarmed* (Doubleday).
Visiak, E. H. *Medusa* (Gollancz).
Vivian, E. Charles. *Woman Dominant* (Ward Lock).
Wallace, Edgar. *Planetoid 127* (Readers Library).
Wells, H. G. *The King Who Was a King: The Book of a Film* [SP] (Benn).
Wright, S. Fowler. *Dawn* (Cosmopolitan; Harrap 1930).
---. *The World Below* (Collins) [rep. *The Dwellers* (Panther 1954)].

GEN

[E] Bernal, J. D. *The World, the Flesh and the Devil* (Kegan Paul).

[FP] H. G. Wells in *AMZ*: "The Lord of the Dynamos" (Feb.).

1930

BIO

b. **'Charles Lewis'** (Roger Dixon), 6 Jan., Portsmouth, Hampshire.
b. **Gerry Davis**, 23 Feb., London.
b. **Douglas Hurd**, 8 Mar., Marlborough, Wiltshire.
b. **R**(onald) **W**(alter) **Mackelworth**, 7 Apr., London.
b. **D**(avid) **G**(uy) **Compton**, 9 Aug., London.
b. **Ted** (i.e. Edward James) **Hughes**, 17 Aug., Mytholmroyd, Yorkshire.
b. **J**(ames) **G**(raham) **Ballard**, 15 Nov., Shanghai, China.
b. **Brian Berry**.
b. **Charles Logan**.
b. **Donald Malcolm**.
b. **Terry Nation**.

*

d. Arthur Conan Doyle, 7 Jul.
d. John Munro, 19 Dec.

FIC

Blair, Hamish. *1957* (Blackwood).
Britton, Lionel. *Brain* [D] (Putnam).
Collier, John. *His Monkey-Wife; or, Married to a Chimp* (P. Davies).
Newman, Bernard. *Armoured Doves: A Peace Book* (Jarrolds).
Newton, Douglas. *The Golden Cat* (Cassell).
'Rohmer, Sax.' *The Day the World Ended* (Cassell).
'Seamark' (J. Austin Small) [P]. *The Avenging Ray* (Hodder & S).
Southwold, Stephen (as 'Miles'). *The Seventh Bowl* (Partridge) [rep. as by 'Neil Bell,' (Collins 1934)].
Stapledon, Olaf. *Last and First Men: A Story of the Near and Far Future* (Methuen).
Tillyard, Aelfrida. *Concrete: A Story of Two Hundred Years Hence* (Hutchinson).
Wells, H. G. *The Autocracy of Mr. Parham: His Remarkable Adventures in This Changing World* (Heinemann).

GEN

[E] Dennis, Geoffrey. *The End of the World* (Eyre & S).

BIO
- b. **Michael** (Aiken) **Elder**, 30 Apr., London.
- b. **Christopher** (Riche) **Evans**, 29 May, Aberdovey, Merioneth, Wales.
- b. **Colin** (Henry) **Wilson**, 26 Jun., Leicester.
- b. **'Ludovic Peters'** (Peter Ludwig Brent), 16 Jul., Beuthen, Germany.
- b. **Bob Shaw**, 31 Dec., Belfast, Northern Ireland.

FIC

Blair, Hamish. *Governor Hardy* (Blackwood).
Collier, John. *No Traveller Returns* (White Owl).
Edmonds, Harry. *The Riddle of the Straits* (Ward Lock).
Garnett, David. *The Grasshoppers Come* (Chatto & W).
Godber, Noel L. *Amazing Spectacles* (J. Long).
Hargrave, John. *The Imitation Man* (Gollancz).
Mitchell, J. Leslie. *The Calends of Cairo* [SS] (Jarrolds).
Southwold, Stephen (as 'Miles'). *The Gas War of 1940* (Partridge) [rep. as by 'Neil Bell' *Valiant Clay* (Collins 1934)].
---. (as 'Neil Bell'). *Precious Porcelain* (Gollancz).
Walsh, J. M. *Vandals of the Void* (Hamilton).
Williams, Charles. *Many Dimensions* (Gollancz).
Wright, S. Fowler. *Dream; or, The Simian Maid* (Harrap).

GEN

[A] Squire, J. C., ed. *If It Had Happened Otherwise: Lapses into Imaginary History* (Longmans) [US *If; or, History Rewritten*].

[FP] Herbert, Benson. "The World Without." *Wonder Stories* (Feb.).
[FP] Wyndham, John (as John Beynon Harris). "Worlds to Barter." *Wonder Stories* (May).
[FP] Groves, J. W. "The Sphere of Death." *AMZ* (Oct.).

1932

BIO

b. **Penelope** (Ann Douglass) **Gilliatt**, 25 Mar., London.
b. **Mark** (i.e. Peter Marcus) **Adlard**, 19 Jun., Seaton Carew, County Durham.
b. **Brian N**(eville) **Ball**, 19 Jun., Cheshire.
b. (Michael) **George Corston**, 14 Jul., Kenton, Middlesex.
b. **Michael G**(reatrex) **Coney**, 28 Sep., Birmingham.
b. **Graham Dunstan Martin**, 21 Oct., Leeds, Yorkshire.
b. **Adrian Mitchell**, 24 Oct., London.

*

d. Edgar Wallace, 10 Feb.
d. John Mastin, 9 Jul.
d. Fergus W. Hume, 12 Jul.

FIC

Furnill, John. *Culmination* (Elkin Mathews & Marrot).
Gloag, John. *To-Morrow's Yesterday* (Allen & U).
Huxley, Aldous. *Brave New World* (Chatto & W).
Lindsay, David. *Devil's Tor* (Putnam).
Mitchell, J. Leslie. *Three Go Back* (Jarrolds).
'Morison, Frank' (A. H. Ross). *Sunset* (Faber).
Nichols, Robert (as 'with Maurice Browne'). *Wings Over Europe* [D] (Chatto & W).
Nicolson, Harold. *Public Faces* (Constable).
Sibson, Francis H. *The Survivors* (Heinemann).
Snell, Edmund. *The Sound Machine* (Skeffington).
---. *The 'Z' Ray* (Skeffington).
Southwold, Stephen (as 'Neil Bell'). *The Disturbing Affair of Noel Blake* (Gollancz).
Stapledon, Olaf. *Last Men in London* (Methuen).
Tillyard, Aelfrida. *The Approaching Storm* (Hutchinson).
Wright, S. Fowler. *Beyond the Rim* (Jarrolds).
--- (as Sydney Fowler). *The New Gods Lead* [SS] (Jarrolds) [rep. & enl. *The Throne of Saturn* (Arkham 1949; Heinemann 1951)].

GEN

[FP] Pragnell, Festus (with R. F. Starzl). "The Venus Germ." *Wonder Stories* (Nov.).

[PUB] *The Passing Show*, 26 Mar., through 25 Feb. 1939.

BIO
- b. **John Boorman**, 18 Jan., Shepperton, Middlesex.
- b. (John) **Edward** (McKenzie) **Lucie-Smith**, 27 Feb., Kingston, Jamaica.
- b. **Martin** (Charles Owen) **Bax**, 13 Aug.
- b. **Barry** (Leslie) **Norman**, 21 Aug.
- b. **Michael Frayn**, 8 Sep., London.
- b. **Maureen Duffy**, 21 Oct., Worthing, Sussex.
- b. **Peter Valentine Timlett**.

FIC

'AE.' *The Avatars: A Futurist Fantasy* (Macmillan).
Aldworth, Frank. *Mr. J. Jay* (Heinemann).
'Arlen, Michael.' *Man's Mortality* (Heinemann).
Beresford, J. D. *The Camberwell Miracle* (Heinemann).
Black, Ladbroke. *The Poison War* (Paul).
Clouston, J. Storer. *Button Brains* (Jenkins).
Collier, John. *Tom's A-Cold* (Macmillan) [US *Full Circle, A Tale*].
Dilnot, Frank Buckland. *I Warmed Both Hands* (Lovat Dickinson).
Edmonds, Harry. *The Death Ship* (J. Lane).
Gloag, John. *The New Pleasure* (Allen & U).
Hilton, James. *Lost Horizon* (Macmillan) [F 1936, 1972].
Hyne, C. J. Cutliffe. *Man's Understanding* [SS] (Ward Lock).
Jaeger, Muriel. *Hermes Speaks* (Duckworth).
'Kendall, John.' *Unborn Tomorrow* (Collins).
Newton, Douglas. *Dr. Odin* (Cassell).
Shiel, M. P. *This Above All* (Vanguard) [rep. *Above All Else* (Lloyd Cole 1943)].
Sibson, Francis H. *Unthinkable* (Methuen).
Southwold, Stephen (as 'Neil Bell'). *The Lord of Life* (Collins).
Wells, H. G. *The Scientific Romances of H. G. Wells* [O] (Gollancz).
---. *The Shape of Things to Come: The Ultimate Revolution* (Hutchinson).
Wheatley, Dennis. *Such Power Is Dangerous* (Hutchinson).
Wright, S. Fowler. *Power* (Jarrolds).

GEN

[FAN] British Interplanetary Society [B.I.S], founded P. E. Cleator, Oct., Liverpool.

[FP] Fearn, John Russell. "The Intelligence Gigantic." *AMZ* (Jun.).

1934

BIO

b. **Raymond** (Redvers) **Briggs**, 18 Jan., London.
b. **Paul Wheeler**, 23 May, Jamaica, West Indies.
b. **John** (Kilian Houston) **Brunner**, 24 Sep., Preston Crowmarsh, Oxfordshire.
b. **Alan Garner**, 17 Oct., Alderley Edge, Cheshire.
b. (Jocelyn) **Pamela Kettle**, 27 Oct.
b. **Alasdair Gray**, 28 Dec., Glasgow, Scotland.
b. **John Griffiths**.
b. **Jon Hartridge**.

*

d. 'F. Anstey,' 10 Mar.
d. Archibald Marshall, 9 Sep.

FIC

Clouston, J. Storer. *The Chemical Baby* (Jenkins).
Curtis, Monica. *Landslide* (Gollancz).
Dalton, Moray. *The Black Death* (Sampson Low).
'Forester, C. S.' *The Peacemaker* (Heinemann).
Gloag, John. *Winter's Youth* (Allen & U).
Hedges, Sid G. *Plague Panic* (H. Jenkins).
Llewellyn, Alun. *The Strange Invaders* (Bell).
McIlraith, Frank & Roy Connolly. *Invasion from the Air: A Prophetic Novel* (Grayson).
Mitchell, J. Leslie. *Gay Hunter* (Heinemann).
O'Neill, Joseph. *Wind from the North* (Cape).
Palmer, John Leslie & Hilary St. G. Saunders (as 'Francis Beeding'). *The One Sane Man* (Hodder & S).
Sibson, Francis H. *The Stolen Continent* (A. Melrose).
Wheatley, Dennis. *Black August* (Hutchinson).
---. *The Fabulous Valley* (Hutchinson).
White, T. H. *Earth Stopped; or, Mr. Marx's Sporting Tour* (Collins).

GEN

[E] Burdekin, Katherine (as 'Murray Constantine'). *Proud Man* (Boriswood).
[E] Stapledon, Olaf. *Waking World* (Methuen).

{[PUB] *Scoops*, ed. F. Haydn Dimmock, 10 Feb., through 23 Jun. (20 issues).}

1935

BIO

b. **D**(onald) **M**(ichael) **Thomas**, 27 Jan., Redruth, Cornwall.
b. **R**(obert) **L**(ionel) **Fanthorpe**, 9 Feb., Dereham, Norfolk.
b. **Douglas** (Arthur) **Hill**, 6 Apr., Brandon, Manitoba, Canada.
b. **Susan Cooper**, 23 May, Burnham, Buckinghamshire.
b. **Josephine** (Mary) **Saxton** (née Howard), 11 Jun., Halifax, Yorkshire.
b. **Keith** (John Kingston) **Roberts**, 20 Sep., Kettering, Northamptonshire.
b. **'Vincent King'** (Rex Thomas Vinson), 22 Oct., Falmouth, Cornwall.
b. **Brenda Pearce**.

*

d. Hamish Blair, 28 Jan.
d. J. Leslie Mitchell, Feb.
d. Edwin Lester Arnold, 1 Mar.
d. 'AE,' 17 Jul.

FIC

Brockway, Fenner. *Purple Plague: A Tale of Love and Revolution* (Low).
Corbett, James. *Devil-Man from Mars* (Jenkins).
Davies, Hugh Sykes. *Petron* (Dent).
Edmonds, Harry. *The Professor's Last Experiment* (Rich & Cowan) [rev. *The Secret Voyage* (Macdonald 1946)].
Houghton, Claude. *This Was Ivor Trent* (Heinemann).
Noel, L. *The Golden Star* (Paul).
'O'Nair, Mairi.' *The Girl with the X-Ray Eyes* (Mills & Boon).
O'Neill, Joseph. *Land Under England* (Gollancz).
Read, Herbert. *The Green Child* (Heinemann).
Shiel, M. P. with 'John Gawsworth.' *The Invisible Voices* [SS] (Richards).
Southwold, Stephen (as 'Neil Bell'). *Mixed Pickles* [SS] (Collins).
Stapledon, Olaf. *Odd John: A Story Between Jest and Earnest* (Methuen).
Wells, H. G. *Things to Come: A Film Story Based on the Material Contained in His History of the Future 'The Shape of Things to Come'* [SP] (Shenval) [rep. *Two Film Stories* (Cresset 1940)].
White, T. H. *Gone to Ground* (Collins).
Wood, S. Andrew. *I'll Blackmail the World* (Hodder & S).
Wright, S. Fowler. *Prelude in Prague: A Story of the War of 1938* (Newnes) [US *The War of 1938* 1936].
--- (as 'Anthony Wingrave') *The Vengeance of Gwa* (Thornton Butterworth).
Wyndham, John (as John Beynon). *The Secret People* (Newnes).

FTV

[F] *The Tunnel* (US *The Transatlantic Tunnel*). Dir. Maurice Elvey. Gaumont. Wr. Kurt Siodmak et al., from novel by Bernhard Kellerman.

GEN

[FAN] [1st.] British Science Fiction Association founded, through 1935.

1936

BIO

b. **George** (Walter) **Locke**, 9 Feb., London.
b. **'Dick Morland'** (Reginald Hill), 3 Apr., West Hartlepool, County Durham.
b. **Hilary Bailey**, 19 Sep., London.
b. **Peter Edwards**.

*

d. Rudyard Kipling, 18 Jan.
d. G. K. Chesterton, 14 Jun.

FIC

Baker, Frank. *The Birds* (Davies).
Balsdon, Dacre. *Sell England?* (Eyre & S).
Beverley, Barrington. *The Space Raiders* (P. Allan).
Edwards, Charman. *Fear Haunts the Roses* (Ward Lock).
Harrison, Michael (as 'Michael Egremont'). *The Bride of Frankenstein* (Queensway).
Herbert, Benson, *Crisis!-1992* (Richards).
Jaeger, Muriel. *Retreat from Armageddon* (Duckworth).
Jameson, Storm. *In the Second Year* (Cassell).
Marsh, John. *Body Made Alive* (S. Smith).
Meredith, E. *Our Stranger: A Kineto-Romance* (Grayson).
O'Neill, Joseph. *Day of Wrath* (Gollancz).
Palmer, J. L. *The Hesperides: A Looking-Glass Fugue* (Secker & W).
Phillpotts, Eden. *The Owl of Athene* (Hutchinson).
Pragnell, Festus. *The Green Man of Kilsona* (P. Allan) [US rev. *The Green Man of Graypec* 1950].
'Smith, Wayland' (Victor Bayley). *The Machine Stops* (Hale).
Stevenson, Dorothy Emily. *The Empty World: A Romance of the Future* (Jenkins) [US *A World in Spell* 1939].
Wells, H. G. *The Croquet Player* (Chatto & W).
---. *The Man Who Could Work Miracles: A Film Story Based on the Material Contained in His Short Story 'Man Who Could Work Miracles'* [SP] (Cresset) [rep. *Two Film Stories* (Cresset 1940)].
Wheatley, Dennis. *They Found Atlantis* (Hutchinson).
Wootton, Barbara. *London's Burning: A Novel for the Decline and Fall of the Liberal Age* (Allen & U).
Wright, S. Fowler. *Four Days' War* (Hale).
Wyndham, John (as John Beynon). *Planet Plane* (Newnes) [rev. *Stowaway to Mars* (Nova 1953)].

FTV

[F] *The Man Who Could Work Miracles*. Dir. Lothar Mendes. London/UA. Wr. Lajos Biro & H. G. Wells, from *story (1898) by H. G. Wells.
[F] *Things to Come*. Dir. William Cameron Menzies. London. Wr. H. G. Wells, from his book *The Shape of Things to Come* (1933).

GEN

[FAN] *Novae Terrae*, 1st ed. Maurice K. Hanson, Mar., through Dec. 1938.

3
British Science Fiction: 1937–1961

Although British scientific romance would, like Wells himself, survive the Second World War, that characteristically American synthesis, 'science fiction,' had started to supersede it long before. Wells's appearance in the new context of the American pulp magazines from April 1926 onward did not, however, make him a 'science-fiction writer' in the eyes of either himself or his contemporary British readers. Only after 1931, in which year John Wyndham published his first story in Gernsback's *Wonder Stories*, did science fiction begin to take shape as an Anglo-American field.

Though Wyndham himself is unquestionably an important figure in the convergence of American science fiction and British scientific romance in this interwar period, the beginnings of a domestic fandom, rather than Wyndham's early work in the American pulps, is a more appropriate starting-point for this section of the chronology. January 1937 is a crucial date, for then was held the first British Science Fiction Conference, at which was formed the Science Fiction Association, with its attendant fanzines. The process of naturalizing American science fiction in Britain had begun.

In a sociological sense, Wyndham's *The Day of the Triffids* (1951) is a key work of this period. In it, the mundane, realistically-depicted British backdrops of Wellsian scientific romance were married with American pulp motifs to produce a bestseller on both sides of the Atlantic. Yet Wyndham's work lacked both the thematic ambition of the better British scientific romance and the ideational energy of the better Campbellian science fiction. The real literary achievements of the period in the field of British science fiction were in the expansion of Wellsian romance in new directions--in C. S. Lewis's Perelandra Trilogy, in George Orwell's *Nineteen Eighty-Four* (1949), in the later Aldous Huxley and in the early Arthur C. Clarke.

BIO
b. **Barrington J**(ohn) **Bayley**, 9 Apr., Birmingham.
b. **Malcolm Levene**, 24 Jun., London.
b. **Colin Spencer**, 17 Jul., London.
b. **Emma** (Christina) **Tennant**, 20 Oct., London.

*

d. Frank Challice Constable, 7 Oct.

FIC
Burdekin, Katherine (as 'Murray Constantine'). *Swastika Night* (Gollancz) [rep. as by KB (Laurence & Wishart 1987)].
{Clark, Charles. *Sky-Raft* (Newnes).}
Gloag, John. *Sacred Edifice* (Cassell).
'Graham, Harvey.' *A Crab Was Crushed* (Rich & Cowan).
Jameson, Storm (as 'William Lamb'). *The World Ends* (Dent).
Large, E. C. *Sugar in the Air* (Cape).
{Low, A. M. *Mars Breaks Through* (H. Joseph).}
Lucas, F. L. *The Woman Clothed with the Sun* [SS] (Cassell).
Powys, John Cowper. *Morwyn; or, The Vengeance of God* (Cassell).
Shiel, M. P. *The Young Men Are Coming!* (Allen & U)
Stapledon, Olaf. *Star Maker* (Methuen).
{Tolkien. J. R. R. *The Hobbit; or, There and Back Again* (Allen & U).}
Wells, H. G. *The Camford Visitation* (Methuen).
---. *Star Begotten: A Biological Fantasia* (Chatto & W).
Wheatley, Dennis. *The Secret War* (Hutchinson).
Wright, S. Fowler. *Megiddo's Ridge* (Hale).
---. *The Screaming Lake* (Hale) [rep. Regal 1953].

GEN
[FAN] First British Science Fiction Conference, 3 Jan., Leeds; formation of the Science Fiction Association, through Sep. 1940, with *Novae Terrae* its official organ; Arthur C. Clarke associate ed. of *Novae Terrae* (Oct.); Clarke's first stories appear in SFA fanzine *Amateur Science Stories*.
[FAN] *Scientifiction*, ed. Walter Gillings, Jan., through Mar. 1938.

[FP] Russell, Eric Frank. "The Saga of Pelican West." *ASF* (Feb.).

[PUB] *Tales of Wonder*, ed. Walter Gillings, Summer, through Spring 1942 (16 Issues).

BIO
b. **Andrew Osmond**, 16 Mar., England.

FIC
Clouston, J. Storer. *Not Since Genesis* (Jarrolds).
Desmond, Shaw. *Chaos* (Hutchinson).
---. *World-Birth* (Methuen).
Large, E. C. *Asleep in the Afternoon* (Cape).
Lewis, C. S. *Out of the Silent Planet* (J. Lane).
Linklater, Eric. *The Impregnable Women* (Cape).
'Marvell, Andrew' (Howell Davies). *Minimum Man; or, Time to Be Gone* (Gollancz).
Neill, A. S. *The Last Man Alive* (H. Jenkins).
Phillpotts, Eden. *Saurus* (Murray).
Priestley, J. B. *The Doomsday Men* (Heinemann).
Southwold, Stephen (as 'Neil Bell'). *One Came Back* (Collins).
Wheatley, Dennis. *Uncharted Seas* (Hutchinson) [*F 1968].
Wright, S. Fowler. *The Adventure of Wyndham Smith* (Jenkins).
---. *The Hidden Tribe* (Hale).

GEN
[FAN] *The Futurian*, ed. J. Michael Rosenblum, Jun., through 1940; as *Futurian War Digest*, 1940-50; as *New Futurian*, 1954-58.

[FP] Temple, William F. "Lunar Lilliput." *Tales of Wonder* (March).
[FP] Gillings, Walter (as 'Thomas Sheridan'). "The Midget from Mars." *Tales of Wonder* (Summer).

[PUB] *Fantasy: Thrilling Science Fiction*, ed. T. Stanhope Sprigg, Jul., through Jul. 1939 (3 issues).

1939

BIO

b. **Peter Nicholls**, 8 Mar., Melbourne, Australia.
b. **Robert Swindells**, 20 Mar., Bradford, Yorkshire.
b. **Sheila MacLeod**, 23 Mar., Stornoway, Isle of Lewis, Scotland.
b. **Michael** (John) **Moorcock**, 18 Dec., Mitcham, Surrey.
b. **James Follett**.

*

d. Ford Madox Hueffer, 26 Jun.

FIC

Bennett, Alfred Gordon. *The Demigods* (Jarrolds).
Chadwick, Philip George. *The Death Guard* (Hutchinson).
Clouston, J. Storer. *The Man in Steel* (Jarrolds).
Craig, Thurlow. *Plague Over London* (Hutchinson).
Huxley, Aldous. *After Many a Summer* (Chatto & W) [US *After Many a Summer Dies the Swan*].
Hyams, Edward. *The Wings of the Morning* (Duckworth).
'Marvell, Andrew.' *Congratulate the Devil* (Gollancz).
---. *Three Men Make a World* (Gollancz).
Parkinson, H. F. *They Shall Not Die* (Constable).
Sherriff, R. C. *The Hopkins Manuscript* (Gollancz) [rep. *The Cataclysm* (Pan 1958)].
Shute, Nevil. *What Happened to the Corbetts* (Heinemann) [US *The Ordeal*].
Todd, Ruthven. *Over the Mountain* (Harrap) [rep. Falcon 1946].
Wells, H. G. *The Holy Terror* (Joseph).
Wheatley, Dennis. *Sixty Days to Live* (Hutchinson).

GEN

[FAN] *The Fantast*, 1st. ed. 'John Christopher' (as C. S. Youd), Apr., through Jul. 1942 (14 issues).
[FAN] *New Worlds*, ed. E. J. Carnell, Apr., through Autumn 1939 (4 issues).

BIO
- b. **Trevor Hoyle**, 25 Feb., Rochdale, Lancashire.
- b. **Angela** (Olive) **Carter** (née Stalker), 7 May, Eastbourne, Sussex.
- b. **John Clute**, Toronto, Ontario, Canada.
- b. **Hugh Darrington**, Bishop's Stortford, Essex.
- b. **Peter Tate**, South Wales.

*

- d. Ladbroke Black, 27 Jul.

FIC

Bridges, T. C. *The Death Star* (Collins).
Gloag, John. *Manna* (Cassell).
'Griff, Alan.' *Lost Men in the Grass* (Oxford).
Horsnell, Horace. *Man Alone* (H. Hamilton).
'Kavan, Anna.' *Asylum Piece* [SS] (Cape).
Noyes, Alfred. *The Last Man* (Murray) [US *No Other Man*].
Shute, Nevil. *An Old Captivity* (Heinemann).
Wells, H. G. *All Aboard for Ararat* (Secker & W).

GEN

[FAN] *Hermes*, ed. Eric Frank Russell, Aug.

BIO
b. **Garry Kilworth**, 5 Jul., York.
b. **Jane Gaskell** (i.e. Jane Gaskell Lynch), 7 Jul., Grange-over-Sands, Lancashire.
b. **Philip** (James) **Harbottle**, 2 Oct., Wallsend-on-Tyne, Northumberland.
b. **Gill Alderman**, Dorset.
b. **Andrew Lovesey**.

*

d. Virginia Woolf, 28 Mar.

FIC
Beresford, J. D. *"What Dreams May Come..."* (Hutchinson).
Bishop, Morchard. *The Star Called Wormwood* (Gollancz).
Warner, Rex. *The Aerodrome: A Love Story* (Lane).

GEN
[FAN] *Zenith*, ed. Harry Turner, Aug., through Apr. 1942 (5 Issues).

1942

BIO

b. **Martin** (Anthony) **Sherwood**, 10 Jan.
b. **Geoffrey Hoyle**, 12 Jan., Scunthorpe, Lincolnshire.
b. (Anthony) **Phillip Mann**, 7 Aug., Northallerton, Yorkshire.
b. **Langdon Jones**, Kent.

FIC

Beresford, J. D. *A Common Enemy* (Hutchinson).
Fearn, John Russell (as 'Dennis Clive'). *Valley of Pretenders* (*Columbia*).
---. ***ca*. 25 novels as JRF, *ca*. 50 as 'Vargo Statten,' *ca*. 12 as 'Volsted Gridban,' et al., through 1960.**
Jameson, Storm. *Then We Shall Hear Singing: A Fantasy in C Major* (Cassell).
Newman, Bernard. *Secret Weapon* (Gollancz).
Sackville-West, Victoria. *Grand Canyon* (Joseph).
Stapledon, Olaf. *Darkness and the Light* (Methuen).

GEN

[FAN] [1st.] British Fantasy Society founded, through 1945.

BIO

- b. **Jean Ure**, 1 Jan.
- b. **Alan Passes** (né Pazolski), 12 Jan.
- b. **James Herbert**, 8 Apr., London.
- b. **Ian Watson**, 20 Apr., North Shields, Northumberland.
- b. **Christopher** (McKenzie) **Priest**, 14 Jul., Cheadle, Cheshire.
- b. **Mick Farren**, 3 Sep., Cheltenham, Gloucestershire.
- b. **Chris** (i.e. Joseph Christopher) **Boyce**, 12 Sep., Glasgow, Scotland.
- b. **Steve Wilson**.

*

- d. 'Christopher Blayre,' 28 Mar.
- d. Earl of Halsbury, 15 Sep.

FIC

Kearney, Chalmers. *Erone* (Biddles).
Lewis, C. S. *Perelandra* (J. Lane) [rep. *Voyage to Venus* (Pan 1953)].
Russell, Eric Frank. *Sinister Barrier* (World's Work).
Todd, Ruthven. *The Lost Traveller* (Grey Walls).

GEN

[CX] "Garth." Cr. Steve Dowling. *Daily Mirror*, 24 Jul., through present.

1944

BIO

b. **Charles** (Nathaniel) **Platt**, 25 Oct., London.
b. **Terry Greenhough**, North Derbyshire.
b. **Peter Weston**.

*

d. C. J. Cutliffe Hyne, 10 Mar.
d. J. Storer Clouston, 23 Jun.
d. T. C. Bridges, Jun.
d. J. L. Palmer, 5 Aug.

FIC

Beresford, J. D. & Esmé Wynne-Tyson. *The Riddle of the Tower* (Hutchinson).
Collins, E. *Mariners of Space* (Lutterworth).
Gloag, John. *99%* (Cassell).
Gunn, Neil M. *The Green Isle of the Great Deep* (Faber).
Huxley, Aldous. *Time Must Have a Stop* (Harper; Chatto & W 1945).
Stapledon, Olaf. *Old Man in New World* [SS] (Allen & U).
---. *Sirius: A Fantasy of Love and Discord* (Secker & W).

BIO

b. **M**(ichael) **John Harrison**, 26 Jul., Rugby, Warwickshire.

*

d. Charles Williams, 15 May.
d. David Lindsay, 16 Jul.
d. E. R. Eddison, 18 Aug.

FIC

Harrison, Michael. *Higher Things* (Macdonald).
'Kavan, Anna.' *I Am Lazarus* [SS] (Cape).
Koestler, Arthur. *Twilight Bar: An Escapade in Four Acts* [D] (Macmillan).
Lewis, C. S. *That Hideous Strength: A Modern Fairy-Tale for Grown-Ups* (J. Lane).
{'Orwell, George.' *Animal Farm: A Fairy Story* (Secker & W) [*F 1954].}
Wheatley, Dennis. *The Man Who Missed the War* (Hutchinson).
Wright, S. Fowler. *Justice, and The Rat* [SS] (Books of Today).
---. *The Witchfinder* [SS] (Books of Today).
--- (as Sydney Fowler). *The Adventure in the Blue Room* (Rich & Cowan).

GEN

[E] Wells, H. G. *Mind at the End of Its Tether* (Heinemann).

1946

BIO
- b. **Julian Barnes**, 19 Jan., Leicester.
- b. **John Gribbin**, 19 Mar., Maidstone, Kent.
- b. **Paul** (Charles William) **Davies**, 22 Apr., London.
- b. **Andrew M**(ichael) **Stephenson**, 8 Oct., Maracaibo, Venezuela.
- b. **Polly Toynbee**, 27 Dec., Isle of Wight.
- b. **Saul** (i.e. Philip M.) **Dunn**.
- b. **Peter Edwards**.
- b. **Jane Palmer**.

*

- d. E. Phillips Oppenheim, 3 Feb.
- d. H. G. Wells, 13 Aug.

FIC

Arnold, Frank Edward. *Wings Across Time* [SS] (Pendulum).
Ashton, Francis. *The Breaking of the Seals* (Dakers).
Chetwynd, Bridget. *Future Imperfect* (Hutchinson).
Gloag, John. *First One and Twenty* [SS] (Allen & U).
Mottram, R. H. *The Visit of the Princess* (Hutchinson).
{Peake, Mervyn. *Titus Groan* (Eyre & S).}
Pragnell, Festus. *The Terror from Timorkal* (Bear, Hudson).
Southwold, Stephen (as 'Neil Bell'). *Alpha and Omega* [SS] (Hale).
--- (as 'Neil Bell'). *Life Comes to Seathorpe* (Eyre & S).
Stapledon, Olaf. *Death Into Life* (Methuen).
'Trevor, Elleston.' *The Immortal Error* (Swan).

GEN

[FAN] Arthur C. Clarke elected chairman of B.I.S., through 1947; also 1950-52.
[FAN] White Horse Tavern circle begin meetings: Frank Edward Arnold, Arthur C. Clarke, William F. Temple, John Wyndham, et al.

[FP] Clarke, Arthur C. "Loophole." *ASF* (Apr.).

[PUB] *New Worlds*, 1st ed. E. J. Carnell, Jul., through Sep. 1979 (216 issues in several formats).
[PUB] *Fantasy: The Magazine of Science Fiction*, ed. Walter Gillings, Dec., through Aug. 1947 (3 issues).
[PUB] *Outlands*, ed. Leslie J. Johnson, Winter (1 issue).

1947

BIO

b. **Stuart** (i.e. Richard) **Gordon**, 18 May, Banff, Scotland.
b. **David S. Garnett**, 15 Jun., Cheshire.
b. (Ahmed) **Salman Rushdie**, 19 Jun., Bombay, India.
b. **Tanith Lee**, 19 Sep., London.
b. **John Brosnan**, Australia.
b. **Michael Butterworth**, Yorkshire.
b. **James Corley**.

*

d. J. D. Beresford, 2 Feb.
d. M. P. Shiel, 14 Feb.
d. E. Charles Vivian, 21 May.
d. 'J. J. Connington,' 1 Jul.
d. 'Arthur Machen,' 15 Dec.

FIC

Heard, H. F. (as Gerald Heard). *Doppelgangers: An Episode of the Fourth, the Psychological, Revolution, 1997* (Vanguard; Cassell 1948).
---. *The Great Fog* [SS] (Cassell).
'Kavan, Anna.' *House of Sleep* (Doubleday) [rep. *Sleep Has His House* (Cassell 1948)].
Nott, Kathleen. *The Dry Deluge* (Hogarth).
Stacpoole, H. de Vere. *The Story of My Village* (Hutchinson).
Staniland, Meaburn. *Back to the Future* (Vane).
Stapledon, Olaf. *The Flames: A Fantasy* (Secker & W).

GEN

[FAN] *Fantasy Review* (later *Science*-), ed. Walter Gillings, Feb., to 1950 (18 issues).

[FP] Rayer, F(rancis) G. "Basic Fundamental." *Fantasy* (Aug.).

1948

BIO

b. **Terry Pratchett**, Apr., Buckinghamshire.
b. **Brian M**(ichael) **Stableford**, 25 Jul., Shipley, Yorkshire.
b. **Robert Holdstock**, 2 Aug., Hythe, Kent.
b. **Snoo Wilson**, 2 Aug., Reading, Berkshire.
b. **Mike** (i.e. Michael Raymond Donald) **Ashley**, Oct., Southall, Middlesex.
b. **Zoë** (Ann) **Fairbairns**, 20 Dec., Tunbridge Wells, Kent.
b. **Richard Doyle**, Channel Isles.
b. **Richard Gill**, Oxford.
b. **John Robert King**.

FIC

Ashton, Francis. *Alas, That Great City* (Dakers).
Colvin, Ian. *Domesday Village* (Falcon).
Farjeon, J. Jefferson. *Death of a World* (Collins).
Gibbs, Henry. *Pawns in Ice* (Jarrolds).
Groom, Pelham. *The Purple Twilight* (Werner Laurie).
Heard, H. F. *The Lost Cavern* [SS] (*Vanguard*; Cassell 1949).
Huxley, Aldous. *Ape and Essence* (*Harper*; Chatto & W 1949).
Newman, Bernard. *The Flying Saucer* (Gollancz).
Parkman, S. *Life Begins Tomorrow* (Hodder & S).
'Sava, George' (as 'George Borodin'). *Spurious Sun* (Werner Laurie).
Shiel, M. P. [P]. *The Best Short Stories of M. P. Shiel* [SS] (Gollancz).
Shute, Nevil. *No Highway* (Heinemann).
Wallis, George C. *The Call of Peter Gaskell* (World's Work).

GEN

[FAN] Science Fantasy Society founded, through 1951.
[FAN] *Slant*, ed. Walter A. Willis, Nov., through Winter 1952/3 (7 issues).

[FP] Phillips, Peter. "Dreams Are Sacred." <u>ASF</u> (Sep.).

1949

BIO

b. **Adrian** (Christopher Synnot) **Cole**, 22 Jul., Plymouth, Devon.
b. **Martin** (Louis) **Amis**, 25 Aug., Oxford.
b. **Peter Ackroyd**, 5 Oct., London.

*

d. Hugh Kingsmill, 15 May.
d. Francis Hernaman-Johnson, 3 Sep.
d. 'Lester Lurgan,' 29 Nov.
d. J. W. Dunne.
d. Horace Horsnell.

FIC

Dahl, Roald. *Sometime-Never: A Fable for Supermen* (Collins).
Desmond, Hugh. *The Terrible Awakening* (Wright & Brown).
Graves, Robert. *Seven Days in New Crete* (Cassell) [US *Watch the North Wind Rise*].
Hyams, Edward. *Not in Our Stars* (Longmans, Green).
Jameson, Storm. *The Moment of Truth* (Macmillan).
Kneale, Nigel. *Tomato Cain* [SS] (Collins).
'Orwell, George.' *Nineteen Eighty-Four* (Secker & W) [*TV 1954; F 1955, *1984].
Phillpotts, Eden. *Address Unknown* (Hutchinson).
Stapledon, Olaf. *Words of Wonder* [O] (*Fantasy*).
Temple, William F. *The Four-Sided Triangle* (J. Long) [*F 1953].
West, Anthony. *On a Dark Night* (Eyre & S).

FTV

[F] *The Perfect Woman*. Dir. Bernard Knowles. Two Cities/ Eagle-Lion. Wr. George & Alfred Black, from play by Wallace Geoffrey and Basil Mitchell.

GEN

[FAN] *Outlaw's Own*, ed. Michael Moorcock, *ca.* 1949/50.

[FP] 'Christopher, John' (as Christopher Youd). "Christmas Tree." *ASF* (Feb.).
[FP] Clark, Ronald. "The Man Who Went Back." *London Evening Standard*.

[PUB] E. J. Carnell sets up Nova Publications.

BIO

d. 'George Orwell,' 21 Jan.
d. Max Pemberton, 22 Feb.
d. Harold E. Gorst, 13 Aug.
d. Olaf Stapledon, 6 Sep.
d. George Bernard Shaw, 2 Nov.

FIC

Barfield, Owen (as 'G. A. L. Burgeon'). *This Ever Diverse Pair* (Gollancz).
Capon, Paul. *The Other Side of the Sun* (Heinemann).
Heard, H. F. *The Black Fox* (Cassell).
Hyams, Edward. *The Astrologer* (Longmans, Green).
{Lewis, C. S. *The Lion, the Witch and the Wardrobe* (Bles).}
{Peake, Mervyn. *Gormenghast* (Eyre & S).}
Stapledon, Olaf. *A Man Divided* (Methuen).

GEN

[CX] "Dan Dare--Pilot of the Future." Cr. Frank Hampson. *Eagle*, 14 Apr., through 1969 (later revived).

[E] Hoyle, Fred. *The Nature of the Universe* (Blackwell).
[E] Low, A. M. *It's Bound to Happen* (Burke) [US *What's the World Coming To?* 1951)].

[FP] McIntosh, J. T. "The Curfew Tolls." *ASF* (Dec.).

[PUB] *Science Fantasy*, 1st. ed. Walter Gillings, Summer, through Feb. 1966 (81 Issues).
[PUB] *Futuristic Science Stories*, ed. John Spencer & Co., Aug., through Apr. 1954 (15 issues).

BIO

b. **Michael Scott Rohan**, Edinburgh, Scotland.
b. **Geoff Ryman**, Canada.

*

d. H. de Vere Stacpoole, 12 Apr.
d. Hilary St. G. Saunders, 16 Dec.
d. Douglas Newton.

FIC

Clarke, Arthur C. *Prelude to Space* (World; rev. Sidgwick & J 1953) [rep. *Master of Space* (Lancer 1961); rep. *The Space Dreamers* (Lancer 1969)].
---. *The Sands of Mars* (Sidgwick & J).
Collier, John. *Fancies and Goodnights* [SS] (Doubleday) [abr. *Of Demons and Darkness* (Corgi 1965)].
Dunsany, Lord. *The Last Revolution* (Jarrolds).
Fraser, Ronald. *Beetle's Career* (Cape).
'Gibbs, Lewis.' *Late Final* (Dent).
'Hawton, Hector.' *Operation Superman* (Ward Lock).
Hay, George. *This Planet for Sale* (Hamilton).
Hyams, Edward. *Sylvester* (Longmans, Green) [US *998*].
Koestler, Arthur. *The Age of Longing* (Collins).
Norwood, Victor. *The Untamed* (Scion).
---. **7+ other novels, through 1962.**
Rayer, Francis G. *Tomorrow Sometimes Comes* (Home & Van Thal).
---. **several other novels, through 1967.**
Russell, Eric Frank. *Dreadful Sanctuary* (Fantasy; Museum 1951) [rev. NEL 1967].
Ryves, T. E. *Bandersnatch* (Gray Walls).
'Sarban.' *Ringstones* [SS] (P. Davies).
Slater, Henry J. *Ship of Destiny* (Jarrolds).
Tubb, E. C. (as 'Gill Hunt'). *Planetfall* (Curtis).
--- (as 'King Lang'). *Saturn Patrol* (Curtis).
---. **60+ other novels as ECT, 5 as 'Volsted Gridban,' 8 as 'Charles Grey,' 18 as 'Gregory Kern,' 3 as 'Edward Thomas,' through 1983.**
West, Anthony. *Another Kind* (Eyre & S).
Wyndham, John. *The Day of the Triffids* (Joseph).

FTV

[F] *The Man in the White Suit*. Dir. Alexander Mackendrick. Ealing. Wr. Roger MacDougall, John Dighton & Alexander Mackendrick, from play by Roger MacDougall.

GEN

[E] Clarke, Arthur C. *The Exploration of Space* (Temple).

[FP] Tubb, E. C. "No Short Cuts." *New Worlds* (Jun.).
[FP] Brunner, John (as 'Gill Hunt'). *Galactic Storm* (Curtis Warren).
[FP] Cooper, Edmund. "The Unicorn." *Everybody's*.

GEN

[PUB] *Authentic Science Fiction* [with title variations], 1st. ed. 'L. G. Holmes' (Gordon Landsborough), Jan., through Oct. 1957 (85 issues in various formats).

[PUB] E. J. Carnell ed. of *Science Fantasy*, Winter, through Apr. 1964.

1952

BIO

b. **Gwyneth** (Ann) **Jones**, 14 Feb., Manchester.
b. **Douglas** (Noel) **Adams**, 11 Mar., Cambridge.
b. **Clive Barker**, Liverpool.

*

d. Norman Douglas, 9 Feb.
d. J. M. Walsh, 29 Aug.
d. Gilbert Frankau, 4 Nov.
d. Cicely Hamilton, 5/6 Dec.
d. C. C. Turner.

FIC

Ashton, Francis & Stephen Ashton. *The Wrong Side of the Moon* (Boardman).
Berry, Bryan. *And the Stars Remain* (Panther).
---. **8 other novels as BB and 'Rolf Garner,' through 1955.**
Bulmer, Kenneth (with A. V. Clarke). *Space Treason* (Panther).
---. **40+ other novels as KB, 30+ as 'Alan Burt Akers,' 4 as 'Tully Zetford,' 4 as 'Philip Kent,' 3 as 'Manning Norvil,' et al., through present.**
Capon, Paul. *The Other Half of the Planet* (Heinemann).
Clarke, Arthur C. *Islands in the Sky* (Sidgwick & J).
Doyle, Sir Arthur Conan [P]. *The Complete Professor Challenger Stories* [O] (Murray).
Duncan, Ronald. *The Last Adam* (Dobson).
Hay, George. *Flight of the "Hesper"* (Hamilton).
{Moore, Patrick. *Master of the Moon* (Museum).}
---. ***ca.* 15 other juveniles, through 1964.**
Niall, Ian. *The Boy Who Saw Tomorrow* (Heinemann).
'Sarban.' *The Sound of His Horn* (P. Davies).
Slater, Henry J. *The Smashed World* (Jarrolds).
'Trevor, Elleston' (as 'Warwick Scott'). *Domesday Story* (Davies) [rep. *Doomsday* (Lion 1953)].
Wheatley, Dennis. *Star of Ill-Omen* (Hutchinson).

GEN

[A] Carnell, John, ed. *No Place Like Earth* (Boardman).

[C] Morton, A. L. *The English Utopia* (Laurence & Wishart).

[FAN] *Hyphen*, 1st. ed. Walter A. Willis, through 1965.

[FP] Morgan, Dan. "Alien Analysis." *New Worlds* (Jan.).
[FP] Wright, Lan. "Operation Exodus." *New Worlds* (Jan.).
[FP] Fanthorpe, R. L. (as 'Lionel Roberts'). "Worlds without End." *Futuristic Science Fiction* (Apr.).
[FP] 'Maine, Charles Eric.' "Spaceways" [BBC Radio Play].

1952 (cont.)

GEN

[PUB] *Nebula Science Fiction*, 1st. ed. Peter Hamilton Jr., Autumn, through Jun. 1959 (41 Issues).
[PUB] H. J. Campbell ed. of *Authentic Science Fiction*, Dec., through Jan. 1956.

[W] *The Exploration of Space* (Arthur C. Clarke): 2nd. International Fantasy Non-Fiction.
[W] *Fancies and Goodnights* (John Collier): 2nd. International Fantasy fiction.

1953

BIO
    b. **David Langford**, 10 Apr., Newport, Wales.
    b. **Sarah Lefanu**.

                        *

    d. Joseph O'Neill, 2 May.
    d. 'Edward Shanks,' 4 May.
    d. Hilaire Belloc, 16 Jul.
    d. 'Martin Swayne,' 30 Aug.

FIC
    Campbell, H. J. *Another Space, Another Time* (Hamilton).
    ---. **Several other sf adventure novels, through 1954.**
    Clarke, Arthur C. *Against the Fall of Night* (Gnome) [rev. *The City and the Stars*, see 1956 entry].
    ---. *Childhood's End* (Ballantine; Sidgwick & J 1954).
    ---. *Expedition to Earth* [SS] (Ballantine; Sidgwick & J 1954).
    Desmond, Hugh. *Fear Rides the Air* (Wright Brown).
    Frankau. Gilbert [P]. *Unborn Tomorrow* (Macdonald).
    Harrison, Michael. *The Brain* (Cassell).
    Heard, H. F. *Wishing Well: An Outline of the Evolution of the Mammals, Told as a Series of Stories* (Faber).
    Kersh, Gerald. *The Great Wash* (Heinemann).
    'Maine, Charles Eric.' *Spaceways* (Hodder & S) [*F 1953] [US *Spaceways Satellite* 1958].
    'McIntosh, J. T.' *World out of Mind* (Doubleday; Museum 1955).
    Priestley, J. B. *The Other Place* [SS] (Heinemann).
    Russell, Bertrand. *Satan in the Suburbs* [SS] (Bodley Head).
    Russell, Eric Frank. *Sentinels from Space* (Bouregy; Museum 1954).
    'Sarban.' *The Doll Maker* [SS] (Davies).
    Shute, Nevil. *In the Wet* (Heinemann).
    Stanford, J. K. *Full Moon at Sweatenham: A Nightmare* (Faber).
    Stapledon, Olaf [P]. *To the End of Time: The Best of Olaf Stapledon* [O] (Funk & Wagnalls).
    Waugh, Evelyn. *Love Among the Ruins* (Chapman & H).
    Wyndham, John. *The Kraken Wakes* (Joseph) [US *Out of the Deeps*].

FTV
    [F] *Four-Sided Triangle*. Dir. Terence Fisher. Hammer. Wr. Paul Tabori & Terence Fisher, from *novel (1949) by William F. Temple.
    [F] *Spaceways*. Dir. Terence Fisher. Hammer. Wr. Paul Tabori & Richard Landau, from radio play (1952) by Charles Eric Maine, *nov. 1953.

    [R] *Journey Into Space*, Wr. & Prod. Charles Chilton, BBC radio, 54 episodes, through 1955.

1953(cont.)

FTV

    [TV] *The Quatermass Experiment.* Prod. Rudolph Cartier. BBC miniseries, 6x35 mins. Wr. Nigel Kneale [*F 1955; *D 1959].

GEN

    [FP] White, James. "Assisted Passage." *New Worlds* (Jan.).
    [FP] 'Sellings, Arthur.' "The Haunting." *Authentic Science Fiction* (Oct.).

1954

BIO

b. **Iain M**(enzies) **Banks**, 16 Feb., Fife, Scotland.
b. **Colin Greenland**, 17 May, Dover, Kent.
b. **David** (John) **Wingrove**, 1 Sep., London.

*

d. James Hilton, 20 Dec.

FIC

Bennett, Margot. *The Long Way Back* (Bodley Head).
Burke, John Frederick. *The Echoing Worlds* (Panther).
---. **10+ other novels, through 1965.**
Capon, Paul. *Down to Earth* (Heinemann).
Carr, Charles. *Colonists of Space* (Ward Lock).
Castle, Jeffery Lloyd. *Satellite E One* (Eyre & S).
Chilton, Charles. *Journey into Space* (Jenkins).
---. **2 other vols. in 'Jet Morgan' trilogy, through 1960.**
'Christopher, John.' *The Twenty-Second Century* [SS] (Grayson).
'Crane, Robert.' *Hero's Walk* (Cresset).
Crowcroft, Peter. *The Fallen Sky* (P. Nevill).
'Dexter, William.' *World in Eclipse* (P. Owen).
Fanthorpe, R. L. *Menace from Mercury* (Spencer).
---. **160+ other novels and short story collections as RLF, 'Lionel Roberts,' 'Leo Brett,' 'Bron Fane,' 'Pel Torro,' 'John E. Muller,' 'Karl Zeigfried,' et al., through 1965.**
Golding, William. *Lord of the Flies* (Faber) [*F 1963].
'Gordon, Rex.' *Utopia 239* (Heinemann).
{Johns, Capt. W. E. *Kings of Space* (Hodder & S).}
---. **8 other juveniles, through 1963.**
MacKenzie, Nigel. *Invasion from Space* (Wright & Brown).
---. **ca. 6 others, through 1960.**
'McIntosh, J. T.' *Born Leader* (Doubleday; Museum 1955) [US rep. *Worlds Apart* 1958].
---. *One in Three Hundred* (Doubleday; Museum 1956).
'Merak, A. J.' *Dark Andromeda* (Hamilton).
---. **ca. 7 others, also as 'J. L. Powers' and 'Rand Le Page,' through 1971.**
Newman, Bernard. *The Wishful Think* (Hale).
Priestley, J. B. *Low Notes on a High Level: A Frolic* (Heinemann).
---. *The Magicians* (Heinemann).
'Rackham, John.' *Jupiter Equilateral* (Pearson).
---. *The Master Weed* (Pearson).
---. *Space Puppet* (Pearson).
---. **16+ more novels as JR and 4 as John T. Phillifent, through 1973.**
Russell, Bertrand. *Nightmares of Eminent Persons* [SS] (J. Lane).
Russell, Eric Frank. *Deep Space* [SS] (*Fantasy*; Eyre & S 1956).
{Tolkien, J. R. R. *The Fellowship of the Ring* (Allen & U).}

1954 (cont.)

FIC

{Tolkien, J. R. R. *The Two Towers* (Allen & U).}
Wilding, Philip. *Spaceflight--Venus* (Hennel Locke).
Wright, S. Fowler. *Spiders' War* (Abelard).
Wyndham, John. *Jizzle* [SS] (Dobson).

FTV

[F] *Animal Farm* (animated). Dir. John Halas & Joy Bachelor. Wr. Lothar Wolff et al., from *novel (1945) by 'George Orwell.'

[TV] *Nineteen Eighty-Four*. Wr. Nigel Kneale, from *novel (1949) by 'George Orwell.'

GEN

[A] Carnell, John, ed. *Gateway to Tomorrow* (Museum).

[CX] "Jeff Hawke." Cr. Eric Souster & Sydney Jordan. *(Junior) Daily Express*, 15 Feb., through 1974.

[E] Stapledon, Olaf [P]. *The Opening of the Eyes* (Methuen).

[FAN] Offtrail Magazine Publishers' Association [OMPA] founded by Kenneth Bulmer, Vincent Clarke & Chuck Harris.

[FP] Bayley, Barrington J. "Combat's End." *Vargo Statten Science Fiction Magazine* (May).
[FP] Aldiss, Brian W. "Criminal Record." *Science Fantasy* (Jul.).
[FP] Shaw, Bob. "Aspect." *Nebula* (Aug.).
[FP] 'Kippax, John.' "Dimple." *Science Fantasy* (Dec.).

[PUB] *Space Fact and Fiction*, Anon. ed., Mar., through Oct. 1954 (8 issues).
[PUB] *Vargo Statten Science Fiction Magazine* (later *British Science Fiction Magazine*; later *British Space Fiction Magazine*), 1st. ed. Alastair Paterson, Jan., through Feb. 1956 (19 issues).

1955

BIO

b. **Paul J. McAuley**, 23 Apr., Stroud, Gloucestershire.
b. **Jen Green.**

*

d. J. Jefferson Farjeon, 6 Jun.
d. Bryan Berry.

FIC

Adams, W. S. *The Fourth Programme* (Lawrence & Wishart).
Ash, Alan. *Conditioned for Space* (Ward Lock).
Atkins, John. *Tomorrow Revealed* (Spearman).
'Barr, Densil Neve.' *The Man with Only One Head* (Rich & Cowan).
Boland, John. *White August* (Joseph).
Bounds, Sydney J. *The Moon Raiders* (Foulsham).
---. **2 others, through 1964.**
Brown, Alec. *Angelo's Moon* (J. Lane).
Carr, Charles. *Salamander War* (Ward Lock).
'Christopher, John.' *The Year of the Comet* (Joseph) [US *Planet in Peril* 1959].
Churchill, R. C. *A Short History of the Future* (Werner Laurie).
Clarke, Arthur C. *Earthlight* (Muller).
Conquest, Robert. *A World of Difference: A Modern Novel of Science and Imagination* (Ward Lock).
'Dexter, William.' *Children of the Void* (P. Owen).
Golding, William. *The Inheritors* (Faber).
Kee, Robert. *A Sign of the Times* (Eyre & S).
Lewis, P. Wyndham. *The Human Age; Monstre Gai; Malign Fiesta* [O] (Methuen).
'Maine, Charles Eric.' *Timeliner* (Hodder & S).
Marsh, John (as 'John Elton'). *The Green Plantations* (Ward Lock).
'McIntosh, J. T.' *The Fittest* (Doubleday; Corgi 1961) [US *The Rule of the Pagbeasts*].
Mead, Harold. *The Bright Phoenix* (Joseph).
Morgan, Dan. *Cee Tee Man* (Panther).
'Savage, Richard.' *When the Moon Died* (Ward Lock).
Sieveking, Lance. *A Private Volcano* (Ward Lock).
Spencer, G. F. *Heavens for All* (Mitre).
{Tolkien, J. R. R. *The Return of the King* (Allen & U).}
Wilding, Philip (as 'John Robert Haynes'). *Scream from Outer Space* (Rich & Cowan).
Wilkins, Vaughan. *Valley Beyond Time* (Cape).
Wyndham, John. *The Chrysalids* (Joseph) [US *Re-Birth*].

FTV

[F] *1984*. Dir. Michael Anderson. Holiday. Wr. William F. Templeton & Ralph Bettinson, from novel *Nineteen Eighty-Four* (1949) by 'George Orwell.'
[F] *The Quatermass Xperiment* (US *The Creeping Unknown*). Dir. Val Guest. Hammer. Wr. Richard Landau & Val Guest, from *TV (1953) by Nigel Kneale.

1955 (cont.)

FTV

[F] *Timeslip*. Dir. Ken Hughes. Anglo-Guild/Amalgamated. Wr. Charles Eric Maine, nov. as *The Isotope Man (1957).

[TV] *Quatermass II*. Prod. Rudolph Cartier. BBC miniseries, 6x35 mins. Wr. Nigel Kneale [*F 1957; *D 1960].

GEN

[A] Carnell, John, ed. *The Best from New Worlds Science Fiction* (Boardman).
[A] ---, ed. *Gateway to the Stars* (Museum).
[A] 'Crispin, Edmund,' ed. *Best SF* (Faber).
---. **6 more annual vols., through 1970.**
[A] Wilson, Angus, ed. *AD 2500* [*Observer* prize stories 1954] (Heinemann).

[C] Gerber, Richard. *Utopian Fantasy: A Study of English Utopian Fiction Since the End of the Nineteenth Century* (Routledge).

[FP] High, Philip E. "The Statics." *Authentic Science Fiction* (Sep.).

[W] "Allamagoosa" (Eric Frank Russell): 2nd. Hugo short story, US.

1956

BIO

b. **Mary Gentle**, 29 Mar., Eastbourne, Sussex.

*

d. 'Michael Arlen,' 23 Jun.
d. A. M. Low, 13 Sep.
d. 'Hugh Addison,' 15 Sep.
d. George C. Wallis, Sep.

FIC

Boland, John. *No Refuge* (Joseph).
Capon, Paul. *Into the Tenth Millennium* (Heinemann).
'Christopher, John.' *The Death of Grass* (Joseph) [US *No Blade of Grass* 1957] [F 1970].
Clarke, Arthur C. *The City and the Stars* (Muller).
---. *Reach for Tomorrow* [SS] (*Ballantine*; Gollancz 1962).
Creasey, John. *The Flood* (Hodder & S).
---. **Several other sf thrillers, through 1973.**
'Gordon, Rex.' *No Man Friday* (Heinemann) [US *First on Mars* 1957].
--- (as Stanley B. Hough). *Extinction Bomber* (Bodley Head).
Hingley, Ronald. *Up, Jenkins!* (Longman).
Large, E. C. *Dawn in Andromeda* (Cape).
Lewis, C. S. "The Shoddy Lands." *FSF* (Feb.)
Lott, S. Makepeace. *Escape to Venus* (Rich & Cowan).
Low, A. M. *Satellite in Space* (Jenkins).
MacLaren, Bernard. *The Day of Misjudgement* (Gollancz).
'Maine, Charles Eric.' *Crisis 2000* (Hodder & S).
---. *Escapement* (Hodder & S) [US *The Man Who Couldn't Sleep*].
Russell, Eric Frank. *Men, Martians and Machines* [SS] (Dobson).
---. *Three To Conquer* (Avalon; Dobson 1957).
'Sellings, Arthur.' *Time Transfer* [SS] (Joseph).
Waller, Robert. *Shadow of Authority* (Cape).
Walter, W. Grey. *Further Outlook* (Duckworth) [US *The Curve of the Snowflake*].
Wilding, Philip. *Shadow over the Earth* (Hennel Locke).
Wyndham, John. *The Seeds of Time* [SS] (Joseph).
---. *Tales of Gooseflesh and Laughter* [SS] (*Ballantine*).

FTV

[F] *X The Unknown*. Dir. Leslie Norman. Hammer/Exclusive. Wr. Jimmy Sangster.

[TV] *The Creature*. Prod. & Wr. Rudolph Cartier & Nigel Kneale. BBC.

GEN

[A] Anon. ed. *Sometime, Never* [Golding/Peake/Wyndham] (Eyre & S).

1956(cont.)

GEN

[FP] Ballard, J. G. "Prima Belladonna." *Science Fantasy* (Dec.).
--- . "Escapement." *New Worlds* (Dec.).

[W] "The Star" (Arthur C. Clarke): 3rd. Hugo short story, US.

1957

BIO

d. P. Wyndham Lewis, 7 Mar.
d. Ronald A. Knox, 24 Aug.
d. Lord Dunsany, 25 Oct.

FIC

Aldiss, Brian. *Space, Time and Nathaniel: Presciences* [SS] (Faber) [US abr. *No Time Like Tomorrow* 1959].
Barlow, James. *One Half of the World* (Cassell).
Castle, Jeffery Lloyd. *Vanguard to Venus* (Dodd Mead).
Clarke, Arthur C. *The Deep Range* (Muller).
---. *Tales from the White Hart* [SS] (Ballantine; Sidgwick & J 1972).
Hoyle, Fred. *The Black Cloud* (Heinemann).
'Maine, Charles Eric.' *High Vacuum* (Hodder & S).
---. *The Isotope Man* (Hodder & S) [*F 1955].
Mead, Harold. *Mary's Country* (Joseph).
Powys, John Cowper. *Up and Out* (Macdonald).
Ray, René. *The Strange World of Planet X* (Jenkins) [*F 1958].
Russell, Eric Frank. *Wasp* (Avalon; Dobson 1958).
Shute, Nevil. *On the Beach* (Heinemann) [F 1959].
Sisson, Marjorie. *The Cave* (Vine).
'Trevor, Elleston.' *The Pillars of Midnight* (Heinemann).
White, James. *The Secret Visitors* (Ace; Digit 1961).
Wright, Lan. *Who Speaks of Conquest?* (Ace; Digit 1963).
---. **6 other novels, through 1968.**
Wyndham, John. *The Midwich Cuckoos* (Joseph) [US rep. *Village of the Damned* 1960] [F *Village of the Damned* 1960; *Children of the Damned* 1963].

FTV

[F] *The Invisible Boy*. Dir. Herman Hoffman. Pan/MGM. Wr. Cyril Hume, from story by Edmund Cooper.
[F] *Quatermass II* (US *Enemy from Space*). Dir. Val Guest. Hammer/UA. Wr. Nigel Kneale & Val Guest, from *T.V. series (1955) by Nigel Kneale.

GEN

[E] Moore, Patrick. *Science and Fiction* (Harrap).

[FAN] Worldcon, London (Loncon I).
[FAN] Michael Moorcock ed. *Tarzan Adventures*, through 1958.

[FP] Bowen, John (as 'Justin Blake'). "Living? Try Death!" *Science Fantasy* (Jun.).
[FP] Moorcock, Michael. "Sojan the Swordsman." *Tarzan Adventures* 7 No. 22 (31 Aug.).
[FP] Locke, George. "The Human Seed." *Authentic Science Fiction* (Oct.).

[PUB] Brian Aldiss literary ed. of the *Oxford Mail*, through 1969.

GEN

[PUB] 'John Christopher' paid *ca.* $80,000 for serialization of *No Blade of Grass* in *Saturday Evening Post*.

[W] *Lord of the Rings* (J. R. R. Tolkien): 6th. International Fantasy Award.

1958

BIO

d. T. C. Wignall, 22 Mar.
d. Alfred Noyes, 28 Jun.
d. Rose Macaulay, 30 Oct.
d. J. C. Squire.

FIC

Aldiss, Brian. *Non-Stop* (Faber) [US *Starship* 1959].
---. *Equator* (Digit) [US *Vanguard from Alpha*].
Blackburn, John F. *A Scent of New-Mown Hay* (Secker & W).
Bowen, John. *After the Rain* (Faber) [rev. *After the Rain: A Play in Three Acts* [D] (Faber 1967)].
Clarke, Arthur C. *The Other Side of the Sky* [SS] (Harcourt; Gollancz 1961).
Cooper, Edmund. *Tomorrow's Gift* [SS] (*Ballantine*).
---. *The Uncertain Midnight* (Hutchinson) [US *Deadly Image*].
Fraser, Ronald. *Jupiter in the Chair* (Cape).
---. *A Visit from Venus* (Cape).
George, Peter (as 'Peter Bryant'). *Two Hours to Doom* (Boardman) [US *Red Alert* 1959] [rev. *Dr. Strangelove; or, How I Learned to Stop Worrying and Love the Bomb* (Corgi 1963)] [rep. *Gregg* 1979] [*F 1963].
Golding, William. *The Brass Butterfly* [D] (Faber).
Jones, Mervyn. *On the Last Day* (Cape).
Kersh, Gerald. *On an Odd Note* [SS] (*Ballantine*).
Leslie, Desmond. *The Amazing Mr. Lutterworth* (Wingate).
Lewis, C. S. "Ministering Angels." *FSF* (Jan.).
MacLeod, Angus. *The Body's Guest* (*Roy*).
'Maine, Charles Eric.' *The Tide Went Out* (Hodder & S) [rev. *Thirst* (Sphere 1977)].
---. *World Without Men* (Ace; Digit 1963) [US rev. *Alph* 1972].
Manvell, Roger. *The Dreamers* (Gollancz).
Phelps, Gilbert. *The Centenarians* (Heinemann).
Russell, Eric Frank. *Six Worlds Yonder* [SS] (Ace).
---. *The Space Willies* (Ace) [rev. *Next of Kin* (Dobson 1959)].
Shute, Nevil. *The Rainbow and the Rose* (Heinemann).
Tonks, Angela. *Mind out of Time* (Gollancz).
'Wallace, Doreen.' *Forty Years On* (Collins).
{White, T. H. *The Once and Future King* (Collins) [US *Camelot*].}

FTV

[F] *Fiend Without a Face*. Dir. Arthur Crabtree. Amalgamated/MGM. Wr. Herbert J. Leder, from short story "The Thought-Monster" by Amelia Reynolds Long.
[F] *First Man Into Space*. Dir. Robert Day. Producers/MGM. Wr. John C. Cooper & Lance Z. Hargreaves, from story by Wyott Ordung.

1958 (cont.)

FTV
- [F] *The Strange World of Planet X* (US *The Cosmic Monster*). Dir. Gilbert Gunn. Eros/DCA. Wr. Paul Ryder & Joe Ambor, from *novel (1957) by René Ray.
- [F] *The Trollenberg Terror* (US *The Crawling Eye*). Dir. Quentin Lawrence. Wr. Jimmy Sangster, from T.V. series by Peter Kay.

- [TV] *Quatermass and the Pit*. Prod. Rudolph Cartier. BBC miniseries, 6x35 mins. Wr. Nigel Kneale [*D 1960; *F 1968].

GEN
- [C] Green, Roger Lancelyn. *Into Other Worlds: Spaceflight in Fiction, from Lucian to Lewis* (Abelard) [rep. Arno 1975].

- [E] Huxley, Aldous. *Brave New World Revisited* (Harper; Chatto & W 1959).
- [E] Young, Michael. *The Rise of the Meritocracy 1870-2033: An Essay on Education and Equality* (Thames & Hudson).

- [FAN] BSFA founded, Eastercon, 4-7 Apr., Kettering.
- [FAN] *Vector* [organ of BSFA], 1st. ed. E. C. Tubb, Summer, through present.
- [FAN] *Science Fiction Adventures*, ed. E. J. Carnell, Mar., through May 1963 (32 issues).

- [FP] Malcolm, Donald. "Lone Voyager." *Nebula Science Fiction* (May).
- [FP] Kapp, Colin. "Life Plan." *New Worlds* (Nov.).

1959

BIO

   b. **Marcus Chown**, London.
   b. **Pete Davies**.
   b. **Kim Newman**, London.

                            *

   d. 'Sax Rohmer,' 1 Jun.
   d. Lady Dorothy Mills, 4 Dec.
   d. Vaughan Wilkins.

FIC

   Aldiss, Brian. *The Canopy of Time* [SS] (Faber) [US rev. *Galaxies Like Grains of Sand* 1960].
   Barr, Tyrone C. *Split Worlds* (Digit).
   Brunner, John. *The Brink* (Gollancz).
   ---. *Echo in the Skull* (Ace) [enl. *Give Warning to the World* (DAW 1974)].
   ---. *The Hundredth Millennium* (Ace) [enl. *Catch a Falling Star* (Ace 1968)].
   ---. *Threshold of Eternity* (Ace).
   ---. *The World Swappers* (Ace).
   Clarke, Arthur C. *Across the Sea of Stars* [O] (Harcourt).
   Cooper, Edmund. *Seed of Light* (Hutchinson).
   Crisp, Frank. *The Ape of London* (Hodder & S).
   'Gordon, Rex.' *First to the Stars* (Ace; Consul 1961 as *The Worlds of Eclos*).
   Hawkes, Jacquetta. *Providence Island: An Archaeological Tale* (Chatto & W).
   Hodder-Williams, Christopher. *Chain Reaction* (Hodder & S).
   Hoyle, Fred. *Ossian's Ride* (Heinemann).
   Kneale, Nigel. *The Quatermass Experiment* [D] (Penguin).
   Laski, Marghanita. *The Offshore Island* [D] (Cresset).
   'Lymington, John.' *The Night of the Big Heat* (Hodder & S) [*F 1967].
   ---. **20+ other novels, through 1984.**
   Mackenzie, Compton. *The Lunatic Republic* (Chatto & W).
   'Maine, Charles Eric.' *Count-Down* (Hodder & S) [US *Fire Past the Future* 1960].
   ---. *Subterfuge* (Hodder & S).
   {Peake, Mervyn. *Titus Alone* (Eyre & S).}
   Wyndham, John (as 'with Lucas Parkes'). *The Outward Urge* (Joseph) [enl. Science Fiction Book Club 1960].

GEN

   [E] Clarke, Arthur C. *The Challenge of the Spaceship: Previews of Tomorrow's World* (Harper).

BIO
- b. **Eric Brown**, 24 May, Haworth, Yorkshire.
- b. **Ian McDonald**, Manchester.

*

- d. Nevil Shute, 12 Jan.
- d. E. Douglas Fawcett, 14 Apr.
- d. John Russell Fearn, 18 Sep.
- d. Shaw Desmond, 23 Dec.
- d. Eden Phillpotts, 29 Dec.

FIC

Aldiss, Brian. *Bow Down to Nul* (Ace; Digit 1961 as *The Interpreter*).
Brunner, John. *The Atlantic Abomination* (Ace).
---. *Sanctuary in the Sky* (Ace).
---. *The Skynappers* (Ace).
---. *Slavers of Space* (Ace) [rev. *Into the Slave Nebula* (Ace 1968); rep. Corgi 1982].
Cooper, Edmund. *Voices in the Dark* [SS] (Digit).
Crisp, Frank R. *The Night Callers* (Long).
Davies, Hugh Sykes. *The Papers of Andrew Melmoth* (Methuen).
Fraser, Ronald. *Trout's Testament* (Cape).
{Garner, Alan. *The Weirdstone of Brisingamen* (Collins).}
Hartley, L. P. *Facial Justice* (H. Hamilton).
Kneale, Nigel. *Quatermass II* [D] (Penguin).
---. *Quatermass and the Pit* [D] (Penguin).
Lawrence, H. L. *The Children of Light* (Macdonald) [*F *The Damned* 1961].
Lewis, Roy. *What We Did to Father* (Hutchinson) [rep. *The Evolution Man* (Penguin 1963)].
'Maine, Charles Eric.' *Calculated Risk* (Hodder & S).
---. *He Owned the World* (Avalon; Hodder & S 1961 as *The Man Who Owned the World*).
'Morel, Dighton.' *Moonlight Red* (Secker & W).
Powys, John Cowper. *All or Nothing* (Macdonald).
Sully, Kathleen M. *Skrine* (P. Davies).
'Trevor, Elleston.' *The Mind of Max Divine* (Swan).
Valentine, Victor. *Cure for Death* (Sidgwick & J).
Wyndham, John. *Trouble with Lichen* (Joseph).

FTV

[F] *Village of the Damned*. Dir. Wolf Rilla. MGM. Wr. Sterling Silliphant, Wolf Rilla & George Barclay, from novel *The Midwich Cuckoos* (1957) by John Wyndham.

GEN

[C] Amis, Kingsley. *New Maps of Hell: A Survey of Science Fiction* (Harcourt; Gollancz 1961).

[FP] Davies, L. P. (as 'Leslie Vardre'). "The Wall of Time." *London Mystery Magazine* (Jun.)

BIO
- d. Claude Houghton, 10 Feb.
- d. Geoffrey Faber, 31 Mar.
- d. Oliver Onions, 9 Apr.
- d. E. Arnot Robertson, 21 Sep.

FIC

Aldiss, Brian. *The Male Response* (Galaxy; Dobson 1963).
---. *The Primal Urge* (Ballantine; Sphere 1967).
Amis, Kingsley. "Something Strange." *FSF* (Jul.).
Brunner, John. *Meeting at Infinity* (Ace).
--- (as 'Keith Woodcott'). *I Speak for Earth* (Ace).
'Cameron, Ian.' *The Lost Ones* (Hutchinson) [US *The Island at the Top of the World*].
Clarke, Arthur C. *A Fall of Moondust* (Gollancz).
Gillon, Diana & Meir. *The Unsleep* (Barrie & Rockliff).
'Gordon, Rex' (as Stanley B. Hough). *Beyond the Eleventh Hour* (Hodder & S).
Hesky, Olga. *The Purple Armchair* (Blond).
'Johnson, L. P. V.' (P. V. LeRoy). *In the Time of the Thetans* (Macmillan).
'Maine, Charles Eric.' *The Mind of Mr. Soames* (Hodder & S).
'McIntosh, J. T.' *200 Years to Christmas* (Ace).
Morgan, Dan. *The Uninhibited* (Digit).
Pape, Richard. *And So Ends the World* (Elek).
Priestley, J. B. *The Thirty-First of June* (Heinemann).
Russell, Eric Frank. *Far Stars* [SS] (Dobson).
Tabori, Paul. *The Green Rain* (Pyramid).
'Wells, Barry' (Dick Richards). *The Day the Earth Caught Fire* (NEL) [*F 1961].
Wilson, Angus. *The Old Men at the Zoo* (Secker & W).
Wyndham, John. *Consider Her Ways* [SS] (Joseph).
---. *The Infinite Moment* [SS] (Ballantine).

FTV

[F] *The Damned* (US *These Are the Damned*). Dir. Joseph Losey. Hammer/Columbia. Wr. Evan Jones, from novel *The Children of Light* (1960) by H. L. Lawrence.
[F] *The Day the Earth Caught Fire*. Dir. Val Guest. British Lion/Pax/Universal. Wr. Wolf Mankowitz & Val Guest. *Nov. 'Barry Wells' (1961).
[F] *Gorgo*. Dir. Eugene Lourie. King/MGM. Wr. John Loring & Daniel Hyatt, from story by Eugene Lourie & Daniel Hyatt.

[TV] *A for Andromeda*. Prod. Michael Hayes & Norman Jones. BBC miniseries, 7x50 mins. Wr. & *nov. (1962) Fred Hoyle & John Elliot.

GEN

[A] Aldiss, Brian, ed. *Penguin Science Fiction* (Penguin).
---. **2 more vols., through 1964.**

GEN
- [A] Amis, Kingsley and Robert Conquest, eds. *Spectrum* (Gollancz).
  ---. **4 more vols., through 1966.**

- [C] Bergonzi, Bernard. *The Early H. G. Wells: A Study of the Scientific Romances* (Manchester UP).
- [C] Clarke, I. F. *Tale of the Future: From the Beginning to the Present Day* (Library Association) [rev. 1972, 1978].

4
New Wave S(peculative) F(iction): 1962-1978

This chapter covers the period known as the 'New Wave, when the abbreviation SF, sometimes decoded as 'speculative fiction,' began to replace the use of 'science fiction' in Britain. Though its starting-point is often associated with the assumption of the editorship of *New Worlds* by Michael Moorcock in 1964, the real beginning of this era is the publication of J. G. Ballard's *The Drowned World* in 1962.

Ballard is to this period as Wells was to the age of scientific romance. That is to say, it is Ballard's artistic achievement, not his sociological importance, which is of primary significance. Ballard's fiction reincorporates the literary tradition into a fiction which confronts the technologically-initiated cultural crises of the nuclear age, while at the same time reincorporating his fiction into the (avant-garde) literary tradition. His is an extreme fiction, yet one perhaps anticipated by the Wells of *Mind at the End of Its Tether* (1945).

The important writers here are those who, like Ballard, understood that the nuclear age needed a fiction that would do more than prostrate itself before the great superseded idols of Technology and Progress. Somehow, the techniques of modernism--by now already mutating into postmodernism--had to be belatedly assimilated. But in Britain the dominant mode of serious fiction was an exhausted realism.

SF came thus to differentiate New Wave fiction from both Anglo-American science fiction and from British realist fiction. The New Wave lasted until it degenerated into mannerism and its most talented writers, aware of the increasing inflexibility of the science-fiction scene, began to return to mainstream publishers. The grip of realism had begun to weaken as a result of the success of ambitious works of fiction in the non-realistic mode by William Golding, Anthony Burgess, John Fowles, Doris Lessing, and others.

1962

BIO

d. J. Henry Harris, 18 Mar.
d. Victoria Sackville-West, 2 Jun.

FIC

Aldiss, Brian. *Hothouse* (Faber) [US enl. *The Long Afternoon of Earth* (NAL)].
Ballard, J. G. *Billenium* [SS] (Berkley).
---. *The Drowned World* (Berkley; Gollancz 1963).
---. *The Voices of Time* [SS] (Berkley).
---. *The Wind from Nowhere* (Berkley; Gollancz 1967).
Barron, D. G. *The Zilov Bombs* (Deutsch).
Brinton, Henry. *Purple-6* (Hutchinson).
Brunner, John. *No Future in It* [SS] (Gollancz).
---. *Secret Agent of Terra* (Ace) [rev. *The Avengers of Carrig* (Dell 1969)].
---. *The Super Barbarians* (Ace).
---. *Times Without Number* (Ace) [rev. and enl. Hamlyn 1974].
--- (as 'Keith Woodcott'). *Ladder in the Sky* (Ace).
Burgess, Anthony. *A Clockwork Orange* (Heinemann) [*F 1971].
---. *The Wanting Seed* (Heinemann).
'Christopher, John.' *The World in Winter* (Eyre & S) [US *The Long Winter*].
Clarke, Arthur C. *From the Ocean, From the Stars* [O] (Harcourt).
---. *Tales of Ten Worlds* [SS] (Harcourt; Gollancz 1963).
'Gordon, Rex.' *First Through Time* (Ace; Gibbs & Phillips 1964 as *The Time Factor*).
Harrison, Helga. *The Catacombs* (Chatto & W).
Hoyle, Fred and John Elliot. *A for Andromeda* (Souvenir) [*TV 1961].
Huxley, Aldous. *Island* (Chatto & W).
MacLeod, Angus. *The Eighth Seal* (Dobson).
'MacTyre, Paul.' *Midge* (Hodder & S) [US *Doomsday 1999*].
'Maine, Charles Eric.' *The Darkest of Nights* (Hodder & S) [US *Survival Margin* 1968] [rev. *The Big Death* (Sphere 1978)].
Mitchison, Naomi. *Memoirs of a Spacewoman* (Gollancz).
Monsarrat, Nicholas. *The Time Before This* (Cassell).
Newman, Bernard. *The Blue Ants* (Hale).
Russell, Eric Frank. *Dark Tides* [SS] (Dobson).
---. *The Great Explosion* (Dobson).
'Sellings, Arthur.' *Telepath* (Ballantine; Dobson 1963 as *The Silent Speakers*).
Temple, William F. *The Automated Goliath, The Three Sons of Amara* (Ace).
Van Greenaway, Peter. *The Crucified City* (New Authors).
White, James. *Hospital Station* [SS] (Ballantine; Corgi 1967).
---. *Second Ending* (Ace).

1962 (cont.)

FTV

[TV] *Andromeda Breakthrough*. Prod. John Elliot. BBC miniseries, 6x50 mins. Wr. & *nov. (1964) Fred Hoyle & John Elliot.

[TV] *The Avengers*. Cr. Sydney Newman. ITV series, through 1968 (later revived).

[TV] *Out of This World*. Prod. Leonard White. ABC anthology series. Story ed. Irene Shubik, from various sf stories.

GEN

[E] Clarke, Arthur C. *Profiles of the Future: An Inquiry Into the Limits of the Possible* (Gollancz).

[FP] Ball, Brian. "The Pioneer." *New Worlds* (Feb.).

[PUB] J. G. Ballard guest ed. of *New Worlds* (May).

[W] The *Hothouse* series (Brian Aldiss): 9th. Hugo short fiction, US.

1963

BIO

d. Victor MacClure, 7 Apr.
d. Geoffrey Dennis, 15 May.
d. John Cowper Powys, 17 Jun.
d. Katherine Burdekin, 10 Aug.
d. Aldous Huxley, 22 Nov.
d. C. S. Lewis, 22 Nov.

FIC

Aldiss, Brian. *Airs of Earth* [SS] (Faber) [rev. *Starswarm* (Panther 1979)] [US *Starswarm* 1964].
Ballard, J. G. *The Four-Dimensional Nightmare* [SS] (Gollancz) [rev. Gollancz 1974 as *The Voices of Time*].
---. *Passport to Eternity* [SS] (Berkley).
Bateman, Robert. *When the Whites Went* (Dobson).
Brunner, John. *The Astronauts Must Not Land* (Ace) [rev. *More Things in Heaven* (Hamlyn 1983)].
---. *Castaway's World* (Ace) [rev. *Polymath* (DAW 1974)].
---. *The Dreaming Earth* (Pyramid; Sidgwick & J 1972).
---. *Listen! The Stars* (Ace) [rev. *The Stardroppers* (DAW 1972; Hamlyn 1982)].
---. *The Rites of Ohe* (Ace).
---. *The Space Time Juggler* (Ace).
--- (as 'Keith Woodcott'). *The Psionic Menace* (Ace).
Clarke, Arthur C. *Dolphin Island: A Story of the People of the Sea* (Gollancz).
Cooper, Edmund. *Tomorrow Came* [SS] (Panther).
{Garner, Alan. *The Moon of Gomrath* (Collins).}
{Gaskell, Jane. *The Serpent* (Hodder & S).}
Hoyle, Fred and Geoffrey Hoyle. *Fifth Planet* (Heinemann).
Ingrey, Derek. *Pig on a Lead* (Faber).
'McIntosh, J. T.' *The Million Cities* (Pyramid).
Temple, William F. *Battle on Venus* (Ace).
White, James. *Star Surgeon* (Ballantine; Corgi 1967).

FTV

[F] *Children of the Damned*. Dir. Anton M. Leader. MGM. Wr. Jack Briley, from novel *The Midwich Cuckoos (1957) by John Wyndham.
[F] *The Day of the Triffids*. Dir. Steve Sekely & Freddie Francis. Allied. Wr. Philip Yordan, from *novel (1951) by John Wyndham.
[F] *Dr. Strangelove; or, How I Learned to Stop Worrying and Love the Bomb*. Dir. Stanley Kubrick. Hawk/Columbia. Wr. Stanley Kubrick, Terry Southern & Peter George, from *novel (1958) by Peter George.
[F] *It Happened Here*. Dir. & Wr. Kevin Brownlow & Andrew Mollo. Rath/Lopert.
[F] *Lord of the Flies*. Dir. Peter Brook. Allen-Hodgdon/Two Arts. Wr. Peter Brook, from *novel (1954) by William Golding.
[F] *Unearthly Stranger*. Dir. John Krish. Independent Artists/AIP. Wr. Rex Carlton.

FTV

[TV] *Dr. Who*. 1st. Prod. Verity Lambert. BBC series. 1st. episode, "An Unearthly Child" 23 Nov., through present. 1st. Wr. Anthony Coburn, from an idea by Sydney Newman & Donald Wilson.

GEN

[E] Huxley, Aldous. *Literature and Science* (Chatto & W).

[FAN] *Zenith Science Fiction/(Zenith) Speculation*, ed. Peter Weston, Oct., through 1973 (33 issues).

[FP] Mackelworth, R. W. "The Statue." *New Worlds* (Jan.).

[FP] Pratchett, Terry. "The Hades Business." *Science Fantasy* (Aug.).

[FP] Bailey, Hilary. "Breakdown." *New Worlds* (Oct.).

1964

BIO

d. T. H. White, 17 Jan.
d. 'Alan Griff," 17 Mar.
d. Stacey Blake, 5 May.
d. Stephen Southwold, 5 Jun.
d. J. B. S. Haldane, 1 Dec.

FIC

Aldiss, Brian. *The Dark Light Years* (Faber).
---. *Greybeard* (Faber).
Ballard, J. G. *The Burning World* (*Berkley*) [enl. *The Drought* (Cape 1965)].
---. *The Terminal Beach* [SS] (Gollancz).
Brooke-Rose, Christine. *Out* (Joseph).
Brunner, John. *Endless Shadow* (Ace).
---. *To Conquer Chaos* (Ace).
---. *The Whole Man* (*Ballantine*) [as *Telepathist* (Faber 1965)].
'Christopher, John.' *Cloud on Silver* (Hodder & S) [US *Sweeney's Island*].
Cooper, Edmund. *Transit* (Faber).
Cooper, Susan. *Mandrake* (Hodder & S).
Davies, L. P. *The Paper Dolls* (Jenkins).
Duke, Madelaine (as 'Maxim Donne'). *Claret, Sandwiches and Sin: A Cartoon* (Four Square).
High, Philip E. *No Truce with Terra* (Ace).
---. *The Prodigal Sun* (Ace; Compact 1965).
Hodder-Williams, Christopher. *The Main Experiment* (Hodder & S).
Hoyle, Fred & John Elliot. *Andromeda Beakthrough* (Souvenir).
Kapp, Colin. *Transfinite Man* (*Berkley*; Corgi 1965 as *The Dark Mind*).
'Lane, Jane.' *A State of Mind* (Muller).
'Maine, Charles Eric.' *Never Let Up* (Hodder & S).
'McIntosh, J. T.' *The Noman Way* (Digit).
Russell, Eric Frank. *With a Strange Device* (Dobson) [US *The Mind Warpers* 1965].
'Sellings, Arthur.' *The Uncensored Man* (Dobson).
White, James. *Deadly Litter* [SS] (*Ballantine*; Corgi 1968).
Wyndham, John [P]. *The John Wyndham Omnibus* [O] (Joseph).

FTV

[F] *The Earth Dies Screaming*. Dir. Terence Fisher. Lippert/Fox. Wr. Henry Cross, from story by Henry Spalding.
[F] *First Men in the Moon*. Dir. Nathan Juran. Columbia. Wr. Nigel Kneale & Jan Read, from *novel by H. G. Wells (1901).

GEN

[A] Aldiss, Brian, ed. *Introducing SF* (Faber).

1964 (cont.)

GEN

[A] Carnell, E. J., ed. *New Writings in SF-1* (Dobson) [through vol. 21, 1972].
[A] ---, ed. *Lambda 1* (*Berkley;* Penguin 1965).

[C] Aldiss, Brian and Harry Harrison, eds. *SF Horizons*, through Winter 1965 (2 issues) [rep. *Arno* 1975].

[FAN] Platt, Charles, ed. *Beyond*.
[FAN] Priest, Christopher, ed. *Con* (Aug.).

[FP] Hill, Ernest. "The Last Generation." *New Worlds* (Jan.).
[FP] Jones, Langdon. "Stormwater Tunnel." *New Worlds* (Jul.).
[FP] Roberts, Keith. "Escapism." *Science Fantasy* (Sep.).
[FP] Platt, Charles. "One of Those Days." *Science Fantasy* (Dec.).
[FP] 'Rankine, John.' "Two's Company." *New Writing in SF-1*.
[FP] Boyce, Chris. "Autodestruct." [*International*] *Storyteller 3* (Omnibus).

[PUB] Moorcock, Michael ed. *New Worlds*, May/Jun., through Mar. 1969.

1965

BIO

d. S. Fowler Wright, 25 Feb.

FIC

Aldiss, Brian. *Best Science Fiction Stories of Brian W. Aldiss* [SS] (Faber) [US *Who Can Replace a Man?*] [enl. 1971].
---. *Earthworks* (Faber).
Allingham, Margery. *The Mind Readers* (Chatto & W).
Ball, Brian N. *Sundog* (Dobson).
---. **15+ other novels, through 1977.**
Brown, Peter (Currell). *Smallcreep's Day* (Gollancz).
Brunner, John. *The Altar on Asconel* (Ace).
---. *Day of the Star Cities* (Ace) [rev. *Age of Miracles* (Sidgwick & J 1973)].
---. *Enigma from Tantalus* (Ace).
---. *The Long Result* (Faber).
---. *Now Then!* [SS] (Mayflower-Dell).
---. *The Repairmen of Cyclops* (Ace).
---. *The Squares of the City* (Ballantine; Penguin 1969).
--- (as 'Keith Woodcott'). *The Martian Sphinx* (Ace).
'Christopher, John.' *The Possessors* (Hodder & S).
---. *A Wrinkle in the Skin* (Hodder & S) [US *The Ragged Edge* 1966].
Clarke, Arthur C. *An Arthur C. Clarke Omnibus* [O] (Sidgwick & J).
---. *Prelude to Mars* [O] (Harcourt).
Compton, D. G. *The Quality of Mercy: A Novel of 1979* (Hodder & S) [rev. Ace 1970].
Daventry, Leonard. *A Man of Double Deed* (Gollancz).
Davies, L. P. *The Artificial Man* (Jenkins) [F 1967 as *Project X*].
---. *Man Out of Nowhere* (Jenkins) [US *Who Is Lewis Pindar?* 1966].
Frayn, Michael. *The Tin Men* (Collins).
{Garner, Alan. *Elidor*. (Collins).}
{Gaskell, Jane. *Atlan* (Hodder & S).}
George, Peter. *Commander-1* (Heinemann).
Gilliatt, Penelope. *One by One* (Secker & W).
Griffiths, John. *The Survivors* (Collins).
'McIntosh, J. T.' *Out of Chaos* (Digit).
Moorcock, Michael. *The Fireclown* (Compact) [US *The Winds of Limbo* 1969] [rep. *The Winds of Limbo* (Sphere 1970)].
---. *The Sundered Worlds* (Compact) [rep. *The Blood-Red Game* (Sphere 1970)].
--- (as 'Edward P. Bradbury'). *Barbarians of Mars* (Compact) [rep. *The Masters of the Pit* (NEL 1971)].
--- (as 'Edward P. Bradbury'). *Blades of Mars* (Compact) [rep. *The Lord of the Spiders* (NEL 1971)].
--- (as 'Edward P. Bradbury'). *Warriors of Mars* (Compact) [rep. *The City of the Beast* (NEL 1971)].
Pincher, Chapman. *Not with a Bang* (Weidenfeld & N).

1965(cont.) 115

FIC

'Ross, Jean.' *A View of the Island* (Hutchinson).
Russell, Eric Frank. *Somewhere a Voice* [SS] (Dobson).
White, James. *Open Prison* (NEL) [US *Escape Orbit*].

FTV

[F] *Dr. Who and the Daleks*. Dir. Gordon Flemyng. Wr. Milton Subotsky, from *T.V. series *Dr. Who* (1963-present).

[TV] *Out of the Unknown*. Prod. Alan Bromly. BBC series, through 1967. Wr. Jack Pulman, et al., from many different stories.

[TVF] *The War Game*. Dir. & Wr. Peter Watkins. BBC/Pathé.

GEN

[A] Moorcock, Michael, ed. *The Best of New Worlds* (Roberts & Vintner).

[E] Clarke, Arthur C. *Voices from the Sky: Previews of the Coming Space Age* (Harper; Gollancz 1966).

[FAN] Worldcon, London (Loncon II).

[FP] Wells, Robert. "Song of the Syren." *Science Fantasy* (Mar.).
[FP] Gordon, Stuart (as Richard Gordon). "A Light in the Sky." *New Worlds* (Jul.).
[FP] Williams, Eric C. "The Desolator." *Science Fantasy* (Aug.).
[FP] Masson, David I. "Traveller's Rest." *New Worlds* (Sep.).
[FP] Saxton, Josephine. "The Wall." *Science Fantasy* (Nov.).
[FP] Stableford, Brian (as 'Brian Craig'). "Beyond Time's Aegis." *Science Fantasy* (Nov.).

BIO
- d. 'Harvey Graham,' 18 Mar.
- d. 'C. S. Forester,' 2 Apr.
- d. Evelyn Waugh, 10 Apr.
- d. Chalmers Kearney, 15 Apr.
- d. Peter George, 1 Jun.
- d. Margery Allingham, 30 Jun.

FIC
Abel, R. Cox, with Charles Barren. *Trivana 1* (Panther).
Aldiss, Brian. *The Saliva Tree and Other Strange Growths* [SS] (Faber).
Amis, Kingsley. *The Anti-Death League* (Gollancz).
Ballard, J. G. *The Crystal World* (Cape).
---. *The Impossible Man* [SS] (Berkley).
Blackburn, John F. *Children of the Night* (Cape).
Brooke-Rose, Christine. *Such* (Joseph).
Brunner, John. *No Other Gods But Me* [SS] (Compact).
---. *A Planet of Your Own* (Ace).
Compton, D. G. *Farewell, Earth's Bliss* (Hodder & S).
---. *The Silent Multitude* (Ace; Hodder & S 1967).
Cooper, Edmund. *All Fools' Day* (Hodder & S).
Davies, L. P. *The Lampton Dreamers* (Jenkins).
---. *Psychogeist* (Jenkins) [F 1967 as *Project X*].
{Gaskell, Jane. *The City* (Hodder & S).}
'Gordon, Rex.' *Utopia Minus X* (Ace; Gibbs 1967 as *The Paw of God*].
Harker, Kenneth. *The Symmetrians* (Compact).
High, Philip E. *The Mad Metropolis* (Ace; Dobson 1970 as *Double Illusion*).
Hoyle, Fred. *October the First Is Too Late* (Heinemann).
Jones, D. F. *Colossus: The Forbin Project* (Hart-Davis). [F 1969].
'Maine, Charles Eric.' *B.E.A.S.T.: Biological Evolutionary Animal Simulation Test* (Hodder & S).
McCutchan, Philip. *A Time for Survival* (Harrap).
---. **6+ other sf thrillers, through 1971.**
Moorcock, Michael. *The Twilight Man* (Compact) [rep. *The Shores of Death* Sphere 1970].
---. (as 'Bill Barclay'). *Printer's Devil* (Compact) [rev. rep. as MM. *The Russian Intelligence* 1980].
---. (as 'Bill Barclay'). *Somewhere in the Night* (Compact) [rev. rep. as MM. *The Chinese Agent* 1970].
---. (as 'James Colvin'). *The Deep Fix* [SS] (Compact).
Morgan, Dan. *The Richest Corpse in Show Business* (Compact).
Peterkiewicz, Jerzy. *Inner Circle* (Macmillan).
Petty, John. *The Last Refuge* (Whiting & Wheaton).
Quest, Rodney. *Countdown to Doomsday* (Harrap).
'Rankine, John.' *Interstellar Two-Five* (Dobson).
---, **20+ other novels and novelizations, 17+ novels as Douglas R. Mason, through 1981.**
Roberts, Keith. *The Furies* (Hart-Davis).
'Sellings, Arthur.' *The Quy Effect* (Dobson).

1966 (cont.)

FIC
- Spencer, Colin. *Asylum* (Blond).
- Temple, William F. *Shoot at the Moon* (Whiting & Wheaton).
- Toynbee, Polly. *Leftovers* (Weidenfeld & N).
- 'Trevor, Elleston.' *The Shoot* (Heinemann).
- White, James. *The Watch Below* (Whiting & Wheaton).

FTV
- [F] *Daleks--Invasion Earth 2150 A.D.* Dir. Gordon Flemyng. Wr. Milton Subotsky, from *TV series *Dr. Who* (1963-present).
- [F] *Invasion.* Dir. Alan Bridges. Merton Park/AIP. Wr. Roger Marshall, from story by Robert Holmes.
- [F] *One Million Years B.C.* Dir. Don Chaffey. Hammer/20C Fox. Wr. Michael Carreras, from US film (1940) dir. Hal Roach.

GEN
- [A] Evans, I. O., ed. *Science Fiction Through the Ages*, 2 vols. (Panther).
- [A] Moorcock, Michael, ed. *SF Reprise* (Compact).
- ---. **4 more vols., through 1966.**

- [C] Clarke, I. F. *Voices Prophesying War 1863-1984* (Oxford UP).

- [E] Lewis, C. S. [P] *Of Other Worlds: Essays and Stories* (Bles).

- [FP] Tate, Peter. "The Post-Mortem People." *New Worlds* (Mar.).
- [FP] Butterworth, Michael. "Girl." *New Worlds* (May).
- [FP] Priest, Christopher. "The Run." *Impulse* (May).
- [FP] Clute, John. "A Man Must Die." *New Worlds* (Nov.).
- [FP] 'King, Vincent.' "Defense Mechanism." *New Writing in SF-9.*

- [PUB] *Impulse* (later *SF Impulse*), 1st. ed. Kyril Bonfiglioli, Mar., through Feb. 1967 (12 issues).

- [W] "The Saliva Tree" (Brian Aldiss): 1st. Nebula novella (joint), US.

1967

BIO
d. F. L. Lucas, 1 Jun.

FIC
Aldiss, Brian. *An Age* (Faber) [US *Cryptozoic!* 1968].
Balchin, Nigel. *Kings of Infinite Space* (Collins).
Ballard, J. G. *The Day of Forever* [SS] (Panther) [rep. Gollancz 1986].
---. *The Disaster Area* [SS] (Cape).
---. *The Overloaded Man* [SS] (Panther).
Brunner, John. *Out of My Mind* [SS] (*Ballantine*) [rev. Four Square 1968).
---. *The Productions of Time* (*Signet*; Penguin 1970).
---. *Quicksand* (*Doubleday*; Sidgwick & J 1969).
Carter, Angela. *The Magic Toyshop* (Heinemann).
'Christopher, John.' *The Little People* (Hodder & S).
Clark, Ronald. *Queen Victoria's Bomb: The Disclosures of Professor Franklin Huxtable, M.A. Cantab.* (Cape).
Clarke, Arthur C. *The Nine Billion Names of God: The Best Short Stories of Arthur C. Clarke* [SS] (*Harcourt*).
Cooney, Michael. *Doomsday England* (Cassell).
Cooper, Edmund. *A Far Sunset* (Hodder & S).
'Cowper, Richard.' *Breakthrough* (Dobson).
Davies, L. P. *Twilight Journey* (Jenkins).
Duke, Madelaine. *This Business of Bomfog: A Cartoon* (Heinemann).
High, Philip E. *Reality Forbidden* (*Ace*; Hale 1968).
---. *These Savage Futurians* (*Ace*; Dobson 1969).
---. *Twin Planets* (*Paperback Library*; Dobson 1968).
Hodder-Williams, Christopher. *The Egg-Shaped Thing* (Hodder & S).
Hoyle, Fred. *Element 79* [SS] (*NAL*).
Jones, D. F. *Implosion* (Hart-Davis).
'Kavan, Anna.' *Ice* (P. Owen).
Martin, D. S. *No Lack of Space* [SS] (Stockwell).
'McIntosh, J. T.' *Time for a Change* (Joseph) [US *Snow White and the Giants* 1968].
Meyers, Roy. *Dolphin Boy* (*Ballantine*; Rapp & W 1968 as *The Dolphin Rider*).
---. **2 sequels, through 1971.**
Moorcock, Michael. *The Wrecks of Time* (*Ace*) [rev. rep. *The Rituals of Infinity* (Arrow 1971)].
Morgan, Dan. *The New Minds* (Corgi).
---. **Sequels, through 1975.**
Peters, Ludovic. *Riot '71* (Hodder & S).
Platt, Charles. *The Garbage World* (*Berkley*; Panther 1968).
'Sellings, Arthur' (as 'Ray Luther'). *Intermind* (*Banner*; Dobson 1969).
Shaw, Bob. *Nightwalk* (*Banner*; NEL 1970) [rev. Gollancz 1977].
Wadsworth, Phyllis Marie. *Overmind* (Sidgwick & J).
Wilson, Colin. *The Mind Parasites* (Barker).

1967(cont.)

FIC
- Young, B. A. *Cabinet Pudding* (H. Hamilton).

FTV
- [F] *Island of Terror*. Dir. Terence Fisher. Planet/Universal. Wr. Alan Ramsen & Edward Andrew Mann.
- [F] *Night of the Big Heat* (US *Island of the Burning Damned*). Dir. Terence Fisher. Planet. Wr. Ronald Liles & Pip & Jane Baker, from *novel (1959) by 'John Lymington.'
- [F] *Privilege*. Dir. Peter Watkins. Worldfilm/Universal. Wr. Norman Bogner, from story by Johnny Speight.

- [TV] *The Prisoner*. Prod. David Tomblin. ITC miniseries, 17x50 mins. Wr. by Patrick McGoohan et al, from idea by Patrick McGoohan.

GEN
- [A] Aldiss, Brian & Harry Harrison, eds. *The Year's Best SF* (Sphere) [US *Best SF*].
  ---. **Annual vols., through 1975.**
- [A] Moorcock, Michael, ed. *Best SF Stories from New Worlds 1* (Panther).
  ---. **7 more vols., through 1974.**

BIO
- d. Bernard Newman, 19 Feb.
- d. Harold Nicolson, 1 May.
- d. Herbert Read, 12 Jun.
- d. Capt. W. E. Johns, 21 Jun.
- d. 'Arthur Sellings,' 24 Sep.
- d. Gerald Kersh, 5 Nov.
- d. Mervyn Peake, 17 Nov.
- d. 'Anna Kavan,' 5 Dec.

FIC

'Alban, Anthony' (?Anthony A. Thompson). *Catharsis Central* (Dobson).
Aldiss, Brian. *Report on Probability A* (Faber).
Ballard, J. G. *Why I Want To Fuck Ronald Reagan* (Unicorn).
Bennett, Margot. *The Furious Masters* (Eyre & S).
Brunner, John. *Bedlam Planet* (Ace; Sidgwick & J 1973).
---. *Father of Lies* (Belmont).
---. *Not Before Time: Science Fiction and Fantasy* [SS] (Four Square).
---. *Stand on Zanzibar* (Doubleday; Macdonald 1969).
Burgess, Anthony. "The Muse." *Hudson Review*.
'Christopher, John.' *Pendulum* (Hodder & S).
Clarke, Arthur C. *An Arthur C. Clarke Second Omnibus* [O] (Sidgwick & J).
---. *The Lion of Comarre* and *Against the Fall of Night* (Harcourt; Gollancz 1970).
---. *2001: A Space Odyssey* (Hutchinson).
Compton, D. G. *Synthajoy* (Hodder & S).
Cooney, Michael. *Ten Years to Oblivion* (Cassell).
Cooper, Colin. *The Thunder and Lightning Man* (Faber).
Cooper, Edmund. *Five to Twelve* (Hodder & S).
---. *News from Elsewhere* [SS] (Mayflower).
Corston, George. *Aftermath* (Hale).
'Cowper, Richard.' *Phoenix* (Dobson).
Davies, L. P. *The Alien* (Jenkins) [rep. *The Groundstar Conspiracy* (Sphere 1972)].
Donson, Cyril. *Born in Space* (Hale).
Durrell, Lawrence. *Tunc* (Faber).
Earnshaw, Brian. *Planet in the Eye of Time* (Hodder & S).
Frayn, Michael. *A Very Private Life* (Collins).
Groves, J. W. *Shellbreak* (Hale).
High, Philip E. *Invader on My Back* (Hale).
---. *The Time Mercenaries* (Ace; Dobson 1969).
Hill, Ernest. *Pity About Earth* (Ace).
Hodder-Williams, Christopher. *Fistful of Digits* (Hodder & S).
{Hughes, Ted. *The Iron Man: A Story in Five Nights* (Faber).}
Hurd, Douglas, with Andrew Osmond. *Send Him Victorious* (Collins).
Jones, Gonner. *The Dome* (Faber).

FIC
Jones, Margaret. *The Day They Put Humpty Together* (Collins) [US *Transplant*].
Kersh, Gerald. *Nightshade and Damnation* [SS] (*Gold Medal*).
Leslie, Peter. *Night of the Trilobites* (Corgi).
Levene, Malcolm. *Carder's Paradise* (Hart-Davis).
Mackelworth, R. W. *Firemantle* (Hale) [US *The Diabols*].
Masson, David I. *The Caltraps of Time* [SS] (Faber).
'McIntosh, J. T.' *Six Gates from Limbo* (Joseph).
Moorcock, Michael. *The Final Programme* (Avon; Allison & B 1969) [rev. Fontana 1979] [*F 1973].
Morgan, Dan & 'John Kippax.' *A Thunder of Stars* (Macdonald).
---. **Series continued, through 1975.**
Roberts, Keith. *Pavane* (Hart-Davis) [US enl. 1968].
'Sellings, Arthur.' *The Long Eureka* [SS] (Dobson).
---. *The Power of X* (Dobson).
Shaw, Bob. *The Two-Timers* (Ace; Gollancz 1969).
Temple, William F. *The Fleshpots of Sansato* (Macdonald).
Thomas, D. M. (SF Poetry), in *Penguin Modern Poets 11* [V] (Penguin).
Van Greenaway, Peter. *The Man Who Held the Queen to Ransom and Sent Parliament Packing* (Weidenfeld & N).
Vansittart, Peter. *The Story Teller* (P. Owen).
Wheeler, Paul. *The Friendly Persuaders* (Hutchinson).
White, James. *All Judgement Fled* (Rapp & W).
Williams, Eric C. *The Time Injection* (Hale).
Wyndham, John. *Chocky* (Joseph).

FTV
[F] *The Lost Continent*. Dir. Michael Carreras. Hammer/20C Fox. Wr. Michael Nash, from novel *Uncharted Seas* (1938) by Dennis Wheatley.
[F] *Quatermass and the Pit* (US *Five Million Years to Earth*). Dir. Roy Ward Baker. Hammer/7 Arts. Wr. Nigel Kneale, from his *T.V. series (1958).
[F] *2001: A Space Odyssey*. Dir. Stanley Kubrick. Wr. Stanley Kubrick & Arthur C. Clarke, from story "The Sentinel" by Arthur C. Clarke.

[TV] *The Year of the Sex Olympics*. Wr. Nigel Kneale. BBC play.

GEN
[A] Merril, Judith, ed. *England Swings SF* (Doubleday) [abr. *The Space-Time Journal* (Panther 1972)].
[A] Moorcock, Michael, ed. *The Traps of Time* (Rapp & W).

[E] Clarke, Arthur C. *The Promise of Space* (Hodder & S).

GEN
- [FP] Harrison, M. John. "Baa Baa Blocksheep." *New Worlds* (Nov.).
- [FP] Holdstock, Robert. "Pauper's Plot." *New Worlds* (Nov.).

- [W] "Behold the Man" (Michael Moorcock): 3rd. Nebula novella, US.

BIO
- d. John Wyndham, 11 Mar.
- d. George Goodchild, 25 Mar.
- d. Paul Capon, 24 Nov.

FIC
Ableman, Paul. *Twilight of the Vilp* (Gollancz).
Aldiss, Brian. *Barefoot in the Head: A European Fantasia* (Faber).
---. *A Brian Aldiss Omnibus* [O] (Sidgwick & J).
---. *Intangibles, Inc.* [SS] (Faber) [US *Neanderthal Planet*].
Brunner, John. *Double, Double* (Ballantine; Sidgwick & J 1971).
---. *The Evil That Men Do* (Belmont).
---. *The Jagged Orbit* (Ace; Sidgwick & J 1970).
---. *Timescoop* (Dell; Sidgwick & J 1972).
Bulmer, Kenneth. *The Ulcer Culture* (Macdonald) [rep. *The Stained-Glass World* (NEL 1976)].
Carter, Angela. *Heroes and Villains* (Heinemann).
Cooper, Edmund. *The Last Continent* (Dell; Hodder & S 1970).
---. *Seahorse in the Sky* (Hodder & S).
'Craig, David.' *Message Ends* (Cape).
Daventry, Leonard. *Reflections in a Mirage* (Hale).
Davies, L. P. *Dimension A* (Barrie & Jenkins).
---. *Genesis Two* (Barrie & Jenkins).
Garnett, David S. *Mirror in the Sky* (Berkley; Hale 1973).
Gaskell, Jane. *A Sweet, Sweet Summer* (Hodder & S).
'Gordon, Rex.' *The Yellow Fraction* (Ace; Dobson 1972).
Groves, J. W. *The Heels of Achilles* (Hale).
Hartridge, Jon. *Binary Divine* (Macdonald).
Hodder-Williams, Christopher. *98.4* (Hodder & S).
Hoyle, Fred & Geoffrey Hoyle. *Rockets in Ursa Major* (Heinemann).
Kettle, Pamela. *The Day of the Women* (Frewin).
'King, Vincent.' *Light a Last Candle* (Ballantine; Rapp & W 1970).
Lauder, G. D. *Our Man for Ganymede* (Dobson).
Leslie, Peter. *The Autumn Accelerator* (Corgi).
Moorcock, Michael. *Behold the Man* (Allison & B).
---. *The Black Corridor* (Mayflower).
---. *The Ice Schooner* (Sphere) [rev. Harper & Row 1977].
---. *The Time-Dweller* [SS] (Hart-Davis).
Robinson, Philip Bedford. *Masque of a Savage Mandarin* (Macdonald).
Ryder, James. *Kark* (Hale).
Saxton, Josephine. *The Hieros Gamos of Sam and An Smith* (Doubleday).
Seymour, Alan. *The Coming Self-Destruction of the United States of America* (Souvenir).
Shaw, Bob. *The Palace of Eternity* (Ace; Gollancz 1970).
---. *Shadow of Heaven* (Avon) [rev. NEL 1970].

1969(cont.)

FIC

Stableford, Brian. *Cradle of the Sun* (Sidgwick & J).
Tabori, Paul. *The Cleft* (Pyramid).
Tate, Peter. *The Thinking Seat* (Doubleday; Faber 1970).
Weatherhead, J. *Transplant* (Harrap).
Wells, Robert. *The Parasaurians* (Berkley).
White, James. *The Aliens Among Us* [SS] (Ballantine; Corgi 1970).
Williams, Eric C. *Monkman Comes Down* (Hale).
---. *To End All Telescopes* (Hale).
Wilson, Colin. *The Philosopher's Stone* (Barker).

FTV

[F] *The Bed-Sitting Room*. Dir. Richard Lester. UA. Wr. John Antrobus et al., from play by John Antrobus and Spike Milligan.
[F] *Invasion of the Body Stealers* (US *Thin Air*). Dir. Gerry Levy. Wr. Mike St. Clair & Peter Marcus.
[F] *Journey to the Far Side of the Sun* (US *Doppelgangers*). Dir Robert Parrish. Century 21/Universal. Wr. Gerry & Sylvia Anderson & Donald James.
[F] *The Mind of Mr. Soames*. Dir. Alan Cooke. Amicus. Wr. Max Rosenberg & Milton Subotsky, from *novel (1951) by 'Charles Eric Maine.'
[F] *Moon Zero Two*. Dir. Roy Ward Baker. Hammer/Warner. Wr. Michael Carreras.
[F] *Scream and Scream Again*. Dir. Gordon Hessler. Amicus/AIP. Wr. Christopher Wicking, from novel *The Disoriented Man* (1967) by 'Peter Saxon.'

[TV] *UFO*. Prod. Reg Hill. ITC/Century 21 miniseries, 50x? mins., through 1970. Wr. Tony Barwick et al., from idea by Gerry & Sylvia Anderson [*F 1980].

GEN

[A] Jones, Langdon, ed. *The New SF* (Hutchinson).
[A] Lucie-Smith, Edward, ed. *Holding Your Eight Hands: An Anthology of Science Fiction Verse* [V] (Doubleday; Rapp & W 1970).
[A] Moorcock, Michael, ed. (as Anon.). *The Inner Landscape* (Allison & B).

[FP] Passes, Alan. "Spoor." *New Worlds* (Jun.).
[FP] Watson, Ian. "Roof Garden Under Saturn." *New Worlds* (Nov.).
[FP] Coney, Michael G. "Symbiote." *New Writing in SF-15*.

[PUB] *Vision of Tomorrow*, ed. Philip Harbottle, Aug., through Sep. 1970 (10 issues).

[W] *Stand on Zanzibar* (John Brunner): 16th. Hugo novel, US.

BIO
　　d. Bertrand Russell, 2 Feb.
　　d. Nigel Balchin, 17 May.
　　d. E. M. Forster, 7 Jun.

FIC
　　Aldiss, Brian. *The Moment of Eclipse* [SS] (Faber).
　　Anderson, Colin. *Magellan* (Gollancz).
　　Ballard, J. G. *The Atrocity Exhibition* [SS] (Cape) [US *Love and Napalm: Export USA* 1972].
　　Bayley, Barrington J. *The Star Virus* (Ace).
　　Bennett, Diana. *Adam and Eve and Newbury* (Hodder & S).
　　Compton, D. G. *Chronocules* (Ace; Joseph 1971 as *Hot Wireless Sets, Aspirin Tablets, the Sandpaper Sides of Used Matchboxes, and Something That Might Have Been Castor Oil*) [rep. *Chronicules* (Arrow 1976)].
　　---. *The Electric Crocodile* (Hodder & S) [US *The Steel Crocodile*].
　　Cooper, Colin. *Outcrop* (Faber).
　　Cooper, Edmund. *Son of Kronk* (Hodder & S) [US *Kronk* 1971] [rep. *Kronk* (Coronet 1975)].
　　Cooper, Hughes. *Sexmax* (NEL).
　　'Craig, David.' *Contact Lost* (Cape).
　　Daventry, Leonard. *The Ticking Is in Your Head* (Hale).
　　Durrell, Lawrence. *Nunquam* (Faber).
　　Egleton, Clive. *Piece of Resistance* (Hodder & S).
　　Elder, Michael. *Paradise Is Not Enough* (Pinnacle).
　　---. **12+ other novels, through present.**
　　Harker, Kenneth. *The Flowers of February* (Hale).
　　Hartridge, Jon. *Earthjacket* (Macdonald).
　　Hoyle, Fred & Geoffrey Hoyle. *Seven Steps to the Sun* (Heinemann).
　　'Kavan, Anna' [P]. *Julia and the Bazooka* [SS] (Owen).
　　Leslie, Peter. *The Plastic Magicians* (Mayflower).
　　Mackelworth, R. W. *Tiltangle* (Ballantine; Hale 1971).
　　MacLeod, Sheila. *The Snow-White Soliloquies* (Secker & W).
　　'McIntosh, J. T.' *Transmigration* (Avon).
　　Mitchell, Adrian. *The Bodyguard* (Cape).
　　Moorcock, Michael. *The Singing Citadel* [SS] (Mayflower).
　　Paget, John.' *World Well Lost* (Hale).
　　Platt, Charles. *The City Dwellers* (Sidgwick & J) [US rev. *Twilight of the City* 1977].
　　Priest, Christopher. *Indoctrinaire* (Faber) [rev. Pan 1979].
　　Roberts, Keith. *The Inner Wheel* (Hart-Davis).
　　Saxton, Josephine. *Vector for Seven: The Weltanschauung of Mrs. Amelia Mortimer and Friends* (Doubleday).
　　'Sellings, Arthur' [P]. *Junk Day* (Dobson).
　　Shaw, Bob. *One Million Tomorrows* (Ace; Gollancz 1971).
　　Stableford, Brian. *The Blind Worm* (Sidgwick & J).
　　Story, Jack Trevor. *One Last Mad Embrace* (Allison & B).
　　Wise, Arthur. *Who Killed Enoch Powell?* (Weidenfeld).

1970 (cont.)

FTV

[F] *When Dinosaurs Ruled the Earth*. Dir. Val Guest. Wr. Val Guest.

[TV] *Doomwatch*. Prod. Terence Dudley. BBC series, 37x50 mins., through 1972. Wr. Kit Pedler & Gerry Davis et al., from their idea.
[TV] *Wine of India*. Wr. Nigel Kneale. BBC play.

GEN

[A] Hay, George, ed. *The Disappearing Future: A Symposium of Speculation* (Panther).

[E] Aldiss, Brian. *The Shape of Further Things: Speculation on Change* (Faber).

[FAN] *Cypher*, ed. James Goddard & Mike Sandow, Jun., through Nov. 1974 (12 issues).
[FAN] *Maya*, 1st. ed. Ian Williams, through 1978 (15 issues).

[PUB] Charles Platt ed. of *New Worlds*.

[W] *Stand on Zanzibar* (John Brunner): BSFA novel.

1971

BIO
    d. R. H. Mottram, 15 Apr.
    d. H. F. Heard, 14 Aug.
    d. J. D. Bernal, 15 Sep.

FIC
    Adlard, Mark. *Interface* (Sidgwick & J).
    Aldiss, Brian. *Brian Aldiss Omnibus 2* [O] (Sidgwick & J).
    Ballard, J. G. *Chronopolis* [SS] (*Putnam*).
    ---. *Vermilion Sands* [SS] (*Berkley*; Cape 1973).
    Brunner, John. *The Dramaturges of Yan* (*Ace*; NEL 1974).
    ---. *The Traveler in Black* (*Ace*; UK 1979).
    ---. *The Wrong End of Time* (*Doubleday*; UK 1975).
    Cooper, Edmund. *Double Phoenix, The Firebird* (*Ballantine*).
    ---. *The Overman Culture* (Hodder & S).
    ---. *Unborn Tomorrow* [SS] (Hale).
    'Cowper, Richard.' *Domino* (Dobson).
    Darrington, Hugh. *Gravitor* (Sidgwick & J).
    Daventry, Leonard. *Terminus* (Hale).
    Golding, William. *The Scorpion God* [SS] (Faber).
    Gutteridge, Lindsay. *Cold War in a Country Garden* (Cape).
    Harrison, M. John. *The Committed Men* (Hutchinson).
    ---. *The Pastel City* (NEL).
    High, Philip E. *Butterfly Planet* (Dobson).
    Hoyle, Fred & Geoffrey Hoyle. *The Molecule Men* and *The Monster of Loch Ness: Two Short Novels* (Heinemann).
    Jones, D. F. *Don't Pick the Flowers* (Panther) [US *Denver Is Missing*].
    'King, Vincent.' *Another End* (*Ballantine*).
    ---. *Candy Man* (Gollancz).
    Lessing, Doris. *Briefing for a Descent into Hell* (Cape).
    'Maine, Charles Eric.' *The Random Factor* (Hodder & S).
    'McIntosh, J. T.' *Flight from Rebirth* (*Avon*; Hale 1973).
    Moorcock, Michael. *A Cure for Cancer* (Allison & B) [rev. Fontana 1979].
    ---. *The Warlord of the Air* (NEL).
    Morgan, Dan. *Inside* (Corgi).
    Pedler, Kit & Gerry Davis. *Mutant 59: The Plastic-Eaters* (Souvenir).
    Platt, Charles. *Planet of the Voles* (*Putnam*).
    Pratchett, Terry. *Carpet People* (Smythe).
    Saxton, Josephine. *Group Feast* (*Doubleday*).
    Shaw, Bob. *Ground Zero Man* (*Avon*; Corgi 1976) [rev. *The Peace Machine* (Gollancz 1985)].
    Sillitoe, Alan. *Travels in Nihilon* (W. H. Allen).
    Stableford, Brian. *The Days of Glory* (Five Star).
    ---. *In the Kingdom of the Beasts* (*Ace*; Quartet 1974).
    ---. *Day of Wrath* (*Ace*; Quartet 1974).
    Story, Jack Trevor. *Hitler Needs You* (Allison & B).

FIC
    Story, Jack Trevor. *Little Dog's Day* (Allison & B).
    ---. *The Wind in the Snottygobble Tree* (Allison & B).
    Tate, Peter. *Gardens 1,2,3,4,5.* (Faber) [US *Gardens One to Five*].
    White, James. *Major Operation* [SS] (Ballantine).
    ---. *Tomorrow Is Too Far* (Ballantine).
    Williams, Eric C. *The Call of Utopia* (Hale).

FTV
    [F] *A Clockwork Orange*. Dir. Stanley Kubrick. Hawk/Warner Bros. Wr. Stanley Kubrick, from *novel (1961) by Anthony Burgess.
    [F] *Quest for Love*. Dir. Ralph Thomas. Wr. Bert Batt, from story "Random Quest" by John Wyndham.
    [F] *Zero Population Growth* (US *Z.P.G.*). Dir. Michael Campus. Sagittarius/Paramount. Wr. Max Ehrlich & Frank DeFelitta.

GEN
    [A] Carnell, E. J., ed. *The Best of New Writings in SF* (Corgi).
    [A] Moorcock, Michael & Langdon Jones, eds. *The Nature of the Catastrophe* (Hutchinson).
    [A] Moorcock, Michael, ed. *New Worlds 1* (Sphere).
    ---. *New Worlds 2* (Sphere).

    [C] Science Fiction Foundation set up at North-East London Polytechnic (later Polytechnic of East London), 1st. administrator Peter Nicholls, through present.

    [FAN] 1st. Novacon, Birmingham; through present.

    [FP] Stephenson, Andrew M. "Holding Action," <u>ASF</u> (Nov.).

    [W] *The Jagged Orbit* (John Brunner): BSFA novel.

BIO
　　d. Lance Sieveking, 6 Jan.
　　d. E. J. Carnell, 23 Mar.
　　d. E. H. Visiak, 30 Aug.
　　d. Francis D. Grierson, 24 Sep.
　　d. Compton Mackenzie, 30 Nov.
　　d. L. P. Hartley, 13 Dec.

FIC
　　{Adams, Richard. *Watership Down* (Rex Collings).}
　　Adlard, Mark. *Volteface* (Sidgwick & J).
　　Aldiss, Brian. *The Book of Brian Aldiss* (DAW; NEL 1973 as *Comic Inferno*).
　　Bayley, Barrington J. *Annihilation Factor* [SS] (Ace; Allison & B 1979 as *The Seed of Evil*).
　　---. *Empire of Two Worlds* (Ace; Hale 1974).
　　Brunner, John. *Entry to Elsewhen* [SS] (DAW).
　　---. *From This Day Forward* [SS] (Doubleday).
　　---. *The Sheep Look Up* (Harper; Dent 1974).
　　Carter, Angela. *The Infernal Desire Machines of Dr. Hoffman* (Hart-Davis) [US *The War of Dreams* 1974].
　　Clarke, Arthur C. *Of Time and Stars: The Worlds of Arthur C. Clarke* [SS] (Gollancz).
　　---. *The Wind from the Sun: Stories of the Space Age* [SS] (Gollancz).
　　Compton, D. G. *The Missionaries* (Ace; Hale 1975).
　　Coney, Michael G. *Mirror Image* (DAW; Gollancz 1973).
　　Cooper, Edmund. *Who Needs Men?* (Hodder & S) [US *Gender Genocide*].
　　'Cowper, Richard.' *Clone* (Gollancz).
　　---. *Kuldesak* (Gollancz).
　　Davies, L. P. *What Did I Do Tomorrow?* (Barrie & Jenkins).
　　Du Maurier, Daphne. *Rule Britannia* (Gollancz).
　　Gordon, Stuart. *Time Story* (NEL).
　　Hitchcock, Raymond. *Venus 13: A Cautionary Space Tale* (W. H. Allen).
　　Jones, Langdon. *The Eye of the Lens* [SS] (Macmillan).
　　Kapp, Colin. *The Patterns of Chaos* (Gollancz).
　　Mackelworth, R. W. *Starflight 3000* (Ballantine; NEL 1976).
　　'McIntosh, J. T.' *The Cosmic Spies* (Hale).
　　---. *The Space Sorcerers* (Hale) [US *The Suiciders* 1973].
　　Moorcock, Michael. *An Alien Heat* (McGibbon & Kee).
　　---. *Breakfast in the Ruins* (NEL).
　　---. *The English Assassin: A Romance of Entropy* (Allison & B) [rev. Fontana 1979].
　　Priest, Christopher. *Fugue for a Darkening Island* (Faber) [US *Darkening Island*].
　　Savarin, Julius Jay. *Lemmus 1: Waiters on the Dance* (Arlington).
　　---. **2 sequels, through 1977.**
　　Shaw, Bob. *Other Days, Other Eyes* (Gollancz).
　　Stableford, Brian. *The Halcyon Drift* (DAW; Dent 1974).

1972 (cont.)

FIC

Stableford, Brian. *To Challenge Chaos* (DAW).
White, James. *Dark Inferno* (Joseph) [US *Lifeboat*].

FTV

[F] *Doomwatch*. Dir. Peter Saady. Tigon. Wr. Clive Exton, from *TV (1970-72).

GEN

[A] Anon., ed. *The Battle of Dorking Controversy* (Cornmarket).
[A] Bulmer, Kenneth, ed. *New Writing in SF-22* (Corgi).
---. **8 more vols., through 1977.**
[A] Locke, George, ed. *Worlds Apart: An Anthology of Interplanetary Fiction* (Cornmarket).
[A] Moorcock, Michael, ed. *New Worlds 3* (Sphere).
[A] ---. *New Worlds 4* (Sphere).

[C] *Foundation: A Review of Science Fiction*, 1st. ed. Charles Barren, Mar., through present.

[E] Clarke, Arthur C. *The Lost Worlds of 2001* (Sidgwick & J).
[E] ---. *Report on Planet Three and Other Speculations* (Gollancz).

[FP] James, Laurence. "And Dug the Dog a Tomb." *New Worlds 3*.

[W] *The Moment of Eclipse* (Brian Aldiss): BSFA fiction.

1973

BIO

d. Neil M. Gunn, 15 Jan.
d. James Barlow, 30 Jan.
d. Robert Bateman, 12 Apr.
d. John Creasey, 9 Jun.
d. J. R. R. Tolkien, 2 Sep.
d. A. S. Neill, 23 Sep.
d. Dorothy E. Stevenson, 30 Dec.

FIC

Aldiss, Brian. *Frankenstein Unbound* (Cape).
Ballard, J. G. *Crash* (Cape).
Barrett, Geoffrey John. *The Brain of Graphicon* (Hale).
---. **ca. 12 others, various pseudonyms, through 1977.**
Bayley, Barrington J. *Collision Course* (*DAW*; Allison & B 1977 as *Collision with Chronos*).
Brunner, John. *The Stone That Never Came Down* (Doubleday; NEL, 1976).
---. *Time Jump* [SS] (Dell).
Clarke, Arthur C. *The Best of Arthur C. Clarke* [SS] (Sidgwick & J) [rev. rep. in 2 vols.: *The Best of Arthur C. Clarke 1937-1955* (Sidgwick & J 1976); *The Best of Arthur C. Clarke 1955-1972* (Sidgwick & J 1977)].
---. *Rendezvous with Rama* (Gollancz).
Coney, Michael G. *Friends Come in Boxes* (*DAW*; Gollancz 1974).
---. *The Hero of Downways* (*DAW*; Futura 1974).
---. *Syzygy* (Elmfield).
Cooper, Edmund. *The Cloud Walker* (Hodder & S).
---. *The Tenth Planet* (Hodder & S).
'Cowper, Richard.' *Time Out of Mind* (Gollancz).
Dickinson, Peter. *The Green Gene* (Hodder & S).
Farren, Mick. *The Texts of Festival* (Hart-Davis).
Frayn, Michael. *Sweet Dreams* (Collins).
{Garner, Alan. *Red Shift* (Collins).}
Gordon, Stuart. *One-Eye* (*DAW*; Sidgwick & J 1974).
---. **2 sequels, through 1976.**
Gutteridge, Lindsay. *Killer Pine* (Cape).
High, Philip E. *Come, Hunt an Earthman* (Hale).
---. *Sold for a Spaceship* (Hale).
Hodder-Williams, Christopher. *Panic O'Clock* (United Writers).
Hoyle, Fred & Geoffrey Hoyle. *The Inferno* (Heinemann).
Hyams, Edward. *The Final Agenda* (Bodley Head).
'McIntosh, J. T.' *Galactic Takeover Bid* (Hale).
Moorcock, Michael. *The Jade Man's Eyes* (Unicorn).
Morgan, Dan. *The High Destiny* (Berkley; Millington 1975).
'Morland, Dick.' *Heart Clock* (Faber).
Roberts, Keith. *Machines and Men* [SS] (Hutchinson).
Shaw, Bob. *Tomorrow Lies in Ambush* [SS] (Gollancz).
Stableford, Brian. *Rhapsody in Black* (*DAW*; Dent 1975).
Swindells, Robert. *When Darkness Comes* (Brockhampton).
Tate, Peter. *Country Love and Poison Rain* (Doubleday).

1973 (cont.)

FIC

Tennant, Emma. *The Time of the Crack* (Faber) [rep. *The Crack* (Penguin 1978)].
Van Greenaway, Peter. *The Medusa Touch* (Gollancz).
Watson, Ian. *The Embedding* (Gollancz).
Williams, Eric C. *Project Renaissance* (Hale).
Wyndham, John [P]. *The Best of John Wyndham* [SS] (Sphere) [rep. *The Man from Beyond* (Joseph 1975)].
--- (as John Beynon) [P]. *Sleepers of Mars* [SS] (Coronet).
--- (as John Beynon) [P]. *Wanderers of Time* [SS] (Coronet).

FTV

[F] *Deathline* (US *Raw Meat*). Dir. Gary Sherman. AIP. Wr. Ceri Jones, from story by Gary Sherman.
[F] *The Final Programme* (US *The Last Days of Man on Earth*). Dir. Robert Fuest. Goodtime/Gladiole/MGM-EMI. Wr. Robert Fuest, from *novel (1968) by Michael Moorcock.
[F] *The Mutations*. Dir. Jack Cardiff. Getty/Columbia. Wr. Robert D. Weinbach & Edward Mann.
[F] *O Lucky Man!* Dir. Lindsay Anderson. Wr. David Sherwin.

[TV] *Moonbase 3*. Prod. Barry Letts. BBC miniseries, 6x30 mins. Wr. Terrance Dicks et al.

[TVF] *Frankenstein: The True Story*. Dir. Jack Smight. NBC/Universal. Wr. Christopher Isherwood & Don Bachardy, from *novel (1818) by Mary Shelley.

GEN

[A] Moorcock, Michael, ed. *New Worlds 5* (Sphere).
--- & Charles Platt, eds. *New Worlds 6* (Sphere).

[C] Aldiss, Brian. *Billion Year Spree: The True History of Science Fiction* (Weidenfeld & N) [rev. as with David Wingrove, *Trillion Year Spree: The History of Science Fiction* (Gollancz 1986)].

[W] "A Meeting with Medusa" (Arthur C. Clarke): 8th. Nebula novella, US.

1974   **133**

BIO
    d. Roy Meyers, 13 Feb.
    d. 'John Kippax,' 17 Jul.
    d. Ronald Fraser, 12 Sep.
    d. Eric Linklater, 7 Nov.
    d. Paul Tabori, 9 Nov.
    d. Olga Hesky.

FIC
    Aldiss, Brian. *The Eighty-Minute Hour: A Space Opera* (Cape).
    Ballard, J. G. *Concrete Island* (Cape).
    Barclay, Alan. *Of Earth and Fire* (Hale).
    ---. **2 more, through 1976.**
    Bayley, Barrington J. *The Fall of Chronopolis* (DAW; Allison & B 1979).
    ---. *The Soul of the Robot* (Doubleday; Allison & B 1976).
    Boorman, John with Bill Stair. *Zardoz* (Pan) [*F 1974]..
    Brunner, John. *Total Eclipse* (Doubleday; Weidenfeld & N 1975).
    ---. *The Web of Everywhere* (Bantam; NEL 1977).
    Carter, Angela. *Fireworks: Nine Profane Pieces* [SS] (Quartet).
    Compton, D. G. *The Continuous Katherine Mortenhoe* (Gollancz) [US *The Unsleeping Eye*] [rep. Magnum 1981 as *Deathwatch*] [F France/Germany 1980 as *La Mort en Direct*, trans. *Deathwatch*].
    Coney, Michael G. *Monitor Found in Orbit* [SS] (DAW).
    ---. *Winter's Children* (Gollancz).
    Cooper, Edmund. *Prisoner of Fire* (Hodder & S).
    ---. *The Slaves of Heaven* (Putnam; Hodder & S 1975).
    'Conrad, Paul.' *Ex Minus* (Hale).
    ---. **15+ other novels, various pseudonyms, through 1975.**
    'Cowper, Richard.' *The Twilight of Briareus* (Gollancz).
    ---. *Worlds Apart* (Gollancz).
    Dickinson, Peter. *The Poison Oracle* (Hodder & S).
    Durrell, Lawrence. *The Revolt of Aphrodite* [O] (Faber).
    Garnett, David S. *Time in Eclipse* (Hale).
    Gordon, Stuart. *The Eyes Trilogy* [O] (Sidgwick & J).
    Griffith, George [P]. *The Raid of 'Le Vengeur'* [SS] (Ferret).
    Harrison, M. John. *The Centauri Device* (Doubleday; Panther 1975).
    Herbert, James. *The Rats* (NEL).
    ---. **10+ sf horror/thrillers, through present.**
    High, Philip E. *Speaking of Dinosaurs* (Hale).
    Hodder-Williams, Christopher. *Coward's Paradise* (United Writers).
    Hoyle, Fred & Geoffrey Hoyle. *Into Deepest Space* (Harper; Heinemann 1975).
    James, Laurence. *Simon Rack: Earth Lies Sleeping* (Sphere).
    ---. **4+ other space operas, through 1975.**

1974 (cont.)

FIC

Jones, D. F. *The Fall of Colossus* (Putnam).
Lessing, Doris. *The Memoirs of a Survivor* (Octagon).
Macey, Peter. *Stationary Orbit* (Dobson).
Moorcock, Michael. *The Hollow Lands* (Harper & Row; Hart-Davis 1975).
---. *The Land Leviathan* (Quartet).
'Morland, Dick.' *Albion! Albion!* (Faber).
Pedler, Kit & Gerry Davis. *Brainrack* (Souvenir).
Priest, Christopher. *Inverted World* (Faber) [US *The Inverted World*].
---. *Real-Time World* [SS] (NEL).
Roberts, Keith. *The Chalk Giants* (Hutchinson).
Stableford, Brian. *The Fenris Device* (DAW; Pan 1978).
---. *The Paradise Game* (DAW; Dent 1976).
---. *Promised Land* (DAW; Dent 1975).
Tate, Peter. *Moon on an Iron Meadow* (Doubleday).
Tennant, Emma. *The Last of the Country House Murders* (Cape).
Timlett, Peter Valentine. *The Seedbearers* (Quartet).
---. **2 other novels in trilogy, through 1977.**
White, James. *The Dream Millennium* (Joseph).

FTV

[F] *Who?* Dir. Jack Gold. Hemisphere & Maclean. Wr. John Gould, from novel (1958) by Algis Budrys.
[F] *Zardoz*. Dir. John Boorman. John Boorman/20C Fox. Wr. & *nov. (1974) John Boorman.

GEN

[A] Hay, George, ed. *Stopwatch* (NEL).
[A] Platt, Charles & Hilary Bailey, eds. *New Worlds 7* (Sphere).

[C/A] Ashley, Mike. *The History of the Science Fiction Magazine: Part 1: 1926-1935* (NEL).
---. **Parts 2-4 through 1978.**

[PUB] *Science Fiction Monthly*, 1st. ed. Patricia Hornsey, Feb., through May 1976 (28 issues).

[W] *Billion Year Spree* (Brian Aldiss): BSFA special award.
[W] *Rendezvous with Rama* (Arthur C. Clarke): 21st. Hugo novel, US; 9th. Nebula novel, US; John W. Campbell Memorial novel (joint); BSFA novel.

1975

BIO
- d. Julian Huxley, 14 Feb.
- d. R. C. Sherriff, 13 Nov.
- d. Edward Hyams, 25 Nov.
- d. Ian Colvin.

FIC

Adlard, Mark. *Multiface* (Sidgwick & J).
Aldiss, Brian. *Excommunication* [SS] (Postcard).
Ballard, J. G. *High-Rise* (Cape).
Boyce, Chris. *Catchworld* (Gollancz).
Brunner, John. *The Shockwave Rider* (Dent).
'Carlton, Roger.' *Beyond Tomorrow* (Hale).
---. **several others, also as D. S. Rowland, through present.**
Clarke, Arthur C. *Imperial Earth: A Fantasy of Love and Discord* (Gollancz) [enl. Harcourt 1976].
Coney, Michael G. *Charisma* (Gollancz).
---. *Hello Summer, Goodbye* (Gollancz) [US *Rax*].
---. *The Jaws That Bite, the Claws That Catch* (DAW; Elmfield 1975 as *The Girl with a Symphony in Her Fingers*).
Cooper, Edmund (as 'Richard Avery'). *The Deathworms of Kratos* (Coronet).
---, **3 sequels, through 1976.**
Gordon, Stuart. *Suaine and the Crow-God* (NEL).
Greenhough, Terry. *Time and Timothy Grenville* (NEL).
Gutteridge, Lindsay. *Fratricide Is a Gas* (Cape).
Harrison, M. John. *The Machine in Shaft Ten* [SS] (Panther).
Hyams, Edward. *Morrow's Ants* (Lane).
Jones, D. F. *The Floating Zombie* (Berkley).
Kapp, Colin. *The Wizard of Anharitte* (Panther).
'Kippax, John' [P] *Where No Stars Guide* (Pan).
Lee, Tanith. *The Birthgrave* (DAW; Futura 1977).
Lewis, Charles. *The Cain Factor* (Harwood-Smart).
Logan, Charles. *Shipwreck* (Gollancz).
Lovesey, Andrew. *The Half-Angels* (Sphere).
Macey, Peter. *Distant Relations* (Dobson).
Mackelworth, R. W. *The Year of the Painted World* (Hale).
Mitchison, Naomi. *Solution Three* (Dobson).
Moorcock, Michael & 'Philip James.' *The Distant Suns* (Unicorn).
Morgan, Dan. *The Country of the Mind* (Corgi).
Norman, Barry. *End Product* (Quartet).
Pearce, Brenda. *Kidnapped into Space* (Dobson).
Pedler, Kit & Gerry Davis. *The Dynostar Menace* (Souvenir).
Penny, David G. *The Sunset People* (Hale).
Rushdie, Salman. *Grimus* (Gollancz).
Russell, Eric Frank. *Like Nothing on Earth* [SS] (Dobson).
Shaw, Bob. *Orbitsville* (Gollancz).
Sherwood, Martin. *Survival* (NEL).

1975 (cont.)

FIC

Spencer, John. *The Electronic Lullaby Meat Market* (Quartet).
Stableford, Brian. *Man in a Cage* (Day).
---. *Swan Song* (DAW; Pan 1978).
Sullivan, Sheila. *Summer Rising* (Weidenfeld & N) [US *The Calling of Bara* 1981].
Tate, Peter. *Seagulls under Glass* [SS] (Doubleday).
Tilley, Patrick. *Fade-Out* (Hodder & S).
Watson, Ian. *The Jonah Kit* (Gollancz).

FTV

[F] *The Land That Time Forgot*. Dir. Kevin Connor. Amicus. Wr. Michael Moorcock & James Cawthorn, from novellas by Edgar Rice Burroughs (1924).

[TV] *Space 1999*. Prod. Ray Austin et al. ITC miniseries. Wr. Christopher Penfold et al., from idea by Gerry & Sylvia Anderson. [*F 1979].
[TV] *Survivors*. Prod. Terence Dudley. BBC series, through 1977. Wr. and *nov. (1976) Terry Nation.

GEN

[A] Bailey, Hilary, ed. *New Worlds 8* (Sphere).
[A] ---, ed. *New Worlds 9* (Corgi).
[A] Moorcock, Michael, ed. *Before Armageddon* (W. H. Allen).

[E] Aldiss, Brian, ed. *Science Fiction Art: The Fantasies of SF* (NEL).

[FP] Kilworth, Garry. "Let's Go to Golgotha." *The Gollancz/Sunday Times Best SF Stories* (Gollancz).

[PUB] *Other Times*, eds. A. Ellsmore et al., Nov., through Feb. 1976 (2 issues).

[W] *Inverted World* (Christopher Priest): BSFA novel.

BIO

d. John Boland, 9 Nov.
d. 'John Rackham,' 16 Dec.
d. Anthony Armstrong.
d. E. C. Large.

FIC

Aldiss, Brian. *The Malacia Tapestry* (Cape).
Amis, Kingsley. *The Alteration* (Cape).
Ballard, J. G. *Low-Flying Aircraft* [SS] (Cape).
Bax, Martin. *The Hospital Ship* (Cape).
Bayley, Barrington J. *The Garments of Caean* (Doubleday; Fontana 1978).
Brunner, John. *The Book of John Brunner* [SS] (DAW).
---. *Interstellar Empire* (DAW; Hamlyn 1989).
Coney, Michael G. *Brontomek!* (Gollancz).
Corley, James. *Benedict's Planet* (Elmfield).
'Cowper, Richard.' *The Custodians* [SS] (Gollancz).
Dickinson, Peter. *King and Joker* (Hodder & S).
Doyle, Richard. *Deluge* (Arlington).
Dunn, Saul. *Steeleye* **Trilogy** (Coronet).
Edwards, Peter. *Terminus* (Macmillan)
Farren, Mick. *The Quest of the DNA Cowboys* (Mayflower).
---. *Synaptic Manhunt* (Mayflower).
Follett, James. *The Doomsday Ultimatum* (Weidenfeld & N).
Garnett, David S. *Cosmic Carousel* [SS] (Hale).
Greenhough, Terry. *The Wandering Worlds* (NEL).
--- (as 'Andrew Lester'). *The Thrice-Born* (NEL).
Haldane, J. B. S. [P]. *The Man with Two Memories* (Merlin).
Hodder-Williams, Christopher. *The Prayer Machine* (Weidenfeld & N).
Holdstock, Robert. *Eye Among the Blind* (Faber).
Kapp, Colin. *The Survival Game* (Ballantine; Dobson 1977).
King, John Robert. *Bruno Lipshitz and the Disciples of Dogma* (Gollancz).
'King, Vincent.' *Timesnake and Superclown* (Futura).
Kneale, Nigel. *The Year of the Sex Olympics and Other TV Plays* [D] (Ferret).
Lee, Tanith. *Don't Bite the Sun* (DAW).
---. *The Storm Lord* (DAW; Futura 1977).
Lindsay, David [P]. *The Violet Apple, and the Witch* (Chicago Review Press; Sidgwick & J 1978).
'McIntosh, J. T.' *Ruler of the World* (Laser).
Moorcock, Michael. *The Adventures of Una Persson and Catherine Cornelius in the Twentieth Century* (Quartet).
---. *The End of All Songs* (Hart-Davis).
---. *Legends from the End of Time* [SS] (W. H. Allen).
---. *The Lives and Times of Jerry Cornelius* [SS] (Allison & B).
---. *Moorcock's Book of Martyrs* [SS] (Quartet) [US *Dying for Tomorrow* 1978].

1976 (cont.)

FIC

Moorcock, Michael, with Michael Butterworth. *The Time of the Hawklords* (Star).
Morgan, Dan. *The Concrete Horizon* (Millington).
Nation, Terry. *Survivors* (Weidenfeld & N).
Pratchett, Terry. *The Dark Side of the Sun* (Smythe).
Priest, Christopher. *The Space Machine: A Scientific Romance* (Faber).
Roberts, Keith. *The Grain Kings* [SS] (Hutchinson).
Shaw, Bob. *Cosmic Kaleidoscope* [SS] (Gollancz) [US enl. 1976].
---. *A Wreath of Stars* (Gollancz).
Shelley, Mary [P]. *Collected Tales and Stories with Original Engravings* [SS] (*Johns Hopkins UP*).
Sherwood, Martin. *Maxwell's Demon* (NEL).
Stableford, Brian. *The Face of Heaven* (Quartet).
---. *The Florians* (*DAW*; Hamlyn 1978).
---. *The Mind Riders* (*DAW*; Fontana 1977).
Stapledon, Olaf [P]. *Four Encounters* [SS] (Bran's Head).
---. *Nebula Maker* (Bran's Head).
Storr, Catherine. *Unnatural Fathers* (Quartet).
Story, Jack Trevor. *Morag's Flying Fortress* (Hutchinson).
Tate, Peter. *Faces in the Flames* (Doubleday).
Tennant, Emma. *Hotel de Dream* (Gollancz).
Watson, Ian. *Orgasmachine* [in French] (Paris: Champ Libre).
Wells, Robert. *Candle in the Sun* (Sidgwick & J).
Wilson, Colin. *The Space Vampires* (Hart-Davis) [*F 1985 as *Life Force*].
Wilson, Steve. *The Lost Traveller: A Motorcycle Grail Quest Epic and Science Fiction Western* (Macmillan).

FTV

[F] *At the Earth's Core*. Dir. Kevin Connor. Amicus/AIP. Wr. Milton Subotsky, from novel (1922) by Edgar Rice Burroughs.
[F] *The Man Who Fell to Earth*. Dir. Nicolas Roeg. British Lion/Cinema V. Wr. Paul Mayersky, from novel (1963) by Walter Tevis.

GEN

[A] Anon., ed. *Supernova 1: SF Introduction* (Faber).
[A] Bailey, Hilary, ed. *New Worlds 10* (Corgi).
[A] Evans, Hilary & Dik, eds. *Beyond the Gaslight: Science in Popular Fiction 1895-1910* (Muller).
[A] Weston, Peter, ed. *Andromeda 1* (Futura).

[C] Nicholls, Peter, ed. *Science Fiction at Large* (Gollancz).

[FAN] *Arena SF*, ed. Geoff Rippington, through 1982.

GEN

[FP] Ryman, Geoff. "Diary of a Translator." *New Worlds 10*.

[PUB] *SF Digest*, ed. Julie Davis (1 issue).

[W] *Orbitsville* (Bob Shaw): BSFA Novel.

BIO
d. I. O. Evans, 13 Feb.
d. W. Grey Walter, 6 May.
d. Henry Brinton, 1 Jun.
d. William Gerhardi, 15 Jul.
d. Dacre Balsdon, 18 Sep.
d. Dennis Wheatley, 11 Nov.

FIC
Aldiss, Brian. *Brothers of the Head* (Pierrot).
---. *Last Orders* [SS] (Cape).
Ballard, J. G. *The Best of J. G. Ballard* [SS] (Futura).
Bayley, Barrington J. *The Grand Wheel* (*DAW*; Fontana 1979).
Butterworth, Michael, with Michael Moorcock. *Queens of Deliria* (Star).
Carter, Angela. *The Passion of New Eve* (Gollancz).
Cooper, Colin. *Dargason* (Dobson).
Dick, Kay. *They: A Sequence of Unease* (Allen Lane).
Farren, Mick. *The Neural Atrocity* (Mayflower).
Hodder-Williams, Christopher. *The Silent Voice* (Weidenfeld & N).
Holdstock, Robert. *Earthwind* (Faber).
Hoyle, Fred & Geoffrey Hoyle. *The Incandescent Ones* (Heinemann).
Hoyle, Trevor. *Blake's Seven* (Sphere).
---. *Q: Seeking the Mythical Future* (Panther).
---. *Q: Through the Eye of Time* (Panther).
Jones, D. F. *Colossus and the Crab* (Berkley).
Kapp, Colin. *The Chaos Weapon* (Ballantine; Dobson 1979).
---. *Manalone* (Panther).
Kilworth, Garry. *In Solitary* (Faber).
Lee, Tanith. *Drinking Sapphire Wine* (*DAW*; Hamlyn 1979).
---. *Volkhavaar* (*DAW*; Hamlyn 1981).
Macey, Peter. *Alien Culture* (Dobson).
MacLeod, Sheila. *Xanthe and the Robots* (Bodley Head).
'McIntosh, J. T.' *Norman Conquest 2066* (Corgi).
---. *This Is the Way the World Begins* (Corgi).
Moorcock, Michael. *The Condition of Muzak* (Allison & B).
---. *The Cornelius Chronicles* [O] (Avon; Fontana 1979 as *Cornelius*).
---. *The Transformation of Miss Mavis Ming* (W. H. Allen) [US *A Messiah at the End of Time* 1978].
Passes, Alan. *Big Step* (Allison & B).
Pearce, Brenda. *Worlds for the Grabbing* (Dobson).
Platt, Charles. *Sweet Evil* (Berkley).
Priest, Christopher. *A Dream of Wessex* (Faber) [US *The Perfect Lover*].
Roberts, Keith. *The Passing of the Dragons* [SS] (Berkley).
Shaw, Bob. *Medusa's Children* (Gollancz).
---. *Who Goes Here?* (Gollancz).

FIC

    Stableford, Brian. *Critical Threshold* (*DAW*; Hamlyn 1979).
    ---. *The Realms of Tartarus* (*DAW*).
    ---. *Wildeblood's Empire* (*DAW*; Hamlyn 1980).
    Stephenson, Andrew M. *Nightwatch* (Futura).
    {Tolkien, J. R. R. [P]. *The Silmarillion* (Allen & U).}
    Watson, Ian. *Alien Embassy* (Gollancz).
    ---. *The Martian Inca* (Gollancz).
    White, James. *Monsters and Medics* [SS] (Corgi).
    Williams, Eric C. *The Drop In* (Elmfield).

FTV

    [F] *The People That Time Forgot*. Dir. Kevin Connor. Amicus. Wr. Patrick Tilley, from novellas (1924) by Edgar Rice Burroughs.

    [TV] *Blake's Seven*. Cr. Terry Nation. Prod. David Maloney. BBC series, 52 episodes, 2 Jan., through 21 Dec. 1981.
    [TV] *1990*. Prod. Prudence Fitzgerald. BBC miniseries. Cr. Wilfred Greatorex.

GEN

    [A] Ashley, Mike, ed. *The Best of British SF* [vols 1 & 2] (Futura).
    [A] Moorcock, Michael, ed. *England Invaded: A Collection of Fantasy Fiction* (W. H. Allen).
    [A] Weston, Peter, ed. *Andromeda 2* (Futura).

    [CX] "2000 A.D." Cr. John Wagner. IPC, 26 Feb., through present.
    [E] Clarke, Arthur C. *The View from Serendip* (*Random House*; Gollancz 1978).

    [PUB] *Vortex*, ed. Keith Seddon, Jan., through May 1977 (5 issues).

    [W] *The Alteration* (Kingsley Amis): John W. Campbell Memorial novel.
    [W] *Brontomek!* (Michael G. Coney): BSFA novel.

BIO
- d. 'Jane Lane,' 6 Jan.
- d. Eric Frank Russell, 28 Feb.
- d. 'Edmund Crispin,' 15 Sep.
- d. Hope Mirrlees.

FIC
- Aldiss, Brian. *Enemies of the System: A Tale of Homo Uniformis* (Cape).
- Ballard, J. G. *The Best Short Stories of J. G. Ballard* [SS] (*Holt Rinehart*).
- Bayley, Barrington J. *The Knights of the Limits* [SS] (Allison & B).
- ---. *Star Winds* (*DAW*).
- Burgess, Anthony. *1985* (Hutchinson).
- Burley, W. J. *The Sixth Day* (Gollancz).
- Clarke, Arthur C. *Four Great SF Novels* [O] (Gollancz).
- Compton, D. G. *A Usual Lunacy* (Borgo).
- Cooper, Edmund. *Merry Christmas, Ms Minerva* (Hale).
- 'Cowper, Richard.' *The Road to Corlay* (Gollancz) [enl. Pocket 1979].
- Deighton, Len. *SS-GB* (Cape).
- Dunn, Saul. *The Cabal* [**Nos. 1 and 2**] (Corgi).
- Farren, Mick. *The Feelies* (Big O).
- High, Philip E. *Fugitive from Time* (Hale).
- Hoyle, Fred & Geoffrey Hoyle. *The Westminster Disaster* (Heinemann).
- Hoyle, Trevor. *Q: The Gods Look Down* (Panther).
- Kapp, Colin. *The Ion War* (Ace; Dobson 1979).
- Kilworth, Garry. *The Night of Kadar* (Faber).
- Lee, Tanith. *Night's Master* (*DAW*; Hamlyn 1982).
- ---. *Quest for the White Witch* (*DAW*; Futura 1979).
- ---. *Vazkor, Son of Vazkor* (*DAW*; Futura 1979 as *Shadowfire*).
- MacLeod, Sheila. *Circuit-Breaker* (Bodley Head).
- Moorcock, Michael. *Gloriana; or, The Unfulfill'd Queen* (Allison & B).
- Russell, Eric Frank. *The Best of Eric Frank Russell* [SS] (*Ballantine*).
- Shaw, Bob. *Ship of Strangers* (Gollancz).
- ---. *Vertigo* (Gollancz).
- Stableford, Brian. *The City of the Sun* (*DAW*; Hamlyn 1980).
- Watson, Ian. *Miracle Vistors* (Gollancz).

FTV
- [F] *The Shout*. Dir. Jerzy Skolimowski. Rank. Wr. Jerzy Skolimowski & Michael Moorcock, from story by Robert Graves.
- [F] *Superman--The Movie*. Dir. R. Donner. Dovemead/International. Wr. Mario Puzo et al., from US comic.
- [F] *Warlords of Atlantis*. Dir. Kevin Connor. EMI. Wr. Brian Hayles.

GEN

[A] Britton, David & Michael Butterworth, eds. *The Savoy Book* (Savoy).
[A] Hay, George, ed. *Pulsar 1* (Penguin).
[A] Priest, Christopher, ed. *Anticipations* (Faber).
[A] Weston, Peter, ed. *Andromeda 3* (Futura).

[C] Aldiss, Brian. *Science Fiction as Science Fiction* (Bran's Head).
[C] Holdstock, Robert, ed. *Encyclopedia of Science Fiction* (Octopus).

[W] *The Jonah Kit* (Ian Watson): BSFA novel.
[W] *The Silmarillion* (J. R. R. Tolkien): 25th Hugo 'Gandalf' fantasy novel, US.

5
The British Fantastic: 1979–1990

If there is British science fiction today, then it is of the kind that conforms to the formulae of, and is usually issued by, American-dominated (though now multinational) publishers. Writers whose earlier work was marketed as science fiction have by now--if they have demonstrated any literary ambition--migrated to, and been reabsorbed by, the mainstream, even though their work may be entirely continuous in subject and theme from their earlier 'science fiction.'

Some would say that the New Wave had decayed before 1979; others, that it was not until the publication of Ballard's *Empire of the Sun* in 1984 that the extent of the British migration from science fiction/SF became clear. Yet 1979 is certainly a watershed year. It saw the last issue of *New Worlds*; it saw the declaration of independence from SF by the most talented of the younger generation of British New Wave writers, Christopher Priest; it saw the publication of the Nicholls *Encyclopedia* at the psychological moment when the field of science fiction had expanded to its maximum extent; and it saw the beginning of the most ambitious attempt to date (though by no means an always artistically successful one) to appropriate and exploit the motifs of science fiction by a writer whose work had, until then, been regarded as 'mainstream': the Canopus Quintet by Doris Lessing.

Hindsight is insufficient to allow an identification of the key works of this period, provisionally entitled here "The British Fantastic." This is intended to suggest a convergence between SF and mainstream literature that, taking its cue from authors as diverse as Poe, Kafka, Nabokov, Borges, the French new novelists and the Latin American magic realists, subverts both realism as literary mode and the reader's confidence in the solidity of consensus reality.

BIO
- d. Nicholas Monsarrat, 8 Aug.
- d. Walter Gillings.

FIC

Adams, Douglas. *The Hitchhiker's Guide to the Galaxy* (Pan) [*TV 1982].
Aldiss, Brian. *New Arrivals, Old Encounters* [SS] (Cape).
---. *Pile: Petals from St Klaed's Computer* [V] (Cape).
Ballard, J. G. *The Unlimited Dream Company* (Cape).
Clarke, Arthur C. *The Fountains of Paradise* (Gollancz).
Compton, D. G. *Windows* (Berkley).
Coney, Michael G. *The Ultimate Jungle* (Millington).
Cooper, Edmund. *Tomorrow Laughs* [SS] (Hodder & S).
'Cowper, Richard.' *Profundis* (Gollancz).
Dickinson, Peter. *The Flight of Dragons* (Pierrot).
Fairbairns, Zoë. *Benefits* (Virago).
Franklin, K. D. *The Worlds of Sector P* (Dobson).
Hackett, Sir John et al. *The Third World War: August 1985* (Macmillan).
High, Philip E. *Blindfold from the Stars* (Dobson).
Hodder-Williams, Christopher. *The Thinktank That Leaked* (United Writers).
Hoyle, Trevor. *Blake's Seven: Project Avalon* (Arrow).
---. *Earth Cult* (Panther) [US *The Sentient Earth*].
Jones, D. F. *Xeno* (Sidgwick & J) [US *Earth Has Been Found*].
Kapp, Colin. *The Unorthodox Engineers* [SS] (Dobson).
Kilworth, Garry. *Split Second* (Faber).
Kneale, Nigel. *Quatermass* (Hutchinson).
Lee, Tanith. *Death's Master* (DAW; Hamlyn 1982).
---. *Electric Forest* (DAW).
Lessing, Doris. *Shikasta* (Cape).
'McIntosh, J. T.' *A Planet Called Utopia* (Zebra).
Orgill, Douglas, with John Gribbin. *The Sixth Winter* (Bodley Head).
Priest, Christopher. *An Infinite Summer* [SS] (Faber).
Roberts, Keith. *Ladies from Hell* [SS] (Gollancz).
Shaw, Bob. *Dagger of the Mind* (Gollancz).
Shiel, M. P. [P] *The Works of M. P. Shiel. Vol. 1.* [O] (PP).
Stableford, Brian. *Balance of Power* (DAW; Hamlyn 1984).
---. *The Paradox of Sets* (DAW).
---. *The Walking Shadow* (Fontana).
Stephenson, Andrew M. *The Wall of Years* (Futura).
Tate, Peter. *Greencomber* (Doubleday).
Watson, Ian. *God's World* [SS] (Gollancz).
---. *The Very Slow Time Machine* [SS] (Gollancz).
White, James. *Ambulance Ship* (Ballantine; Corgi 1980).
---. *Underkill* (Corgi).
Wyndham, John [P]. *Web* (Joseph).
--- (as John Beynon) [P]. *Exiles on Asperus* (Severn House).

FTV

[F] *Alien*. Dir. Ridley Scott. Fox/Brandywine. Wr. Dan O'Bannon.

[TVF] *The Quatermass Conclusion*. Dir. Piers Haggard. Euston. Wr. Nigel Kneale.

GEN

[A] Grant, John, ed. *Aries 1* (David & C).
[A] Hay, George, ed. *Pulsar 2* (Penguin).
[A] Holdstock, Robert & Christopher Priest, eds. *Stars of Albion* (Pan).

[C] Nicholls, Peter, ed. *The Encyclopedia of Science Fiction* (Granada).

[E] Aldiss, Brian. *This World and Nearer Ones: Essays Exploring the Familiar* (Weidenfeld & N).

[FAN] Worldcon, Brighton (Seacon I).

[PUB] Last issue, *New Worlds* (Sep.) [vol. 61 No. 216].

[W] *Gloriana; or, The Unfulfill'd Queen* (Michael Moorcock): John W. Campbell Memorial novel; World Fantasy Award novel.

BIO
- d. John Collier, 6 Apr.
- d. Margot Bennett, 6 Dec.

FIC
- Adams, Douglas. *The Restaurant at the End of the Universe* (Pan).
- Aldiss, Brian. *Moreau's Other Island* (Cape) [US *An Island Called Moreau* 1981].
- Amis, Kingsley. *Russian Hide-and-Seek: A Melodrama* (Hutchinson).
- Ballard, J. G. *The Venus Hunters* [SS] (Panther).
- Boyce, Chris. *Brainfix* (Panther).
- Brunner, John. *Foreign Constellations: The Fantastic Worlds of John Brunner* [SS] (*Everest House*).
- ---. *The Infinitive of Go* (Ballantine).
- ---. *Players at the Game of People* (Ballantine).
- Compton, D. G. *Ascendancies* (Gollancz).
- Cooper, Edmund. *A World of Difference* (Hale).
- 'Cowper, Richard.' *Out There Where the Big Ships Go* [SS] (*Pocket*).
- ---. *The Web of the Magi* [SS] (Gollancz).
- Evans, Christopher. *Capella's Golden Eye* (Faber).
- Harrison, M. John. *A Storm of Wings* (Sphere).
- Hoban, Russell. *Riddley Walker* (Cape).
- Kapp, Colin. *The Timewinders* (Dobson).
- Lee, Tanith. *Day by Night* (DAW).
- ---. *Kill the Dead* (DAW).
- ---. *Sabella; or, The Blood-Stone* (DAW; Unwin 1988).
- Lessing, Doris. *The Marriages Between Zones Three, Four and Five* (Cape).
- Moorcock, Michael. *The Golden Barge* (Savoy).
- ---. *My Experiences in the Third World War* [SS] (Savoy).
- Roberts, Keith. *Molly Zero* (Gollancz).
- Saxton, Josephine. *The Travails of Jane Saint* (Virgin) [enl. Women's 1986 as *The Travails of Jane Saint and Other Stories*].
- Shiel, M. P. [P]. *The New King* (PP).
- Stableford, Brian. *Optiman* (DAW; Pan 1981 as *War Games*).
- Stapledon, Olaf [P]. *Far Future Calling: Uncollected Science Fiction and Fantasies* [SS] (*Oswald Train*).
- Vyse, Michael. *The Outer Reaches* [SS] (Faber).
- ---. *Overworld* (Faber).
- Watson, Ian. *The Gardens of Delight* (Gollancz).

FTV
- [F] *The Falls*. Wr. & Dir. Peter Greenaway. BFI.
- [F] *Flash Gordon*. Dir. Michael Hodges. Starling/Famous. Wr. Lorenzo Semple, Jr.
- [F] *Inseminoid* (US *Horror Planet*). Dir. Norman J. Warren. Jupiter. Wr. Nick & Gloria Maley.

1980 (cont.)

[F] *Saturn 3*. Dir. Stanley Donen. ITC/Transcontinental. Wr. Martin Amis, from story by John Barry. Novelized as *Saturn Three* by Steve Gallagher (Sphere 1980).
[F] *Superman II*. Dir. Richard Lester. Dovemead/International. Wr. Mario Puzo et al.

GEN

[PUB] *Something Else*, ed. Charles Partington, Spring, through Spring 1984 (3 issues).

[W] *The Fountains of Paradise* (Arthur C. Clarke): 27th. Hugo novel, US; 15th. Nebula novel, US.
[W] *The Unlimited Dream Company* (J. G. Ballard): BSFA novel.

BIO
- d. David Garnett, 17 Feb.
- d. D. F. Jones, 1 Apr.
- d. Kit Pedler, 27 May.
- d. Francis G. Rayer, 11 Jul.
- d. John Gloag, 17 Jul.

FIC
Aldiss, Brian. *Foreign Bodies* (Singapore: *Chopmen*).
Ballard, J. G. *Hello America* (Cape).
Cole, Adrian. *The Lucifer Experiment* (Hale).
---. *Wargods of Ludorbis* (Hale).
Coney, Michael G. *Neptune's Cauldron* (Tower).
'Cowper, Richard.' *A Dream of Kinship* (Gollancz).
Duffy, Maureen. *Gor Saga* (Methuen).
Evans, Christopher. *The Insider* (Faber).
Farren, Mick. *The Song of Phaid the Gambler* (NEL).
Gordon, Stuart. *Smile on the Void* (Putnam; Arrow 1982).
Gray, Alasdair. *Lanark* (Canongate).
Hoyle, Trevor. *Blake's Seven: Scorpio Attack* (BBC).
Kapp, Colin. *Search for the Sun* (NEL).
Kilworth, Garry. *Gemini God* (Faber).
Lee, Tanith. *Delusion's Master* (DAW; Arrow 1987).
---. *The Silver Metal Lover* (Nelson Doubleday).
Lessing, Doris. *The Sirian Experiments* (Cape).
Mackelworth, R. W. *Shakehole* (Hale).
Moorcock, Michael. *Byzantium Endures* (Secker & W).
---. *The Entropy Tango* (NEL).
---. *The Steel Tsar* (Mayflower).
---. *The Warhound and the World's Pain* (Pocket; NEL 1982).
Pratchett, Terry. *Strata* (Smythe).
Priest, Christopher. *The Affirmation* (Faber).
Shaw, Bob. *The Ceres Solution* (Gollancz).
---. *Galactic Tours* (Proteus).
Stableford, Brian. *The Castaway of Tanagar* (DAW).
Thomas, D. M. *The White Hotel* (Gollancz).
Watson, Ian. *Deathhunter* (Gollancz).
--- & Michael Bishop. *Under Heaven's Bridge* (Gollancz).

FTV
- [F] *The Memoirs of a Survivor*. Dir. David Gladwell. Memorial/EMI. Wr. David Gladwell & Kerry Grabbe, from *novel (1974) by Doris Lessing.
- [F] *Outland*. Wr. & Dir. Peter Hyams. Ladd.
- [F] *The Time Bandits*. Dir. Terry Gilliam. Avco Embassy/HandMade. Wr. Terry Gilliam & Michael Palin.

GEN
- [A] Watson, Ian, ed. *Pictures at an Exhibition* (Greystoke Mobray).

BIO

    d. Edmund Cooper, 11 Mar.
    d. Ronald Duncan, 3 Jun.
    d. John Hargrave, 21 Nov.

FIC

    Adams, Douglas. *Life, the Universe and Everything* (Pan).
    Aldiss, Brian. *Helliconia Spring* (Cape).
    Ballard, J. G. *Myths of the Near Future* [SS] (Cape).
    ---. *News from the Sun* (Interzone).
    Bayley, Barrington J. *Pillars of Eternity* (DAW).
    Burgess, Anthony. *The End of the World News* (Hutchinson).
    Clarke, Arthur C. *2010: Odyssey Two* (Granada) [F 1984].
    Coney, Michael G. *Cat Karina* (Ace; Gollancz 1983).
    'Cowper, Richard.' *A Tapestry of Time* (Gollancz).
    Hackett, Sir John, et al. *The Third World War: The Untold Story* (Sidgwick & J).
    Harrison, M. John. *In Viriconium* (Gollancz) [US *The Floating Gods* 1983].
    Hemingway, Amanda. *Pzyche* (Faber).
    Holdstock, Robert. *In the Valley of the Statues* [SS] (Faber).
    ---. *Where Time Winds Blow* (Faber).
    Kapp, Colin. *The Lost World of Cronus* (NEL).
    ---. *The Tyrant of Hades* (NEL).
    Langford, David. *The Space Eater* (Arrow).
    Lee, Tanith. *Cyrion* [SS] (DAW).
    Lessing, Doris. *The Making of the Representative for Planet 8* (Cape).
    Mann, Phillip. *The Eye of the Queen* (Gollancz).
    Moorcock, Michael. *The Brothel in Rosenstrasse* (NEL).
    Rohan, Mike Scott. *Run to the Stars* (Arrow).
    Shaw, Bob. *A Better Mantrap* (Gollancz).
    Stableford, Brian. *Journey to the Center* (DAW).
    Tennant, Emma. *Queen of Stones* (Cape).
    Van Greenaway, Peter. *Manrissa Man* (Gollancz).
    Watson, Ian. *Sunstroke* [SS] (Gollancz).
    White, James. *Future Past* [SS] (*Ballantine*).

FTV

    [F] *Xtro*. Dir. H. Bromley Davenport. Ashley Amalgamated. Wr. Iain Cassie & Robert Smith.

GEN

    [CX] Briggs, Raymond. *When the Wind Blows* (H. Hamilton).

    [PUB] *Extro Science Fiction*, ed. Paul Campbell, Feb./Mar., through Jul./Aug. (3 issues).
    [PUB] *Interzone*, eds. David Pringle et al., Spring, through present.

GEN
- [W] *Riddley Walker* (Russell Hoban): John W. Campbell Memorial.

BIO
d. Arthur Koestler, 3 Mar.
d. 'John Lymington,' 3 Aug.

FIC
Aldiss, Brian. *Helliconia Summer* (Cape).
Bayley, Barrington J. *The Zen Gun* (DAW; Methuen 1984).
Berry, Adrian. *Koyama's Diamond: A Novel of the Far Future* (Book Guild).
Brunner, John. *The Crucible of Time* (Ballantine; Arrow 1984).
Coney, Michael G. *The Celestial Steam Locomotive* (Houghton M).
Dunstan, Frederick. *Habitation One* (Fontana).
Fullerton, Alexander. *Regenesis* (Joseph).
Gentle, Mary. *Golden Witchbreed* (Gollancz).
Gordon, Stuart. *Fire in the Abyss* (Berkley; Arrow 1984).
Harrison, M. John. *The Ice Monkey* [SS] (Gollancz).
Hoyle, Trevor. *The Last Gasp* (Crown; Sphere 1984).
Lee, Tanith. *Anackire* (DAW; Futura 1986).
---. *Red as Blood; or, Tales from the Sisters Grimmer* [SS] (DAW).
---. *Sung in Shadow* (DAW).
Lessing, Doris. *The Sentimental Agents in the Volyen Empire* (Cape).
Mitchison, Naomi. *Not by Bread Alone* (Boyars).
Moorcock, Michael. *The Dancers at the End of Time* [O] (Granada).
Pratchett, Terry. *The Colour of Magic* (Smythe).
Shaw, Bob. *Orbitsville Departure* (Gollancz).
Stableford, Brian. *The Gates of Eden* (DAW).
Van Greenaway, Peter. *graffiti* (Gollancz).
Watson, Ian. *Chekhov's Journey* (Gollancz).
White, James. *Sector General* [SS] (Ballantine).

FTV
[F] *The Dark Crystal*. Dir. Jim Henson & Frank Oz. Henson/ITC. Wr. David Odell from story by Jim Henson.
[F] *Krull*. Dir. Peter Yates. Columbia. Wr. Stanford Sherman.
[F] *Superman III*. Dir. Richard Lester. Dovemead/Cantharus. Wr. David Newman & Leslie Newman.

[TV] *The Hitch-Hiker's Guide to the Galaxy*. BBC series, 7x60 mins., from *novel (1979) by Douglas Adams.

GEN
[A] Moorcock, Michael, ed. *New Worlds: An Anthology* (Flamingo).

GEN

[C] Greenland, Colin. *The Entropy Exhibition: Michael Moorcock and the British 'New Wave' in Science Fiction* (Routledge).

[C] Suvin, Darko. *Victorian Science Fiction in the U.K.: The Discourses of Knowledge and of Power* (G. K. Hall).

[CX] "Judge Dredd." Cr. John Wagner, drawn by John Bolland. *Eagle* and elsewhere, Nov., through present.

[W] *Helliconia Spring* (Brian Aldiss): John W. Campbell Memorial novel; BSFA novel.

1984

BIO

d. Douglas Orgill, Feb.
d. J. B. Priestley, 14 Aug.
d. 'Ludovic Peters,' Dec.
d. Hugh Sykes Davies.

FIC

Adams, Douglas. *So Long, and Thanks for All the Fish* (Pan).
Aldiss, Brian. *Seasons in Flight* [SS] (Cape).
Ballard, J. G. *Empire of the Sun* (Gollancz).
Banks, Iain. *The Wasp Factory* (Macmillan).
Berry, Adrian. *Labyrinth of Lies* (Book Guild).
Brunner, John. *The Tides of Time* (Ballantine; Penguin 1988).
Carter, Angela. *Nights at the Circus* (Chatto & W).
Coney, Michael G. *Gods of the Greataway* (Houghton M).
'Cowper, Richard.' *The Tithonian Factor* [SS] (Gollancz).
Farren, Mick. *Protectorate* (Ace).
Greenland, Colin. *Daybreak on a Different Mountain* (Unwin).
Harrison, M. John. *Viriconium Nights* [O] (Ace; rev. Gollancz 1985).
Hodder-Williams, Christopher. *The Chromosome Game* (Mithras).
Holdstock, Robert. *Mythago Wood* (Gollancz).
Jones, Gwyneth. *Divine Endurance* (Allen & U).
Kilworth, Garry. *The Songbirds of Pain* [SS] (Gollancz).
---. *A Theatre of Timesmiths* (Gollancz).
Langford, David. *The Leaky Establishment* (Muller).
Lee, Tanith. *The Beautiful Biting Machine* [SS] (*Cheap Street*).
---. *The Dragon Hoard* (Ace; Beaver 1989).
---. *Tamastara; or, The Indian Nights* (DAW).
Moorcock, Michael. *The Laughter of Carthage* (Secker & W).
---. *The Nomad of Time* [O] (Panther).
---. *The Opium General* [SS] (NEL).
Priest, Christopher. *The Glamour.* (Cape)
Shaw, Bob. *Fire Pattern* (Gollancz).
Tilley, Patrick. *The Amtrak Wars Book 1: Cloud Warrior* (Severn House).
Watson, Ian. *The Book of the River* (Gollancz).
---. *The Book of the Stars* (Gollancz).
---. *Converts* (Granada).
Wells, H. G. [P]. *The Man with a Nose and Other Uncollected Stories of H. G. Wells* (Athlone).
Wilson, Snoo. *Spaceache* (Chatto & W).

FTV

[F] *Electric Dreams*. Dir. Steve Barron. Virgin/MGM/UA/Fox. Wr. Rusty Lemorade.

1984 (cont.)

FTV

[F] *Greystoke: The Legend of Tarzan of the Apes*. Dir. Hugh Hudson. WEA/Warner. Wr. Robert Towne & Michael Austin, from novel *Tarzan of the Apes* (1914) by Edgar Rice Burroughs.

[F] *1984*. Dir. and Wr. Michael Radford. Virgin/Umbrella/Rosenblum. From novel *Nineteen Eighty-Four* (1949) by 'George Orwell.'

GEN

[A] Britton, David & Michael Butterworth, eds. *Savoy Dreams* (Savoy).

[E] Clarke, Arthur C. *1984: Spring: A Choice of Futures* (Granada).

BIO

d. Robert Graves, 7 Dec.
d. Kyril Bonfiglioli.

FIC

Ackroyd, Peter. *Hawksmoor* (H. Hamilton).
Aldiss, Brian. *Helliconia Winter* (Cape).
Banks, Iain. *Walking on Glass* (Macmillan)
Barker, Clive. *The Damnation Game* (Weidenfeld & N).
Bayley, Barrington. *The Rod of Light* (Methuen).
Carter, Angela. *Black Venus* [SS] (Chatto & W).
Compton, D. G. *Scudder's Game* (Munich: *Heyne*; Kerosina 1988).
Evans, Christopher. *In Limbo* (Granada).
Forbes, Caroline. *The Needle on Full* [SS] (Onlywomen).
Fowles, John. *A Maggot* (Cape).
Household, Geoffrey. *Arrows of Desire* (Joseph).
Hoyle, Fred. *Comet Halley* (Joseph).
Lee, Tanith. *Days of Grass* (DAW).
---. *The Gorgon and Other Beastly Tales* [SS] (*DAW*).
Noyes, Ralph. *A Secret Property* (Quartet).
Palmer, Jane. *The Planet Dweller* (Women's).
Powys, John Cowper [P]. *Three Fantasies* [SS] (Carcanet).
Roberts, Keith. *Kiteworld* (Gollancz).
Ryman, Geoff. *The Warrior Who Carried Life* (Allen & U).
Saxton, Josephine. *The Power of Time* (Chatto & W).
Shaw, Bob. *The Peace Machine* (Gollancz).
Stableford, Brian & David Langford. *The Third Millennium: A History of the World: AD 2000-3000* (Sidgwick & J).
Tilley, Patrick. *The Amtrak Wars Book 2: First Family* (Sphere).
Watson, Ian. *The Book of Being* (Gollancz).
---. *The Book of Ian Watson* [SS & E] (*Ziesing*).
---. *Slow Birds* [SS] (Gollancz).
White, James. *Star Healer* (*Ballantine*).
Wilson, Snoo. *Inside Babel* (Chatto & W).

FTV

[F] *Brazil*. Dir. Terry Gilliam. Brazil/Fox. Wr. Terry Gilliam, Tom Stoppard & Charles McKeown.
[F] *Life Force*. Dir. Tobe Hooper. London/Cannon. Wr. Dan O'Bannon & Don Jakoby, from novel *The Space Vampires* (1976) by Colin Wilson.
[F] *Morons from Outer Space*. Dir. Mike Hodges. Thorn/EMI. Wr. Mel Smith & Griff Rhys Jones.

GEN

[A] Clute, John, et al. *Interzone: The First Anthology* (Dent).
[A] Green, Jen & Sarah Lefanu, eds. *Despatches from the Frontiers of the Female Mind* (Women's).

1985(cont.)

GEN

[C] Stableford, Brian. *Scientific Romance in Britain 1890-1950* (4th Estate).

[E] Aldiss, Brian. *The Pale Shadow of Science* (*Serconia*).

[W] *Mythago Wood* (Robert Holdstock): World Fantasy novel; BSFA novel.

BIO
    d. Rex Warner, 24 Jun.
    d. Storm Jameson, 30 Sep.
    d. Cyril Donson, 13 Nov.

FIC

    Banks, Iain. *The Bridge* (Macmillan).
    Barnes, Julian. *Staring at the Sun* (Cape).
    Brooke-Rose, Christine. *Xorandor* (Carcanet).
    Butler, David. *The Man Who Mastered Time* (Heinemann).
    Clarke, Arthur C. *The Songs of Distant Earth* (Grafton).
    'Cowper, Richard.' *Shades of Darkness* (Kerosina).
    Davies, Pete. *The Last Election* (Deutsch).
    Jones, Gwyneth. *Escape Plans* (Allen & U).
    Mann, Phillip. *Master of Paxwax* (Gollancz).
    Martin, Graham Dunstan. *Time-Slip* (Allen & U).
    Moorcock, Michael. *The City in the Autumn Stars* (Grafton).
    Palmer, Jane. *The Watcher* (Women's).
    Pratchett, Terry. *The Light Fantastic* (Smythe).
    Roberts, Keith. *Kaeti and Company* (Kerosina).
    ---. *The Lordly Ones* [SS] (Gollancz).
    Ryman, Geoff. *The Unconquered Country* (Unicorn).
    Saxton, Josephine. *Little Tours of Hell* (Pandora).
    ---. *Queen of the States* (Women's).
    Shaw, Bob. *The Ragged Astronauts* (Gollancz).
    Watson, Ian. *The Books of the Black Current* [O] (*Nelson Doubleday*).
    ---. *Queenmagic, Kingmagic* (Gollancz).

GEN

    [E] Aldiss, Brian. *And the Lurid Glare of the Comet* (*Serconia*).

    [W] *Helliconia Winter* (Brian Aldiss): BSFA novel.

BIO

    d. Ronald Clark, 9 Mar.
    d. Roger Lancelyn Green, 8 Oct.
    d. Frank Edward Arnold, 14 Nov.
    d. Roger Manvell, 30 Nov.
    d. Anthony West, 27 Dec.

FIC

    Adams, Douglas. *Dirk Gently's Holistic Detective Agency* (Heinemann).
    Aldiss, Brian. *Cracken at Critical* (Kerosina) (US *The Year Before Yesterday*).
    ---. *The Magic of the Past* (Kerosina).
    ---. *Ruins* (Hutchinson).
    Amis, Martin. *Einstein's Monsters* [SS] (Cape).
    Ballard, J. G. *The Day of Creation* (Gollancz).
    Banks, Iain M. *Consider Phlebas* (Macmillan).
    Barker, Clive. *Weaveworld* (Collins).
    Beebee, Chris. *The Hub* (Macdonald).
    Brunner, John. *The Shift Key* (Methuen).
    Burgess, Anthony. *A Clockwork Orange: A Play with Music* [D] (Hutchinson).
    Constantine, Storm. *The Enchantments of Flesh and Spirit* (Macdonald).
    Davies, Paul. *Fireball* (Heinemann).
    Gentle, Mary. *Ancient Light* (Gollancz).
    Gordon, Stuart. *Archon* (Orbit).
    Greenland, Colin. *The Hour of the Thin Ox* (Unwin).
    Kilworth, Garry. *Spiral Winds* (Bodley Head).
    Langford, Dave & John Grant. *Earthdoom!* (Grafton).
    Mann, Phillip. *The Fall of the Families* (Gollancz).
    Martin, Graham Dunstan. *The Dream Wall* (Unwin).
    Moorcock, Michael. *The Dragon in the Sword* (Grafton).
    Platt, Charles. *Less Than Human* (Grafton).
    Pratchett, Terry. *Equal Rites* (Gollancz).
    ---. *Mort* (Gollancz).
    Roberts, Keith. *Gráinne* (Kerosina).
    Tilley, Patrick. *The Amtrak Wars Book 3: The Iron Master* (Sphere).
    Watson, Ian. *Evil Water* [SS] (Gollancz).
    ---. *The Power* (Headline).
    Webster, Lyn. *The Illumination of Alice J. Cunningham* (Dedalus).
    Wilson, Colin. *Spider World: The Tower* (Grafton).
    ---. *Spider World: The Delta* (Grafton).

GEN

    [A] Evans, Christopher & Robert Holdstock, eds. *Other Edens* (Unwin).
    [A] Kaveney, Roz, ed. *Tales from the Forbidden Planet* (Titan).

    [C] Moorcock, Michael. *Wizardry and Wild Romance* (Gollancz).

GEN

[E] Arthur C. Clarke. *Arthur C. Clarke's July 20, 2019: A Day in the Life of the Twenty-First Century* (Grafton).

[FAN] Worldcon, Brighton (Conspiracy).

[W] *The Ragged Astronauts* (Bob Shaw): BSFA novel.
[W] *Trillion Year Spree* (Brian Aldiss with David Wingrove): Hugo non-fiction, US.

BIO
- d. Marghanita Laski, 6 Feb.
- d. Fenner Brockway, 28/29 Apr.
- d. Barbara Wootton, 11 Jul.
- d. Geoffrey Household, 4 Oct.

FIC
- Adams, Douglas. *The Long Dark Tea-Time of the Soul* (Heinemann).
- Aldiss, Brian. *Best SF Stories of Brian W. Aldiss* [SS] (Gollancz) [rep. Gollancz 1989 as *Man in His Time: Best SF Stories*].
- ---. *Science Fiction Blues* [D] (Avernus).
- Ballard, J. G. *Memories of the Space Age* [SS] (Arkham House).
- ---. *Running Wild* (Hutchinson).
- Banks, Iain M. *The Player of Games* (Macmillan).
- Brosnan, John. *The Sky Lords* (Gollancz).
- Brunner, John. *The Best of John Brunner* [SS] (Ballantine).
- ---. *The Days of March* (Kerosina).
- Clarke, Arthur C. *2061: Odyssey Three* (Grafton).
- --- & Gentry Lee. *Cradle* (Gollancz).
- Constantine, Storm. *The Bewitchments of Love and Hate* (Macdonald).
- Dickinson, Peter. *Eva* (Gollancz).
- Farren, Mick. *Their Master's War* (Sphere).
- ---. *Vickers* (Ace).
- Ferguson, Neil. *Putting Out* (H. Hamilton).
- Fowler, Christopher. *Roofworld* (Legend).
- Gordon, Stuart. *The Hidden World* (Orbit).
- Greenland, Colin. *Other Voices* (Unwin).
- Gribbin, John & Marcus Chown. *Double Planet* (Gollancz).
- Holdstock, Robert. *Lavondyss* (Gollancz).
- Jones, Gwyneth. *Kairos* (Unwin).
- Kilworth, Garry. *Abandonati* (Unwin).
- ---. *Cloudrock* (Unwin).
- Lee, Tanith. *The Book of the Beast* (Unwin).
- ---. *The Book of the Damned* (Unwin).
- ---. *The White Serpent* (DAW).
- Lessing, Doris. *The Fifth Child* (Cape).
- Mann, Philip. *Pioneers* (Gollancz).
- Martin, Graham Dunstan. *Half a Glass of Moonshine* (Unwin).
- McAllister, Angus. *The Krugg Syndrome* (Grafton).
- McAuley, Paul J. *Four Hundred Billion Stars* (Gollancz).
- McDonald, Ian. *Desolation Road* (Bantam).
- ---. *Empire Dreams* [SS] (Bantam).
- Moorcock, Michael. *Mother London* (Secker & W).
- Platt, Charles. *Free Zone* (Avon).
- ---. *Plasm* (Grafton).
- Pratchett, Terry. *Sourcery* (Gollancz).
- ---. *Wyrd Sisters* (Gollancz).
- Shaw, Bob. *The Wooden Spaceships* (Gollancz).
- Stableford, Brian. *The Empire of Fear* (Simon & S).

1988 (cont.)

FIC

Thompson, E. P. *The Sykaos Papers* (Bloomsbury).
Tilley, Patrick. *The Amtrak Wars Book 4: Blood River* (Sphere).
Watson, Ian. *The Fire Worm* (Gollancz).
---. *Meat* (Headline).
---. *Whores of Babylon* (Grafton).
White, James. *Federation World* (Ballantine; Orbit 1990).
Wright, Helen. *A Matter of Oaths* (Methuen).

GEN

[A] Clute, John, et al. eds., *Interzone: The Second Anthology* (Simon & S).
---. *Interzone: The Third Anthology* (Simon & S).
[A] Evans, Christopher & Robert Holdstock, eds. *Other Edens II* (Unwin).
[A] Garnett, David S., ed. *Orbit Science Fiction Year Book 1* (Orbit).

[PUB] *Fear: The World of Fantasy and Horror* [and *Science Fiction* from May/Jun. 1989], 1st. ed. John Gilbert, Jul./Aug., through present.

[W] *Gráinne* (Keith Roberts): BSFA novel.

BIO
  d. 'Sarban,' 11 Apr.
  d. Daphne Du Maurier, 19 Apr.
  d. William F. Temple, 15 Jul.

FIC
  Alderman, Gill. *The Archivist: A Black Romance* (Unwin).
  Aldiss, Brian. *A Romance of the Equator: Best Fantasy Stories* [SS] (Gollancz).
  Banks, Iain [M]. *Canal Dreams* (Macmillan).
  ---. *The State of the Art* [SS] (*Ziesing*).
  Barnes, Julian. *A History of the World in 10 Chapters* (Cape).
  Beebee, Chris. *The Main Event* (Orbit).
  Britton, David. *Lord Horror* (Savoy).
  Brosnan, John. *War of the Sky Lords* (Gollancz).
  Brunner, John. *Victims of the Nova* [O] (Arrow).
  'Christchild, Ravan' (Keith Seddon). *The Agonies of Time* (Dunscaith).
  Clarke, Arthur C. *Tales from Planet Earth* [SS] (Legend).
  --- & Gentry Lee. *Rama II* (Gollancz).
  Cole, Adrian. *Mother of Storms* (Unwin).
  ---. *Thief of Dreams* (Unwin).
  Constantine, Storm. *The Fulfilments of Fate and Desire: The Third Book of Wraeththu* (Drunken Dragon).
  Elton, Ben. *Stark* (Sphere).
  Farren, Mick. *Exit Funtopia* (Sphere).
  ---. *Last Stand of the DNA Cowboys* (*Ballantine*; Orbit 1990).
  Fowler, Christopher. *The Bureau of Lost Souls* [SS] (Century).
  Gentle, Mary. *Scholars and Soldiers* [SS] (Macdonald).
  Gill, Richard. *Time Keepers* (Merlin).
  Gribbin, John. *Father to the Man* (Gollancz).
  Hill, Douglas. *The Fraxilly Fracas* (Gollancz).
  Kilworth, Garry. *In the Hollow of the Deep-Sea Wave: A Novel and Seven Stories* (Bodley Head).
  Lee, Samantha. *Childe Roland* (Futura).
  Lee, Tanith. *Forests of the Night* [SS] (Unwin).
  ---. *Women as Demons: The Male Perceptions of Women Through Space and Time* [SS] (Women's).
  McAuley, Paul J. *Secret Harmonies* (Gollancz) [US *Of the Fall*].
  McDonald, Ian. *Out on Blue Six* (Bantam; Bantam 1990).
  Moorcock, Michael. *Casablanca* (Gollancz).
  'Naylor, Grant.' *Red Dwarf: Infinity Welcomes Careful Drivers* (Penguin).
  Newman, Kim. *The Night Mayor* (Simon & S).
  Pratchett, Terry. *Guards! Guards!* (Gollancz).
  ---. *Pyramids* (Gollancz).
  Roberts, Keith. *Winterwood and Other Hauntings* [SS] (Morrigan).
  Ryman, Geoff. *The Child Garden* (Unwin).

1989(cont.)

FIC
- Saxton, Josephine. *Jane Saint and the Backlash* (Women's).
- Shaw, Bob. *Dark Night in Toyland* (Gollancz).
- ---. *The Fugitive Worlds* (Gollancz).
- Tilley, Patrick. *The Amtrak Wars Book 5: Death-Bringer:* (Sphere).
- Ure, Jean. *Plague 99* (Methuen).
- Watson, Ian. *Salvage Rites* [SS] (Gollancz).
- Wingrove, David. *Chung Kuo: The Middle Kingdom* (NEL).

GEN
- [A] Clute, John et al. *Interzone: The Fourth Anthology* (Simon & S).
- [A] Evans, Christopher & Robert Holdstock, eds. *Other Edens III* (Unwin).
- [A] Garnett, David S, ed. *Orbit Science Fiction Year Book 2* (Orbit).
- ---. *Zenith: The Best in New British Science Fiction* (Sphere).

- [E] Clarke, Arthur C. *Astounding Days: A Science-Fictional Autobiography* (Gollancz).
- [E] Roberts, Keith. *The Natural History of the P. H.* (Kerosina).
- [E] Stableford, Brian. *The Way to Write Science Fiction* (Elm Tree).

- [W] *Four Hundred Billion Stars* (Paul J. McAuley): 7th. Philip K. Dick (joint), US.
- [W] *Lavondyss* (Robert Holdstock): BSFA novel.

BIO
- d. Lawrence Durrell, 7 Nov.
- d. Roald Dahl, 23 Nov.

FIC
- Alderman, Gill. *The Land Beyond: A Fable* (Unwin).
- Ballard, J. G. *War Fever* [SS] (Collins).
- Banks, Iain M. *Use of Weapons* (Orbit).
- Brooke-Rose, Christine. *Verbivore* (Carcanet).
- Brown, Eric. *The Time-Lapsed Man* [SS] (Pan).
- Brunner, John. *Children of the Thunder* (Orbit).
- Cole, Adrian. *Labyrinth of Worlds* (Unwin).
- ---. *Warlord of Heaven* (Unwin).
- Constantine, Storm. *The Monstrous Regiment* (Orbit).
- Fowler, Christopher. *Rune* (Century).
- Gentle, Mary. *Rats and Gargoyles* (Bantam).
- Greenland, Colin. *Take Back Plenty* (Unwin).
- Hill, Douglas. *The Colloghi Conspiracy* (Gollancz).
- 'Kavan, Anna' [P]. *My Madness: The Selected Writings of Anna Kavan* [O] (Picador).
- Lee, Tanith. *The Blood of Roses* (Legend).
- Mann, Phillip. *Wulfsyarn* (Gollancz).
- 'Naylor, Grant.' *Better Than Life* (Viking).
- Newman, Kim. *Bad Dreams* (Simon & S).
- Palmer, Jane. *Moving Moosevan* (Women's).
- Platt, Charles. *Soma* (Grafton).
- Pratchett, Terry. *Diggers* (Doubleday).
- ---. *Eric* (Gollancz).
- ---. *Moving Pictures* (Gollancz).
- Priest, Christopher. *The Quiet Woman* (Bloomsbury).
- Rohan, Mike Scott. *Chase the Morning* (Orbit).
- Shaw, Bob. *Orbitsville Judgement* (Gollancz).
- Slade, Derek. *England 1940: Invasion* (Oriflamme).
- Stableford, Brian. *The Werewolves of London* (Simon & S).
- Watson, Ian. *The Flies of Memory* (Gollancz).
- Wingrove, David. *Chung Kuo: The Broken Wheel* (NEL).

GEN
- [A] Barrett, David V., ed. *Digital Dreams* (NEL).
- [A] Garnett, David S., ed. *Zenith 2* (Orbit).
- [A] Kaveney, Roz, ed. *More Tales from the Forbidden Planet* (Titan).

- [E] Aldiss, Brian. *Bury My Heart at W. H. Smith's: A Writing Life* (Hodder & S).

- [W] *The Child Garden* (Geoff Ryman): Arthur C. Clarke; John W. Campbell Memorial.
- [W] *Pyramids* (Terry Pratchett): BSFA novel.

Author Index

Abbott, Edwin A. (*1839-1926*): 1884
Abel, R. Cox: 1966
Ableman, Paul (*1927-*): 1969
Ackroyd, Peter (*1949-*): 1985
Adam, R. J., see 'MacTyre, Paul': 1924
Adams, Douglas (*1952-*): 1979, 1980, 1982, 1984, 1987, 1988
Adams, J., see 'Kuppord, Skelton': 1902
Adams, Richard (*1920-*): 1972
Adams, W. S.: 1955
'Addison, Hugh' (*1882-1956*): 1923
Adlard, Mark (*1932-*): 1971, 1972, 1975
'AE' (*1867-1935*): 1933
Aiken, John Kempton, see 'Paget, John': 1913
'Akers, Alan Burt,' see Bulmer, Kenneth: **1952**
'Alban, Antony': 1968
Alderman, Gill (*1941-*): 1989, 1990
Aldiss, Brian [W.] (*1925-*): 1954[FP], 1957, 1957[PUB], 1958, 1959, 1960, 1961, 1961[A], 1962, 1962[W], 1963, 1964, 1964[A], 1964[C], 1965, 1966, 1966[W], 1967, 1967[A], 1968, 1969, 1970, 1970[E], 1971, 1972, 1972[W], 1973, 1973[C], 1974, 1974[W], 1975, 1975[E], 1976, 1977, 1978, 1978[C], 1979, 1979[E], 1980, 1981, 1982, 1983, 1983[W], 1984, 1985, 1985[E], 1986[E], 1986[W], 1987, 1987[W], 1988, 1989, 1990[E]
Aldworth, Frank: 1933
Allen, Grant (*1848-99*): 1884, 1886, 1887, 1889, 1890, 1893, 1895, 1896
Allingham, Margery (*1904-66*): 1965
Amis, Kingsley (*1922-*): 1960[C], 1961, 1961[A], 1966, 1976, 1977[W], 1980
Amis, Martin (*1949-*): 1987
Anderson, Colin: 1970
Anon.: 1755, 1763, 1954[PUB], 1956[A], 1972[A], 1977[A]
'Anstey, F' (*1856-1934*): 1891, 1900

'Arlen, Michael' (*1895-1956*): 1933
Armstrong, Anthony (*1897-1976*): 1925
Arnold, Edwin Lester (*1857-1935*): 1890, 1895, 1901, 1905
Arnold, Frank Edward (*1914-87*): 1946, 1946[FAN]
Ash, Alan: 1955
'Ash, Fenton,' see Atkins, Francis Henry: 1840, 1905
'Ashley, Fred,' see Atkins, Francis Henry: 1840, 1905
Ashley, Mike (*1948-*): 1974[C/A], 1977[A]
Ashton, Francis (*1904-*): 1946, 1948, 1952
Ashton, Stephen: 1951 under Ashton, Francis
Atkins, Francis Henry (*1840-1927*): 1896, 1899, 1903, 1905
Atkins, John (*1916-*): 1955
'Aubrey, Frank,' see Atkins, Francis Henry: 1840, 1896, 1899, 1903
'Avery, Richard,' see Cooper, Edmund: **1975**

Bacon, Francis (*1561-1626*): 1627
Bailey, Hilary (*1936-*): 1963[FP], 1974[A] under Platt, Charles, 1975[A], 1976[A]
Baker, Frank (*1908-*): 1936
Balchin, Nigel (*1908-70*): 1967
Baldwin, Oliver, see 'Hussingtree, Martin': 1924
Ball, Brian (*1932-*): 1962[FP], **1965**
Ballard, J. G. (*1930-*): 1956[FP], 1962, 1962[PUB], 1963, 1964, 1966, 1967, 1968, 1970, 1971, 1973, 1974, 1975, 1976, 1977, 1978, 1979, 1980, 1980[W], 1981, 1982, 1984, 1987, 1988, 1990
Balsdon, Dacre (*1901-77*): 1936
Banks, Iain [M.] (*1954-*): 1984, 1985, 1986, 1987, 1988, 1989, 1990
'Barclay, Bill,' see Moorcock, Michael: 1966
Barfield, Owen (*1898-*): 1950
Barker, Clive (*1952-*): 1985, 1987
Barlow, James (*1921-73*): 1957
Barlow, James William (*1826-1913*): 1891
Barnes, Julian (*1946-*): 1986, 1989
'Barr, Densil Neve' (*1918-*): 1955
Barr, Robert (*1850-1912*): 1892[PUB], 1894
Barr, Tyrone C.: 1959
Barren, Charles (*1913-*): 1966 under Abel, R. Cox, 1972[C]
Barrett, David V.: 1990[A]
Barron, D. G. (*1922-*): 1962
Bateman, Robert (*1922-73*): 1963
Bax, Martin (*1933-*): 1976
Bayley, Barrington J. (*1937-*): 1954[FP], 1970, 1972, 1973, 1974, 1976, 1977, 1978, 1979, 1982, 1983, 1985
Bayley, Victor, see 'Smith, Wayland': 1936
Beebee, Chris: 1987, 1989
'Beeding, Francis,' see Palmer, John Leslie: 1934
'Bell, Neil,' see Southwold, Stephen: 1930, 1931, 1932, 1933, 1935, 1938, 1946
Belloc, Hilaire (*1870-1953*): 1928
Bennett, Alfred Gordon (*1901-*): 1939

Bennett, Diana: 1970
Bennett, Margot (*1912-80*): 1954, 1968
Benson, Robert Hugh (*1871-1914*): 1907, 1911
Beresford, J. D. (*1873-1947*): 1911, 1913, 1915[C], 1918, 1921, 1928, 1929, 1933, 1941, 1942, 1944
Beresford, Leslie: 1910, 1918, 1921, 1924
Bergonzi, Bernard (*1929-*): 1961[C]
Bernal, J. D. (*1901-71*): 1929[E]
Berry, Adrian: 1983, 1984
Berry, Bryan (*1930-55*): **1952**
Besant, Walter (*1836-1901*): 1882, 1888
Beverley, Barrington: 1936
Beynon, John, see Wyndham, John: 1935, 1936, 1979
Bishop, Morchard: 1941
Bishop, Michael: 1981 under Watson, Ian
Black, Ladbroke (*1877-1940*): 1933
Blackburn, John F. (*1923-*): 1958, 1966
Blair, Andrew (*?-1885*): 1874
Blair, Hamish (*1872-1935*): 1930, 1931
'Blake, Justin,' see Bowen, John: 1957[FP]
Blake, Mrs. Muirson, see Delaire, Jean: 1888
Blake, Stacey (*1878-1964*): 1920
'Blayre, Christopher' (*1861-1943*): 1921, 1923
Boland, John (*1913-76*): 1955, 1956
Bolland, John: 1983[CX]
Bonfiglioli, Kyril (*1928-1985*): 1966[PUB]
Boorman, John (*1933-*): 1974
'Borodin, George,' see 'Sava, George': 1948
Bounds, Sydney J. (*1920-*): **1955**
Bowen, John (*1924-*): 1957[FP], 1958
Boyce, Chris (*1943-*): 1964[FP], 1975, 1980
'Bradbury, Edward P.,' see Moorcock, Michael: 1965
Brash, Margaret Maud, see 'Kendall, John': 1888
Bray, John Francis: 1842
Brent, Peter Ludwig, see 'Peters, Ludovic': 1931
'Brett, Leo,' see Fanthorpe, R. L.: **1954**
Bridges, T. C. (*1868-1944*): 1940
Briggs, Raymond (*1934-*): 1982[CX]
Brinton, Henry (*1901-77*): 1962
Britton, David: 1978[A], 1984[A], 1989
Britton, Lionel (*1888-*): 1930
Brockway, Fenner (*1888-1988*): 1935
Brooke-Rose, Christine (*1923-*): 1964, 1966, 1986, 1990
Broomhead, Reginald: 1923
Brosnan, John (*1947-*): 1988, 1989
Brown, Alec: 1955
Brown, Charles R.: 1892 under Morgan, Arthur
Brown, Eric (*1960-*): 1990
Brown, Peter: 1965
'Browne, Maurice,' see Nichols, Robert: 1932
Brunner, John (*1934-*): 1951[FP], 1959, 1960, 1961, 1962, 1963, 1964, 1965, 1966, 1967, 1968, 1969, 1969[W], 1970[W], 1971, 1971[W], 1972, 1973, 1974, 1975, 1976, 1980, 1983, 1984, 1987, 1988, 1989, 1990
'Brunt, Captain Samuel': 1727

'Bryant, Peter,' see George, Peter: 1958
Buchanan, Robert (*1841-1901*): 1898
Bulmer, Kenneth (*1921-*): **1952**, 1954[PUB], 1969, 1972[A]
Bulwer-Lytton, Edward (*1803-73*): 1871
Burdekin, Katherine (*1896-1963*): 1927, 1929, 1934[E], 1937
'Burgeon, G. A. L.,' see Barfield, Owen: 1950
Burgess, Anthony (*1917-*): 1962, 1968, 1978, 1982, 1987
Burke, John (*1922-*): **1954**
Burley, W. J.: 1978
Butler, David: 1986
Butler, Samuel (*1612-80*): 1759
Butler, Samuel (*1835-1902*): 1872, 1901
Butterworth, Michael (*1947-*): 1966[FP], 1976 under Moorcock,
    Michael, 1977, 1978[A] under Britton, David, 1984[A]
    under Britton, David
Buttrey, Douglas Norton, see 'Barr, Densil Neve': 1918
Buxton, Richard, see 'Shanks, Edward': 1892

'Cameron, Ian' (*1924-*): 1961
Campbell, H. J. (*1925-*): 1952[PUB], **1953**
Campbell, Paul: 1982[PUB]
Capon, Paul (*1912-1969*): 1950, 1952, 1954, 1956
'Carlton, Roger' (*1928-*): **1975**
Carnell, E. J[ohn] (*1912-72*): 1939[PUB], 1946[PUB],
    1949[PUB], 1951[PUB], 1952[A], 1954[A], 1955[A],
    1958[FAN], 1964[A], 1971[A]
Carr, Charles: 1954, 1955
'Carroll, Lewis'(*1832-98*): 1865, 1872
Carter, Angela (*1940-*): 1967, 1969, 1972, 1974, 1977, 1984,
    1985
Castle, Jeffery Lloyd (*1898-?*): 1954, 1957
Cawthorn, James, see 'James, Philip': 1929
Chadwick, Philip George: 1939
Chance, John Newton, see 'Lymington, John': 1911
Charkin, Paul (*1907-*): 1963
Chesney, George T. (*1830-95*): 1871, 1879
'Chesney, Weatherby,' see Hyne, C. J. Cutliffe: 1898
Chesterton, G. K. (*1874-1936*): 1904
Chetwynd, Bridget (*1910-*): 1946
Childers, Erskine (*1870-1922*): 1903
Chilton, Charles (*1927-*): **1954**
Chown, Marcus (*1959-*): 1988 under Gribbin, John
'Christchild, Ravan': 1989
'Christopher, John' (*1922-*): 1939[FAN], 1949[FP], 1954,
    1955, 1956, 1957[PUB], 1962, 1964, 1965, 1967, 1968
Churchill, R. C. (*1916-*): 1955
Clark, Charles: 1937
Clark, Ronald (*1916-87*): 1949[FP], 1967
Clarke, Arthur C. (*1917-*): 1937[FAN], 1946[FAN], 1946[FP],
    1951, 1951[E], 1952, 1952[W], 1953, 1955, 1956,
    1956[W], 1957, 1958, 1959, 1959[E], 1961, 1962,
    1962[E], 1963, 1965, 1965[E], 1967, 1968, 1968[E],
    1972, 1972[E], 1973, 1973[W], 1974[W], 1975, 1977[E],

Clarke, Arthur C. (cont.): 1979, 1980[W], 1982, 1984[E],
    1986, 1987, 1988, 1989, 1989[E]
Clarke, George Sydenham, see 'Seaforth, A. Nelson': 1892
Clarke, I. F. (*1918-*): 1961[C], 1966[C]
Clarke, Vincent: 1952 under Bulmer, Kenneth, 1954[FAN]
Cleator, P. E.: 1933[FAN]
'Clive, Denis,' see Fearn, John Russell: **1942**
Clouston, J. Storer (*1870-1944*): 1916, 1933, 1934, 1937,
    1938
Clowes, W. Laird (*1856-1905*): 1892, 1893, 1894
Clute, John (*1940-*): 1966[FP], 1985[A], 1988[A], 1989[A]
Cobban, James MacLaren (*1849-1903*): 1890
Cole, Adrian (*1949-*): 1981, 1989, 1990
Cole, Robert William (*fl. 1900-08*): 1900
Collier, John (*1901-80*): 1930, 1931, 1933, 1951, 1952[W]
Collins, E.: 1944
Colomb, Philip H. (*1831-1899*): 1893
Colvin, Ian (*1912-75*): 1948
'Colvin, James,' see Moorcock, Michael: 1966
Compton, D. G. (*1930-*): 1965, 1966, 1968, 1970, 1972, 1974,
    1978, 1979, 1980, 1985
Coney, Michael G. (*1932-*): 1969[FP], 1972, 1973, 1974, 1975,
    1976, 1977[W], 1979, 1981, 1982, 1984,
'Connington, J. J.' (*1880-1947*): 1923
Connolly, Roy: 1934 under McIlraith, Frank
Conquest, Robert (*1917-*): 1955, 1961[A] under Amis, Kingsley
Conrad, Joseph (*1857-1924*): 1901
'Conrad, Paul': **1974**
Constable, Frank Challice (*1846-1937*): 1895
'Constantine, Murray,' see Burdekin, Katherine: 1896,
    1934[E], 1937
Constantine, Storm: 1987, 1988, 1989, 1990
Cooney, Michael (*1921-*): 1967, 1968
Cooper, Colin (*1926-*): 1968, 1970, 1977
Cooper, Edmund (*1926-1982*): 1951[FP], 1958, 1959, 1960,
    1963, 1964, 1966, 1967, 1968, 1969, 1970, 1971, 1972,
    1973, 1974, **1975**, 1978, 1979, 1980
Cooper, Hughes: 1970
Cooper, Susan (*1935-*): 1964
Corbett, James: 1935
'Corelli, Marie' (*1855-1924*): 1886, 1918
Corley, James (*1947-*): 1976
Corston, George (*1932-*): 1968
Cotes, May, 1886 under Allen, Grant
Cove, J. W., see 'Gibbs, Lewis': 1891
'Cowper, Richard' (*1926-*): 1967, 1968, 1971, 1972, 1973,
    1974, 1976, 1978, 1979, 1980, 1981, 1982, 1984, 1986
'Craig, Brian,' see Stableford, Brian M.: 1965[FP]
'Craig, David' (*1929-*): 1969, 1970
Craig, Thurlow: 1939
'Crane, Robert' (*1908-*): 1954
Creasey, John (*1908-73*): **1956**
Creswick, Paul (*1866-?*): 1928
Crisp, Frank R. (*1915-*): 1959, 1960
'Crispin, Edmund' (*1921-78*): 1955[A]

Critten, Stephen H., see Southwold, Stephen: 1887
Croly, George (*1780-1860*): 1828
Cromie, Robert (*1856-1907*): 1889, 1890, 1895, 1896, 1897, 1902
Crowcroft, Peter (*1923-*): 1954
Curtis, Monica (*1892-?*): 1934
Curwen, Henry (*1845-1892*): 1887
Curzon, Virginia, see 'Hawton, Hector': 1901

Dahl, Roald (*1916-90*): 1949
Dakers, Elaine, see 'Lane, Jane': 1905
Dalton, Moray: 1934
'Dare, Alan,' see Goodchild, George: 1927
Darrington, Hugh (*1940-*): 1971
Darwin, Charles (*1809-82*): 1859[E]
Darwin, Erasmus (*1731-1802*): 1791, 1794[E], 1803
Daventry, Leonard (*1915-*): 1965, 1969, 1970, 1971
Davidson, John (*1857-1909*): 1896
Davies, Howell, see 'Marvell, Andrew': 1938
Davies, Hugh Sykes (*1909-84*): 1935, 1960
Davies, L. P. (*1914-*): 1960[FP], 1964, 1965, 1966, 1967, 1968, 1969, 1972
Davies, Paul (*1946-*): 1987
Davies, Pete (*1959-*): 1986
Davis, Gerry (*1930-*): 1971, 1974, 1975 all under Pedler, Kit
Davis, Julie: 1976[PUB]
Defoe, Daniel (*1660/1-1731*): 1705, 1719, 1722
Deighton, Len (*1929-*): 1978
Delaire, Jean (*1888-?*): 1904
Dennis, Geoffrey (*1892-1963*): 1930[E]
Dent, Guy: 1926
Desmond, Hugh: 1949, 1953
Desmond, Shaw (*1877-1960*): 1926, 1938
'Dexter, William' (*1909-*): 1954, 1955
Dick, Kay (*1915-*): 1977
Dick-Lauder, G., see Lauder, G. D.: 1917
Dickinson, Peter (*1927-*): 1973, 1974, 1976, 1979, 1988
Dilnot, Frank Buckland (*1875-?*): 1933
Dimmock, F. Haydn: 1934[PUB]
Dixie, Lady Florence (*1857-1905*): 1890, 1903
Dixon, Roger, see 'Lewis, Charles': 1930
Dodgson, Charles Lutwidge, see 'Carroll, Lewis': 1832
'Donne, Maxim,' see Duke, Madelaine: 1964
Donson, Cyril (*1919-86*): 1968
Douglas, Norman (*1868-1952*): 1927
Dowling, Steve: 1943[CX]
Doyle, Arthur Conan (*1859-1930*): 1889, 1890, 1891, 1893, 1894, 1908, 1911, 1912, 1913, 1918, 1919, 1926, 1929, 1952
Doyle, Richard (*1948-*): 1976
Dudley-Smith, T., see 'Trevor, Elleston': 1920
Du Maurier, Daphne (*1907-89*): 1972
Du Maurier, George (*1834-96*): 1898

Duffy, Maureen (*1933-*): 1981
Duke, Madelaine (*1925-*): 1964, 1967
Duncan, Ronald (*1914-82*): 1952
Dunn, Philip M., see Dunn, Saul: 1946
Dunn, Saul (*1946-*): **1976**, **1978**
Dunne, J. W. (*1875-1949*): 1927[E]
Dunsany, Lord (*1878-1957*): 1951
Dunstan, Frederick: 1983
Durrell, Lawrence (*1912-90*): 1968, 1970, 1974

Earnshaw, Brian (*1929-*): 1968
Eddison, E. R. (*1882-1945*): 1922
Edmonds, Harry: 1931, 1933, 1935
Edwards, Charman (*1896-?*): 1936
Edwards, F. A., see Edwards, Charman: 1936
Edwards, Peter (*1946-*): 1976
Egleton, Clive (*1927-*): 1970
'Egremont, Michael,' see Harrison, Michael: 1936
Elder, Michael (*1931-*): **1970**
Elliot, John (*1918-*): 1962, 1964 both under Hoyle, Fred
Ellis, T. Mullett (*fl. 1893-1916*): 1895
Ellsmore, A.: 1975[PUB]
Elmore, Ernest (*1901-*): 1928
Elton, Ben: 1989
'Elton, John,' see Marsh, John: 1907
Erskine, Thomas (*1788-1870*): 1817
Evans, Christopher (*1931-*): 1980, 1981, 1985, 1987[A], 1988[A], 1989[A]
Evans, Constance Mary, see 'O'Nair, Mairi': 1889
Evans, Dik: 1977[A] under Evans, Hilary
Evans, Hilary: 1977[A]
Evans, I. O. (*1894-1977*): 1966[A]

Faber, Geoffrey (*1889-1961*): 1925
Fairbairns, Zoë (*1948-*): 1979
'Fane, Bron,' see Fanthorpe, R. L.: **1954**
Fanthorpe, R. L. (*1935-*): 1952[FP], **1954**
Farjeon, J. Jefferson (*1883-1955*): 1948
Farncombe, Frank E.: 1925, 1927 both under Hadfield, Robert L.
Farren, Mick (*1943-*): 1973, 1976, 1977, 1978, 1981, 1984, 1988, 1989
Fawcett, E. Douglas (*1866-1960*): 1893, 1894
Fearn, John Russell (*1908-60*): 1933[FP], **1942**
Ferguson, Neil: 1988
Flack, I. H., see 'Graham, Harvey': 1912
Flecker, J. Elroy (*1884-1915*): 1908
Fleming, Brandon: 1913
'Folingsby, Kenneth': 1891
Follett, James (*1939-*): 1976
Forbes, Caroline: 1985

Ford, D. M.: 1910
'Forester, C. S.' (*1899-1966*): 1934
Forster, E. M. (*1879-1970*): 1909
Fowler, Christopher: 1988, 1989
Fowler, Sydney, see Wright, S. Fowler: 1932, 1945
Fowles, John (*1926-*): 1985
Frankau, Gilbert (*1884-1952*): 1953
Franklin, K. D. (*1929-*): 1979
Fraser, Ronald (*1888-1974*): 1924, 1951, 1958, 1960
Frayn, Michael (*1933-*): 1965, 1968, 1973
Fullerton, Alexander: 1983
Furnill, John: 1932
Fytton-Armstrong, T. I., see 'Gawsworth, John': 1912

Ganthony, Richard: 1912 under 'Lurgan, Lester'
Garner, Alan (*1934-*): 1960, 1963, 1973
'Garner, Rolf,' see Berry, Bryan: **1952**
Garnett, David (*1892-1981*): 1931
Garnett, David S. (*1947-*): 1969, 1988[A], 1989[A], 1990[A]
Gaskell, Jane (*1941-*): 1963, 1965, 1966, 1969
'Gawsworth, John' (*1912-*): 1935 under Shiel, M. P.
Gayton, Bertram: 1922
Gentle, Mary (*1956-*): 1983, 1987, 1989, 1990
George, Peter (*1924-66*): 1958, 1965
George, W. L.: 1926
Gerber, Richard: 1955[C]
Gerhardi, William (*1895-1977*): 1928
Gibbs, Henry: 1948
'Gibbs, Lewis' (*1891-?*): 1951
Gifford, H. G., see Halsbury, Earl of: 1880
Gilbert, John: 1988[PUB]
Gill, Richard (*1948-*): 1989
Gilliatt, Penelope (*1932-*): 1965
Gillings, Walter (*1912-79*): 1937[FAN], 1937[PUB], 1938[FP], 1946[PUB], 1947[FAN], 1950[PUB]
Gillon, Diana (*1915-*): 1961
Gillon, Meir (*1907-*): 1961 under Gillon, Diana
Glasby, John S., see 'Merak, A. J.': 1928
Glemser, Bernard, see 'Crane, Robert': 1908
Glendon, George: 1910
Gloag, John (*1896-1981*): 1932, 1933, 1934, 1937, 1940, 1944, 1946
Godber, Noel L. (*1881-?*): 1931
Goddard, James: 1970[FAN]
Godwin, Francis (*1562-1633*): 1638
Golding, William (*1911-*): 1954, 1955, 1958, 1971
'Gonsales, Domenico,' see Godwin, Francis: 1638
Goodchild, George (*1888-1969*): 1927
'Gordon, Rex' (*1917-*): 1954, 1956, 1959, 1961, 1962, 1966, 1969
Gordon, Richard, see Gordon, Stuart: 1947, 1965
Gordon, Stuart (*1947-*): 1965[FP], 1972, 1973, 1974, 1975, 1981, 1983, 1987, 1988

Gorst, Harold E. (*1868-1950*): 1898
'Graham, Harvey' (1912-66): 1937
Graham, Mrs. Constantine, see Tillyard, Aelfrida: 1883
Graham, P. Anderson (?-*1925*): 1923
Grant, John: 1979[A], 1987 under Langford, David
Graves, Robert (*1895-1985*): 1949
Gray, Alasdair (*1934-*): 1981
Green, A. Lincoln: 1901
Green, Jen (*1955-*): 1985[A]
'Green, Nunsowe': 1882
Green, Roger Lancelyn (*1918-87*): 1958[C]
Greenhough, Terry (*1944-*): 1975, 1976
Greenland, Colin (*1954-*): 1983[C], 1984, 1987, 1988, 1990
Greer, Tom (*1846-1904*): 1885
Greg, Percy (*1836-89*): 1880
Gregory, Owen: 1918
'Grey, Charles,' see Tubb, E. C.: **1951**
Gribbin, John (*1946-*): 1979 under Orgill, Douglas, 1988, 1989
'Gridban, Volsted,' see Fearn, John Russell: 1942, or Tubb, E. C.: 1951
Grierson, Francis D. (*1888-1972*): 1928
'Griff, Alan' (*1900-64*): 1940
Griffith, George (*1857-1906*): 1893, 1894, 1895, 1897, 1898, 1899, 1901, 1903, 1904, 1905, 1906, 1907, 1908, 1911, 1974
Griffith-Jones, G. C., see Griffith, George: 1857
Griffiths, John (*1934-*): 1965
Groom, Pelham: 1948
Grove, W.: 1889
Groves, J. W. (*1910-*): 1931[FP], 1968, 1969
Gubbins, Herbert: 1914
Guest, Ernest: 1929
Gull, Ranger, see 'Thorne, Guy': 1906, 1915, 1919, 1921
Gunn, Neil M. (*1891-1973*): 1944
Guthrie, Thomas Anstey, see 'Anstey, F.': 1856
Gutteridge, Lindsay (*1923-*): 1971, 1973, 1975

Hackett, Sir John (*1910-*): 1979, 1982
Hadfield, Robert L.: 1925, 1927
Haggard, H. Rider (*1856-1925*): 1885, 1886, 1887, 1891, 1894, 1895, 1904, 1905, 1906, 1908, 1910, 1911, 1918, 1919, 1921, 1923, 1924, 1927
Haldane, J. B. S. (*1892-1964*): 1923[E], 1927[E], 1976
Halsbury, Earl of (*1880-1943*): 1926
Hamilton, Cicely (*1872-1952*): 1922
Hamilton, Lord Frederick: 1893[PUB]
Hamilton, Peter: 1952[PUB]
Hampson, Frank: 1950[CX]
Hanson, Maurice K.: 1936[FAN]
Harbottle, Philip (*1941-*): 1969[PUB]
Hargrave, John (*1894-1982*): 1923, 1931
Harker, Kenneth (*1927-*): 1966, 1970

Harris, Chuck: 1954[PUB]
Harris, J. Henry (*1875-1962*): 1906
Harris, John Beynon, see Wyndham, John: 1931[FP]
Harris, John Wyndham Parkes Lucas Beynon, see Wyndham, John: 1903
Harrison, Harry: 1964[C], 1967[A] both under Aldiss, Brian
Harrison, Helga: 1962
Harrison, M. John (*1945-*): 1968[FP], 1971, 1974, 1975, 1980, 1982, 1983, 1984
Harrison, Michael (*1907-*): 1945, 1953
Hartley, L. P. (*1895-1972*): 1960
Hartridge, Jon (*1934-*): 1969, 1970
Hawkes, Jacquetta (*1910-*): 1959
'Hawton, Hector' (*1901-*): 1951
Hay, George (*1922-*): 1951, 1952, 1970[A], 1974[A], 1978[A], 1979[A]
Hay, W. Delisle (*fl. 1880-1893*): 1880, 1881
'Haynes, John Robert,' see Wilding, Philip: 1955
Haywood, Eliza (*?1693-1756*): 1736
Heard, H. F. (*1889-1971*): 1947, 1948, 1950, 1953
Hedges, Sid G. (*1897-?*): 1934
Hemingway, Amanda: 1982
Henham, E. G., see 'Trevena, John': 1890
Herbert, Benson (*1912-*): 1931[FP], 1936
Herbert, James (*1943-*): **1974**
Hernaman-Johnson, Francis (*1879-1949*): 1906
Heron-Allen, Edward, see 'Blayre, Christopher': 1861
Hesky, Olga (*?-1974*): 1961
High, Philip E. (*1914-*): 1955[FP], 1964, 1966, 1967, 1968, 1971, 1973, 1974, 1978, 1979
Hill, Douglas (*1935-*): 1989, 1990
Hill, Ernest (*1915-*): 1964[FP], 1968
Hill, Reginald, see 'Morland, Dick': 1936
Hilton, James (*1900-54*): 1933
Hind, C. Lewis: 1868[PUB]
Hingley, Ronald (*1920-*): 1956
Hinton, C. Howard (*1853-1907*): 1886, 1895, 1896, 1907
Hitchcock, Raymond (*1922-*): 1972
Hoban, Russell (*1925-*): 1980, 1982[W]
Hodder-Williams, Christopher (*1926-*): 1959, 1964, 1967, 1968, 1969, 1973, 1974, 1976, 1977, 1979, 1984
Hodgson, William Hope (*1877-1918*): 1907, 1908, 1909, 1912
Holdstock, Robert (*1948-*): 1968[FP], 1976, 1977, 1978[C], 1979[A], 1982, 1984, 1985[W], 1987[A] under Evans, Christopher, 1988, 1988[A] under Evans, Christopher, 1989[A] under Evans, Christopher, 1989[W]
'Holmes, L. G.': 1951[PUB]
Holt-White, William: 1909
Horne, Richard Henry (*1803-84*): 1849
Horner, Donald W.: 1910, 1912
Hornsey, Patricia: 1974[PUB]
Horsnell, Horace (*1883-1949*): 1940
Hough, Stanley B., see 'Gordon, Rex': 1917, 1956, 1961
Houghton, Claude (*1889-1961*): 1935
Household, Geoffrey (*1900-88*): 1985

Author Index 177

Hoyle, Fred (*1915-*): 1950[E], 1957, 1959, 1962, 1963, 1964, 1966, 1967, 1969, 1970, 1971, 1973, 1974, 1977, 1978, 1985
Hoyle, Geoffrey (*1942-*): 1963, 1969, 1970, 1971, 1973, 1974, 1977, 1978 all under Hoyle, Fred
Hoyle, Trevor (*1940-*): 1977, 1978, 1979, 1981, 1983
Hudson, W. H. (*1841-1922*): 1887
Hueffer, Ford Madox (*1873-1939*): 1901 under Conrad, Joseph
Hughes, Ted (*1930-*): 1968
Hume, Fergus W. (*1859-1932*): 1891
'Hunt, Gill,' see Brunner, John: 1951[FP]
Hurd, Douglas (*1930-*): 1968
'Hussingtree, Martin': 1924
Huxley, Aldous (*1894-1963*): 1932, 1939, 1944, 1948, 1958[E], 1962, 1963[E]
Huxley, Julian (*1887-1975*): 1926
Hyams, Edward (*1910-75*): 1939, 1949, 1950, 1951, 1973, 1975
Hynam, John Charles, see 'Kippax, John': 1915
Hyne, C. J. Cutliffe (*1865-1944*): 1889, 1892, 1893, 1898, 1900, 1904, 1910, 1929, 1933

Ingrey, Derek: 1963

Jacomb, Charles Ernest (*1888-?*): 1926
Jaeger, Muriel (*?1893-?*): 1926, 1927, 1933, 1936
James, Laurence: 1972[FP], **1974**
'James, Philip': 1975 under Moorcock, Michael
Jameson, Storm (*1891-1986*): 1936, 1937, 1942, 1949
Jane, Fred T. (*1870-1916*): 1895, 1896, 1897, 1899
Jefferies, Richard (*1848-87*): 1885
Jerome, Jerome K. (*1859-1927*): 1891, 1892[PUB], 1893
Johns, Capt. W. E. (*1893-1968*): **1954**
Johnson, Leslie J.: 1946[PUB]
'Johnson, L. P. V.': 1961
Johnson, Samuel (*1709-84*): 1759
Jones, Arthur Llewellyn, see 'Machen, Arthur': 1863
Jones, D. F. (*1918-1981*): 1966, 1967, 1971, 1974, 1975, 1977, 1979
Jones, Gonner: 1968
Jones, Gwyneth (*1952-*): 1984, 1986, 1988
Jones, Langdon (*1942-*): 1964[FP], 1969[A], 1971 under Moorcock, Michael, 1972
Jones, Margaret: 1968
Jones, Mervyn (*1922-*): 1958
Jordan, Sydney: 1954[CX]

Kapp, Colin (*1929-*): 1958[FP], 1964, 1972, 1975, 1976, 1977, 1978, 1979, 1980, 1981, 1982
'Kavan, Anna' (*1901-68*): 1940, 1945, 1947, 1967, 1970

Kaveney, Roz: 1987[A], 1990[A]
Kearney, Chalmers (*1881-1966*): 1943
Kee, Robert (*1919-*): 1955
'Kendall, John,' (*1888-?*): 1933
Kennedy, R. A.: 1912
'Kent, Philip,' see Bulmer, Kenneth: **1952**
'Kern, Gregory,' see Tubb, E. C.: **1951**
Kerry, Peter: 1890[PUB]
Kersh, Gerald (*1911-68*): 1953, 1958, 1968
Kettle, Pamela (*1934-*): 1969
Kilworth, Garry (*1941-*): 1975[FP], 1977, 1978, 1979, 1981, 1984, 1987, 1988, 1989
King, John Robert (*1948-*): 1976
'King, Vincent' (*1935-*): 1966[FP], 1969, 1971, 1976
Kingsmill, Hugh (*1889-1949*): 1924, 1929
Kipling, Rudyard (*1865-1936*): 1905, 1912
'Kippax, John' (*1915-74*): 1954[FP], **1968** under Morgan, Dan, 1975
Kneale, Nigel (*1922-*): 1949, 1959, 1960, 1976, 1979
Knowles, Mabel Winifred, see 'Lurgan, Lester': 1875
Knox, G. D.: 1923 under Wignall, T. C.
Knox, Ronald A. (*1888-1957*): 1923
Koestler, Arthur (*1905-1983*): 1945, 1951
'Kuppord, Skelton': 1902

Lach-Szyrma, W. S. (*1841-1915*): 1874, 1892
'Lamb, William,' see Jameson, Storm: 1891, 1937
Landsborough, Gordon, see 'Holmes, L. G.': 1951[PUB]
'Lane, Jane' (*1905-78*): 1964
Lang, Andrew (*1844-1912*): 1886
'Lang, King', see Tubb, E. C.: **1951**
Langford, David (*1953-*): 1982, 1984, 1985 under Stableford, Brian, 1987
Large, E. C. (*?-1976*): 1937, 1938, 1956
Laski, Marghanita (*1915-88*): 1959
Lauder, G. D. (*1917-*): 1969
Lawrence, H. L. (*1908-*): 1960
Lee, Gentry: 1989, 1990 both under Clarke, Arthur C.
Lee, Samantha: 1989
Lee, Tanith (*1947-*): 1975, 1976, 1977, 1978, 1979, 1980, 1981, 1982, 1983, 1984, 1985, 1988, 1989, 1990
Lefanu, Sarah (*1953-*): 1985[A]
'Le Page, Rand,' see 'Merak, A. J.': **1954**
Le Queux, William (*1864-1927*): 1894, 1895, 1897, 1898, 1899, 1906, 1910, 1915, 1916, 1920
LeRoy, P. V., see 'Johnson, L. P. V.': 1961
Leslie, Desmond (*1921-*): 1958
Leslie, Peter (*1922-*): 1968, 1969, 1970
Lessing, Doris (*1919-*): 1971, 1974, 1979, 1980, 1981, 1982, 1983, 1988
'Lester, Andrew,' see Greenhough, Terry: 1976
Levene, Malcolm (*1937-*): 1968

Lewis, C. S. (*1898-1963*): 1938, 1943, 1945, 1950, 1956, 1958, 1966[E]
'Lewis, Charles' (*1930-*): 1975
Lewis, Matthew Gregory (*1775-1818*): 1795
Lewis, P. Wyndham (*1882-1957*): 1928, 1955
Lewis, Roy (*1913-*): 1960
Ley, Arthur Gordon, see 'Sellings, Arthur': 1921
Lindsay, David (*1878-1945*): 1920, 1922, 1923, 1932, 1976
Linklater, Eric (*1899-1974*): 1938
Llewellyn, Alun (*1903-*): 1934
Locke, George (*1936-*): 1957[FP], 1972[A]
Logan, Charles (*1930-*): 1975
Lott, S. Makepeace: 1956
Loudon, Jane (*1807-58*): 1827
Lovesey, Andrew (*1941-*): 1975
Low, A. M. (*1888-1956*): 1937, 1950[E], 1956
Lucas, F. L. (*1894-1967*): 1937
Lucie-Smith, Edward (*1933-*): 1969[A]
Lunn, Hugh Kingsmill, see Kingsmill, Hugh: 1889
'Lurgan, Lester' (*1875-1949*): 1912
'Luther, Ray,' see 'Sellings, Arthur': 1967
'Lymington, John' (*1911-1983*): **1959**
Lynch, Bohun (*1884-1928*): 1925
Lynch, Jane Gaskell, see Gaskell, Jane: 1941
Lytton, Edward Bulwer, see Bulwer-Lytton, Edward: 1803

Macaulay, Rose (*1881-1958*): 1919
MacClure, Victor (*1887-1963*): 1924
MacColl, Hugh: 1889
MacDonald, George (*1824-1905*): 1858, 1871, 1895
MacGregor, James Murdoch, see 'McIntosh, J. T.': 1925
Macey, Peter: 1974, 1975, 1977
'Machen, Arthur' (*1863-1947*): 1894, 1917
Mackay, Mary, see 'Corelli, Marie': 1855
Mackelworth, R. W. (*1930-*): 1963[FP], 1968, 1970, 1972, 1975, 1981
Mackenzie, Compton (*1883-1972*): 1959
MacKenzie, Nigel: **1954**
MacLaren, Bernard: 1956
MacLeod, Angus (*1906-*): 1958, 1962
MacLeod, Sheila (*1939-*): 1970, 1977, 1978
'MacTyre, Paul' (*1924-*): 1962
'Maine, Charles Eric' (*1921-*): 1952[FP], 1953, 1955, 1956, 1957, 1958, 1959, 1960, 1961, 1962, 1964, 1966, 1971
Maitland, Edward (*1824-1897*): 1873
Malcolm, Donald (*1930-*): 1958[FP]
Mann, Phillip (*1942-*): 1982, 1986, 1987, 1988, 1990
Manvell, Roger (*1909-87*): 1958
Marlowe, Christopher (*1564-1593*): 1604
Marsh, John (*1907-*): 1936, 1955
Marshall, Archibald (*1866-1934*): 1915
Martin, D. S. (*1913-*): 1967
Martin, Graham Dunstan (*1932-*): 1986, 1987, 1988

'Marvell, Andrew': 1938, 1939
Mason, Douglas R., see 'Rankine, John': 1918, **1966**
Masson, David I. (*1921-*): 1965[FP], 1968
Mastin, John (*1865-1932*): 1905, 1907, 1909
Maturin, Charles R. (*1782-1824*): 1820
'Maurice, Michael' (*1889-?*): 1923
McAllister, Angus: 1988
McAuley, Paul J. (*1955-*): 1988, 1989, 1989[W]
McCutchan, Philip (*1920-*): **1966**
'McDermot, Murtagh': 1728
McDonald, Ian (*1960-*): 1988, 1989
McIlraith, Frank: 1934
McIlwain, David, see 'Maine, Charles Eric': 1921
'McIntosh, J. T.' (*1925-*): 1950[FP], 1953, 1954, 1955, 1961, 1963, 1964, 1965, 1967, 1968, 1970, 1971, 1972, 1973, 1976, 1977, 1979
Mead, Harold (*1910-*): 1955, 1957
Mears, A(melia) Garland: 1895
'Merak, A. J.' (*1928-*): **1954**
Meredith, E.: 1936
Merril, Judith: 1968[A]
Meyers, Roy (*1910-1974*): **1967**
'Miles,' see Southwold, Stephen: 1930, 1931
Milkomane, A. M., see 'Sava, George': 1903
Mills, Lady Dorothy (*?-1959*): 1924
Milton, John (*1608-74*): 1667
Minto, William (*1845-1893*): 1886
Mirrlees, Hope (*1887-1978*): 1926
Mitchell, Adrian (*1932-*): 1970
Mitchell, J. Leslie (*1901-35*): 1931, 1932, 1934
Mitchison, Naomi (*1897-*): 1962, 1975, 1983
Monsarrat, Nicholas (*1910-79*): 1962
Montgomery, Robert Bruce, see 'Crispin, Edmund': 1921
Moorcock, Michael (*1939-*): 1949[FAN], 1957[FAN], 1957[FP], 1964[PUB], 1965, 1965[A], 1966, 1966[A], 1967, 1967[A], 1968, 1968[A], 1968[W], 1969, 1969[A], 1970, 1971, 1971[A], 1972, 1972[A], 1973, 1973[A], 1974, 1975, 1975[A], 1976, 1977, 1977[A], 1978, 1979[W], 1980, 1981, 1982, 1983, 1983[A], 1984, 1986, 1987, 1987[C], 1988, 1989
Moore, Patrick (*1923-*): **1952**, 1957[E]
More, Thomas (*1478-1535*): 1516
'Morel, Dighton' (*1915-*): 1960
Morgan, Arthur: 1892
Morgan, Dan (*1925-*): 1952[FP], 1955, 1961, 1966, **1967**, **1968**, 1971, 1973, 1975, 1976
'Morison, Frank' (*1881-?*): 1932
'Morland, Dick' (*1936-*): 1973, 1974
'Morris, Ralph': 1751
Morris, William (*1834-96*): 1890, 1896
Morton, A. L. (*1903-*): 1952[C]
Mottram, R. H. (*1883-1971*): 1946
'Muller, John E.,' see Fanthorpe, R. L.: **1954**
Munro, H. H., see 'Saki': 1870
Munro, John (*1849-1930*): 1897

'Muralto, Onuphrio,' see Walpole, Horace: 1764
Murray, V. T.: 1925
Murry, John Middleton, Jr., see 'Cowper, Richard': 1926

Nation, Terry (*1930-*): 1976
'Naylor, Grant': 1989
Neill, A. S. (*1883-1973*): 1938
'Netterville, Luke' (*1846-1928*): 1900
Newman, Bernard (*1897-1968*): 1930, 1942, 1948, 1954, 1962
Newman, Kim (*1959-*): 1989, 1990
Newnes, Sir George: 1891[PUB]
Newton, Douglas (*1884-1951*): 1914, 1930, 1933
Niall, Ian: 1952
Nicholls, Peter (*1939-*): 1971[C], 1976[C], 1979[C]
Nichols, Robert (*1893-?*): 1932
Nicoll, Maurice, see 'Swayne, Martin': 1884
Nicolson, Harold (*1886-1968*): 1932
Noel, L.: 1935
Norman, Barry (*1933-*): 1975
'Norvil, Manning,' see Bulmer, Kenneth: **1952**
Norway, Nevil Shute, see Shute, Nevil: 1899
Norwood, Victor (*1920-*): **1951**
Nott, Kathleen (*1910-*): 1947
Noyes, Alfred (*1880-1958*): 1940
Noyes, Ralph: 1985

O'Grady, Standish James, see 'Netterville, Luke': 1846
'O'Nair, Mairi' (*1889-?*): 1935
O'Neill, Joseph (*1886-1953*): 1934, 1935, 1936
Odle, E. V.: 1923
Oldfield, Claude Houghton, see Houghton, Claude: 1889
Oliphant, Mrs. [M]. (*1828-97*): 1880
Onions, Oliver (*1873-1961*): 1918
Oppenheim, E. Phillips (*1866-1946*): 1925
Orgill, Douglas (*1922-84*): 1979
'Orwell, George' (*1903-50*): 1945, 1949
Osmond, Andrew (*1938-*): 1968 under Hurd, Douglas
Owen, Harry Collinson, see 'Addison, Hugh': 1882

'Paget, John' (*1913-*): 1970
Pain, Barry (*1864-1928*): 1911
Pallander, Edwin: 1896, 1902
Palmer, Jane (*1946-*): 1985, 1986, 1990
Palmer, J. L. (*1885-1944*): 1934, 1936
Paltock, Robert (*1697-1767*): 1751
'Pan,' see Beresford, Leslie: 1918, 1921
Pape, Richard (*1916-*): 1961
Parkes, Lucas, see Wyndham, John: 1959
Parkinson, H. F.: 1939

Parkman, S. (*1895-*): 1948
Partington, Charles: 1980[PUB]
Passes, Alan (*1943-*): 1969[FP], 1977
Paterson, Alastair: 1954[PUB]
Payn, James (*1830-98*): 1879, 1888
Payne, Donald Gordon, see 'Cameron, Ian': 1924
Peake, Mervyn (*1911-68*): 1946, 1950, 1959
Pearce, Brenda (*1935-*): 1975, 1977
Pearson, C. Arthur: 1896[PUB]
Pedler, Kit (*1927-1981*): 1971, 1974, 1975
Pemberton, Max (*1863-1950*): 1895, 1902
Peterkiewicz, Jerzy (*1916-*): 1966
'Peters, Ludovic' (*1931-84*): 1967
Petty, John (*1919-*): 1966
Phelps, Gilbert (*1915-*): 1958
Phillifent, John T., see 'Rackham, John': 1916, **1954**
Phillips, Peter (*1921-*): 1948[FP]
Phillpotts, Eden (*1862-1960*): 1901, 1929, 1936, 1938, 1949
Pincher, Chapman (*1914-*): 1965
Pinkerton, T. A.: 1902
Platt, Charles (*1944-*): 1964[FAN], 1964[FP], 1967, 1970, 1970[PUB], 1971, 1973[A] under Moorcock, Michael, 1974[A], 1977, 1987, 1988, 1990
Pocock, Roger (*1865-?*): 1911
'Powers, J. L.,' see 'Merak, A. J.': **1954**
Powys, John Cowper (*1872-1963*): 1957, 1960, 1985
Pragnell, Festus (*1905-*): 1932[FP], 1936, 1946
Pratchett, Terry (*1948-*): 1963[FP], 1981, 1986, 1987, 1988, 1989, 1990, 1990[W]
Priest, Christopher (*1943-*): 1964[FAN], 1966[FP], 1970, 1972, 1974, 1975[W], 1976, 1977, 1978[A], 1979, 1979[A] under Holdstock, Robert, 1981, 1984, 1990
Priestley, J. B. (*1894-1984*): 1927, 1938, 1953, 1954, 1961
Pringle, David: 1982[PUB]
Pritchard, W. T., see 'Dexter, William': 1909

Quest, Rodney (*1897-?*): 1966

'Rackham, John' (*1916-76*): **1954**
Ranger-Gull, C. A. E., see 'Thorne, Guy': 1876
'Rankine, John' (*1918-*): 1964[FP], **1966**
Raphael, John N.: 1913
Rash, Dora, see 'Wallace, Doreen': 1897
Ray, René: 1957
Ray, Robert: 1950[FP]
Rayer, Francis G. (*1921-1981*): 1947[FP], **1951**
Read, Herbert (*1893-1968*): 1935
Richards, Alfred Bate (*1820-76*): 1870
Richards, Dick, see 'Wells, Barry': 1961
Rippington, Geoff: 1977[FAN]

Roberts, Keith (*1935-*): 1964[FP], 1966, 1968, 1970, 1973, 1974, 1976, 1977, 1979, 1980, 1985, 1986, 1987, 1988[W], 1989, 1989[E]
'Roberts, Lionel,' see Fanthorpe, R. L.: 1952[FP], **1954**
Robertson, E. Arnot (*1903-61*): 1929
Robinson, Philip Bedford (*1926-*): 1969
Roe, Ivan, see 'Savage, Richard': 1917
Rohan, Mike Scott (*1951-*): 1982, 1990
'Rohmer, Sax' (*1883-1959*): **1913**, 1930
Rosenblum, J. Michael: 1938[FAN]
Ross, A. H., see 'Morison, Frank': 1881
'Ross, Jean': 1965
Rowland, D. S., see 'Carlton, Roger': 1928, **1975**
Rushdie, Salman (*1947-*): 1975
Russell, Bertrand (*1872-1970*): 1953, 1954
Russell, Eric Frank (*1905-78*): 1937[FP], 1940[FAN], 1943, 1951, 1953, 1954, 1955[W], 1956, 1957, 1958, 1961, 1962, 1964, 1965, 1975, 1978
Russell, George William, see 'AE': 1867
Russen, David (*fl. 1702-5*): 1703
Ryder, James: 1969
Ryman, Geoff (*1951-*): 1976[FP], 1985, 1986, 1989, 1990[W]
Ryves, T. E.: 1951

Sackville-West, Victoria (*1892-1962*): 1942
Sandow, Mike: 1970[FAN]
'Saki' (*1870-1916*): 1914
'Sarban' (*1910-1989*): 1951, 1952, 1953
Saunders, Hilary St. G. (*1898-1951*): 1934
'Sava, George' (*1903-*): 1948
'Savage, Richard' (*1917-*): 1955
Savarin, Julius Jay: **1972**
Saxton, Josephine (*1935-*): 1965[FP], 1969, 1970, 1971, 1980, 1985, 1986, 1989
'Scott, Warwick,' see 'Trevor, Elleston': 1952
Scrymsour, Ella: 1922
'Seaforth, A. Nelson': 1892
'Seamark' (*?-1929*): 1930
Seddon, Keith: 1977[PUB]
'Sellings, Arthur' (*1921-68*): 1953[FP], 1956, 1962, 1964, 1966, 1967, 1968, 1970
Seymour, Alan (*1927-*): 1969
Seymour, Cyril: 1906
Shakespeare, William (*1564-1616*): 1623
'Shanks, Edward' (*1892-1953*): 1920
Shaw, Bob (*1931-*): 1954[FP], 1967, 1968, 1969, 1970, 1971, 1972, 1973, 1975, 1976, 1976[W], 1977, 1978, 1979, 1981, 1982, 1983, 1984, 1985, 1986, 1987[W], 1988, 1989, 1990
Shaw, George Bernard (*1856-1950*): 1921
Shelley, Mary Wollstonecraft (*1797-1851*): 1818, 1826, 1891, 1976
'Sheridan, Thomas,' see Gillings, Walter: 1938[FP]

Sherriff, R. C. (*1896-1975*): 1939
Sherwood, Martin (*1942-*): 1975, 1976
Shiel, M. P. (*1865-1947*): 1896, 1897 (under Tracy, Louis), 1898, 1901, 1905, 1906, 1909, 1911, 1913, 1933, 1935, 1937, 1948, 1979, 1980
Shute, Nevil (*1899-1960*): 1939, 1940, 1948, 1953, 1957, 1958
Sibson, Francis H. (*1899-*): 1932, 1933, 1934
Sieveking, Lance (*1896-1972*): 1924, 1925, 1955
Sillitoe, Alan (*1928-*): 1971
Sisson, Marjorie: 1957
Skinner, Rev. C. A., see 'Maurice, Michael': 1889
'Skorpios, Antares,' see Barlow, James William: 1891
Slade, Derek: 1990
Slater, Henry J.: 1951, 1952
Small, J. Austin, see 'Seamark': 1930
Smith, C. L. T., see 'Forester, C. S.': 1899
'Smith, Wayland': 1936
Snell, Edmund (*1889-?*): 1928, 1932
Souster, Eric: 1954[CX]
Southwold, Stephen (*1887-1964*): 1930, 1931, 1932, 1933, 1935, 1938, 1946
Spanner, E. F. (*1888-?*): 1926
Spencer, Colin (*1937-*): 1966
Spencer, G. F.: 1955
Spencer, John: 1950[PUB]
Spencer, John: 1975
Sprigg, T. Stanhope (*1903-*): 1938
Squire, J. C. (*1884-1958*): 1931[A]
Stableford, Brian M. (*1948-*): 1965[FP], 1969, 1970, 1971, 1972, 1973, 1974, 1975, 1976, 1977, 1978, 1979, 1980, 1981, 1982, 1983, 1985, 1985[C], 1988, 1989[E], 1990
Stables, Gordon (*1840-1910*): 1891, 1903, 1906
Stacpoole, H. de Vere (*1865-1951*): 1947
Stair, Bill: 1974 under Boorman, John
Stanford, J. K. (*1892-?*): 1953
Staniland, Meaburn: 1947
Stanley, William (*1829-1909*): 1903
Stapledon, Olaf (*1886-1950*): 1930, 1932, 1934[E], 1935, 1937, 1942, 1944, 1946, 1947, 1949, 1950, 1953, 1954[E], 1976, 1980
Starzl, R. F.: 1932[FP] under Pragnell, Festus
'Statten, Vargo,' see Fearn, John Russell: **1942**
Stephenson, Andrew M. (*1946-*): 1971[FP], 1977, 1979
Stevenson, Dorothy Emily (*1892-1973*): 1936
Stevenson, Robert Louis (*1850-94*): 1886
Stewart, Alfred Walter, see 'Connington, J. J.': 1880
Stoker, Bram (*1847-1912*): 1897
Storr, Catherine (*1913-*): 1976
Story, Jack Trevor (*1917-*): 1970, 1971, 1976
Suddaby, W. D., see 'Griff, Alan': 1900
Sullivan, Sheila: 1975
Sully, Kathleen M. (*1910-*): 1960
Suvin, Darko: 1983[C]
'Swayne, Martin' (*1884-1953*): 1918
Swift, Jonathan (*1667-1745*): 1726

Swindells, Robert (*1939-*): 1973

Tabori, Paul (*1908-74*): 1961, 1969
Tate, Peter (*1940-*): 1966[FP], 1969, 1971, 1973, 1974, 1975, 1976, 1979
Tayler, J. Lionel: 1924
Temple, William F. (*1914-1989*): 1938[FP], 1946[FAN], 1949, 1962, 1963, 1966, 1968
Tennant, Emma (*1937-*): 1973, 1974, 1976, 1982
Thomas, D. M. (*1935-*): 1968, 1981
'Thomas, Edward,' see Tubb, E. C.: **1951**
Thompson, Anthony A., see 'Alban, Antony': 1968
Thompson, E. P. (*1924-*): 1988
'Thorne, Guy' (*1876-1923*): 1904, 1906, 1908, 1915, 1916, 1919, 1921, 1924
Tilley, Patrick (*1928-*): 1975, 1984, 1985, 1987, 1988, 1989
Tillyard, Aelfrida (*1883-?*): 1930, 1932
Timlett, Peter Valentine (*1933-*): **1974**
Todd, Ruthven (*1914-*): 1939, 1943
Tolkien, J. R. R. (*1892-1973*): 1937, 1954, 1955, 1957[W], 1977, 1978[W]
Tonks, Angela: 1958
'Torro, Pel,' see Fanthorpe, R. L.: **1954**
Toynbee, Polly (*1946-*): 1966
Tracy, Louis (*1863-1928*): 1896, 1897, 1898, 1901, 1906
'Trevena, John' (*1890-?*): 1911
'Trevor, Elleston' (*1920-*): 1946, 1952, 1957, 1960, 1966
Trollope, Anthony (*1815-82*): 1882
'Trueman, Chrysostom': 1864
Tubb, E. C. (*1919-*): 1951[FP], **1951**, 1958[FAN]
Tucker, Allan James, see 'Craig, David': 1929
Turner, C. C. (*1870-1952*): 1923, 1927
Turner, Harry: 1941[FAN]
Turner, Lady, see Robertson, E. Arnot: 1903

Ure, Jean (*1943-*): 1989

Valentine, Victor: 1960
Van Greenaway, Peter (*1924-*): 1962, 1968, 1973, 1982, 1983
Vansittart, Peter (*1920-*): 1968
'Vardre, Leslie,' see Davies, L. P.: 1960[FP]
Vinson, Rex Thomas, see 'King, Vincent': 1935
Visiak, E. H. (*1878-1972*): 1929
Vivian, E. Charles (*1882-1947*): 1925, 1929
Vyse, Michael: 1980

Wadsworth, Phyllis Marie: 1967

Wagner, John: 1977[CX], 1983[CX]
Wall, John W., see 'Sarban': 1910
'Wallace, Doreen'(*1897-?*): 1958
Wallace, Edgar (*1875-1932*): 1912, 1913, 1915, 1919, 1922, 1926, 1929
Waller, Robert (*1913-*): 1956
Wallis, George C. (*1871-1946*): 1901, 1928[FP], 1948
Walpole, Horace (*1717-1797*): 1764
Walsh, J. M. (*1897-1952*): 1931
Walter, W. Grey (*1910-77*): 1956
Ward, Arthur H. S., see 'Rohmer, Sax': 1883
Warner, Kenneth Lewis, see 'Morel, Dighton': 1915
Warner, Rex (*1905-86*): 1941
Watson, H. B. Marriott (*1863-1921*): 1888
Watson, Ian (*1943-*): 1969[FP], 1973, 1975, 1976, 1977, 1978, 1978[W], 1979, 1980, 1981, 1981[A], 1982, 1983, 1984, 1985, 1986, 1987, 1988, 1989, 1990
Waugh, Evelyn (*1903-66*): 1953
Weatherhead, J.: 1969
Webster, Lyn: 1987
'Wells, Barry': 1961
Wells, H. G. (*1866-1946*): 1887, 1888, 1891[E], 1893, 1893[E], 1894, 1894[E], 1895, 1896, 1896[E], 1897, 1898, 1899, 1901, 1901[E], 1902, 1902[E], 1903, 1904, 1905, 1906, 1908, 1911, 1914, 1921, 1921[E], 1923, 1924, 1926, 1926[FP], 1927, 1927[FP], 1928, 1928[FP], 1929, 1929[FP], 1930, 1933, 1935, 1936, 1937, 1939, 1940, 1945[E], 1984
Wells, Robert (*1929-*): 1965[FP], 1969, 1976
West, Anthony (*1914-1987*): 1949, 1951
Westall, William (*1834-1903*): 1886, 1887, 1888, 1901
Weston, Peter (*1944-*): 1963[FAN], 1976[A], 1977[A], 1978[A]
Wheatley, Dennis (*1897-1977*): 1933, 1934, 1936, 1937, 1938, 1939, 1945, 1952
Wheeler, Paul (*1934-*): 1968
White, Fred M. (*1859-?*): 1900
White, James (*1928-*): 1953[FP], 1957, 1962, 1963, 1964, 1965, 1966, 1968, 1969, 1971, 1972, 1974, 1977, 1979, 1982, 1983, 1985, 1988
White, T. H. (*1906-64*): 1934, 1935, 1958
Wicks, Mark: 1911
Wignall, T. C. (*1883-1958*): 1923
Wilding, Philip: 1954, 1955, 1956
Wilkins, John (*1614-72*): 1638[E], 1648[E]
Wilkins, Vaughan (*1890-1959*): 1955
Williams, Charles (*1886-1945*): 1931
Williams, Eric C. (*1918-*): 1965[FP], 1968, 1969, 1971, 1973, 1977
Williams, Ian: 1970[FAN]
Willis, G. A. A., see Armstrong, Anthony: 1897
Willis, Walter A.: 1948[FAN], 1952[FAN]
Wilson, Angus (*1913-91*): 1955[A], 1961
Wilson, Colin (*1931-*): 1967, 1969, 1976, 1987
Wilson, John Anthony Burgess, see Burgess, Anthony: 1917
Wilson, Snoo (*1948-*): 1984, 1985

Wilson, Steve (*1943-*): 1976
Wilson, William: 1851[C]
'Wingrave, Anthony,' see Wright, S. Fowler: 1935
Wingrove, David (*1954-*): 1973[C] under Aldiss, Brian, 1987[W], 1989, 1990
Winsor, G. MacLeod: 1919
Wise, Arthur (*1923-*): 1970
Wood, S. Andrew (*1890-?*): 1935
'Woodcott, Keith,' see Brunner, John: 1961, 1962, 1963, 1965
Woods, Helen, see 'Kavan, Anna': 1901
Woolf, Virginia (*1882-1941*): 1928
Wootton, Barbara (*1897-1988*): 1936
Wright, Helen: 1988
Wright, Lan (*1923-*): 1952[FP], **1957**
Wright, S. Fowler (*1874-1965*): 1925, 1927, 1928, 1929, 1931, 1932, 1933, 1935, 1936, 1937, 1938, 1945, 1954
Wyndham, John (*1903-69*): 1931[FP], 1935, 1936, 1946[FAN], 1951, 1953, 1954, 1955, 1956, 1957, 1959, 1960, 1961, 1968, 1973, 1979
Wynne-Tyson, Esmé (*1898-*): 1944 under Beresford, J. D.

Youd, C. S., see 'Christopher, John': 1922, 1939[FAN], 1949[FP]
Young, B. A. (*1912-*): 1967
Young, Michael (*1915-*): 1958[E]

'Zeigfried, Karl,' see Fanthorpe, R. L.: **1954**
'Zetford, Tully,' see Bulmer, Kenneth: **1952**

Title Index

'1925' (Wallace): 1926
1944 (Halsbury): 1926
1957 (Blair): 1930
1984 (Orwell), see *Nineteen Eighty-Four*
1984: Spring (Clarke): 1984[E]
1985 (Burgess): 1978
200 Years to Christmas (McIntosh): 1961
"2000 A.D.": 1977[CX]
2001 (Clarke): 1968
2010 (Clarke): 1982
2061 (Clarke): 1988
98.4 (Hodder-Williams): 1969
99% (Gloag): 1944
998 (Hyams): 1951

A for Andromeda (Hoyle & Elliot): 1962
Abandonati (Kilworth): 1988
Abbs (Hyne): 1929
Above All Else (Shiel): *1933*
Across the Sea of Stars (Clarke): 1959
Across the Zodiac (Greg): 1880
Across the Zodiac (Pallander): 1896
AD 2500 (ed. Wilson): 1955[A]
Adam and Eve and Newbury (Bennett): 1970
Adam in Moonshine (Priestley): 1927
Address Unknown (Phillpotts): 1949
"Advent of the Flying Man, The" (Wells): 1893
Adventure in the Blue Room, The (Wright): 1945
Adventure of Wyndham Smith, The (Wright): 1938
Adventures of a Micro-Man, The (Pallander): 1902
Adventures of a Solicitor, The (Hyne): 1898
Adventures of an Engineer, The (Hyne): 1898

Title Index

Adventures of Eovaai, The (Haywood): 1736
Adventures of Una Persson, The (Moorcock): 1976
"Aepyornis Island" (Wells): 1894, 1927[FP]
Aerodrome, The (Warner): 1941
Affirmation, The (Priest): 1981
After London (Jefferies): 1885
After Many a Summer (Huxley): 1939
After Many a Summer Dies the Swan (Huxley): 1939
After the Rain (Bowen): 1958
After the Rain: A Play: (Bowen): *1958*
Aftermath (Corston): 1968
Against the Fall of Night (Clarke): 1953, 1968
Age of Longing, The (Koestler): 1951
Age of Miracles (Brunner): *1965*
Age, An (Aldiss): 1967
Agonies of Time, The (Christchild): 1989
Air Pirate, The (Thorne): 1919
Airs of Earth (Aldiss): 1963
Alas, That Great City (Ashton): 1948
Albion! Albion! (Morland): 1974
Aleriel (Lach-Szyrma): 1874
Alice's Adventures in Wonderland (Carroll): 1865
"Alien Analysis" (Morgan): 1952[FP]
Alien Culture (Macey): 1977
Alien Embassy (Watson): 1977
Alien Heat, An (Moorcock): 1972
Alien, The (Davies): 1968
Aliens Among Us, The (White): 1969
All Aboard for Ararat (Wells): 1940
All Fools' Day (Cooper): 1966
All Judgement Fled (White): 1968
All or Nothing (Beresford): 1928
All or Nothing (Powys): 1960
"Allamagoosa" (Russell): 1955[W]
Allan and the Ice-Gods (Haggard): 1927
Allan Quatermain (Haggard): 1887
Alph (Maine): *1958*
Alpha and Omega (Southwold): 1946
Altar on Asconel, The (Brunner): 1965
Alteration, The (Amis): 1976, 1977[W]
Amateur Science Stories: 1937[FAN]
Amazing Mr. Lutterworth, The (Leslie): 1958
Amazing Spectacles (Godber): 1931
Ambrosio, or The Monk, see *Monk, The*
Ambulance Ship (White): 1979
American Emperor, An (Tracy & Shiel): 1897
Amphibians, The (Wright): 1925
Amtrak Wars: Book 1 (Tilley): 1984
Amtrak Wars: Book 2 (Tilley): 1985
Amtrak Wars: Book 3 (Tilley): 1987
Amtrak Wars: Book 4 (Tilley): 1988
Amtrak Wars: Book 5 (Tilley): 1989
Anackire (Lee): 1983
Ancient Light (Gentle): 1987
And a New Earth (Jacomb): 1926

Title Index

"And Dug the Dog a Tomb" (James): 1972[FP]
And It Came to Pass (Thorne): 1916
And So Ends the World (Pape): 1961
And the Lurid Glare of the Comet (Aldiss): 1986[E]
And the Stars Remain (Berry): 1952
Andromeda 1 (ed. Weston): 1976[A]
Andromeda 2 (ed. Weston): 1977[A]
Andromeda 3 (ed. Weston): 1978[A]
Andromeda Breakthrough (Hoyle & Elliot): 1964
Angel of the Revolution, The (Griffith): 1893
Angel, The (Thorne): 1908
Angelo's Moon (Brown): 1955
Animal Farm (Orwell): 1945
Annals of the Twenty-Ninth Century (Blair): 1874
Annihilation Factor, The (Bayley): 1972
Another End (King): 1971
Another Kind (West): 1951
Another Space, Another Time (Campbell): 1953
Anti-Death League, The (Amis): 1966
Anticipations (ed. Priest): 1978[A]
Anticipations (Wells): 1901[E]
Ape and Essence (Huxley): 1948
Ape of London, The (Crisp): 1959
Apes, The (Phillpotts): 1929
"Apple, The" (Wells): 1896
Approaching Storm, The (Tillyard): 1932
Archivist, The (Alderman): 1989
Archon (Gordon): 1987
Arena SF: 1976[FAN]
"Argonauts of the Air, The" (Wells): 1895
Aries 1 (ed. Grant): 1979[A]
Ark of the Covenant, The (MacClure): 1924
Armata (Erskine): 1817
Armoured Doves (Newman): 1930
Arms of the Sun, The (Mills): 1924
Around a Distant Star (Delaire): 1904
Arrows of Desire (Household): 1985
Arthur C. Clarke Omnibus, An (Clarke): 1965
Arthur C. Clarke Second Omnibus, An (Clarke): 1967
Arthur C. Clarke's July 20, 2019 (Clarke): 1987[E]
Artificial Man, The (Davies): 1965
"As Easy as ABC" (Kipling): 1912
Ascendancies (Compton): 1980
Asleep in the Afternoon (Large): 1938
"Aspect" (Shaw): 1954[FP]
"Assisted Passage" (White): 1953[FP]
Astounding Days (Clarke): 1989[E]
Astrologer, The (Hyams): 1950
Astronauts Must Not Land, The (Brunner): 1963
Asylum (Spencer): 1966
Asylum Piece (Kavan): 1940
At the Back of the North Wind (MacDonald): 1871
At the End of the World (Guest): 1929
Atlan (Gaskell): 1965
Atlantic Abomination, The (Brunner): 1960

Atoms (Wignall): 1923
Atoms of Empire (Hyne): 1904
Atrocity Exhibition, The (Ballard): 1970
Authentic Science Fiction: 1951[PUB], 1952[PUB]
Autocracy of Mr. Parham, The (Wells): 1930
"Autodestruct" (Boyce): 1964[FP]
Automated Goliath, The (Temple): 1962
Autumn Accelerator, The (Leslie): 1969
Avatars, The (AE): 1933
Avengers of Carrig, The (Brunner): *1962*
Avenging Ray, The (Seamark): 1930
Ayesha (Haggard): 1905

B.E.A.S.T. (Maine): 1966
"Baa Baa Blocksheep" (Harrison): 1968[FP]
Back to Methuselah (Shaw): 1921
Back to the Future (Staniland): 1947
Bad Dreams (Newman): 1990
Balance of Power (Stableford): 1979
Bandersnatch (Ryves): 1950
Barbarians of Mars (*Moorcock*): 1965
Barefoot in the Head (Aldiss): 1969
"Basic Fundamental" (Rayer): 1947[FP]
Battle of Dorking Controversy, The (ed. Anon): 1972[A]
"Battle of Dorking, The" (*Chesney*): 1871
Battle of London, The (Addison): 1923
Battle on Venus (Temple): 1963
Beautiful Biting Machine, The (Lee): 1984
Beckoning Hand, The (Allen): 1887
Bedlam Planet (Brunner): 1968
Beetle's Career (Fraser): 1951
Before Armageddon (ed. Moorcock): 1975[A]
Behold the Man (Moorcock): 1969
"Behold the Man" (Moorcock): 1968[W]
Beleagured City, A (Oliphant): 1880
Beneath Your Very Boots (Hyne): 1889
Benedict's Planet (Corley): 1976
Benefits (Fairbairns): 1979
Benita (Haggard): 1906
Best from New Worlds Science Fiction (ed. Carnell): 1955[A]
Best of Arthur C. Clarke 1937-1955, The (Clarke): *1973*
Best of Arthur C. Clarke 1955-1972, The (Clarke): *1973*
Best of Arthur C. Clarke, The (Clarke): 1973
Best of British SF, The (ed. Ashley): 1977[A]
Best of Eric Frank Russell, The (Russell): 1978
Best of J. G. Ballard, The (Ballard): 1977
Best of John Brunner, The (Brunner): 1988
Best of John Wyndham, The (Wyndham): 1973
Best of New Worlds, The (ed. Moorcock): 1965[A]
Best of New Writings in SF, The (ed. Carnell): 1971[A]
Best Science Fiction Stories (Aldiss): 1965
Best SF (ed. Crispin): 1955[A]
Best SF (eds. Aldiss & Harrison): 1967[A]

Best SF Stories (Aldiss): 1988
Best SF Stories from New Worlds (ed. Moorcock): 1967[A]
Best Short Stories of J. G. Ballard, The (Ballard): 1978
Best Short Stories of M. P. Shiel, The (Shiel): 1948
Better Mantrap, A (Shaw): 1982
Bewitchments of Love and Hate, The (Constantine): 1988
Beyond the Blue (Blake): 1920
Beyond the Eleventh Hour (Gordon): 1961
Beyond the Gaslight (eds. Evans & Evans): 1976[A]
Beyond the Rim (Wright): 1932
"Beyond Time's Aegis" (*Stableford*): 1965[FP]
Beyond Tomorrow (Carlton): 1975
Beyond: 1964[FAN]
Big Death, The (Maine): *1962*
Big Step (Passes): 1977
Billenium (Ballard): 1962
Billion Year Spree (Aldiss): 1973[C], 1974[W]
Binary Divine (Hartridge): 1969
Birds, The (Baker): 1936
Birthgrave, The (Lee): 1975
B.I.S., see British Interplanetary Society
Black August (Wheatley): 1934
Black Cloud, The (Hoyle): 1957
Black Corridor, The (Moorcock): 1969
Black Death, The (Dalton): 1934
Black Doctor, The (Doyle): 1919
Black Fox, The (Heard): 1950
Black Venus (Carter): 1985
Blades of Mars (Moorcock): 1965
Blake of the 'Rattlesnake' (Jane): 1895
Blake's Seven (Hoyle): 1977
Blake's Seven: Project Avalon (Hoyle): 1979
Blake's Seven: Scorpio Attack (Hoyle): 1981
Blind Worm, The (Stableford): 1970
Blindfold from the Stars (High): 1979
Blood of Roses, The (Lee): 1990
Blood-Red Game, The (Moorcock): *1965*
Blue Ants, The (Newman): 1962
Blue Germ, The (Swayne): 1918
Boats of the 'Glen Carrig', The (Hodgson): 1907
Body Made Alive (Marsh): 1936
Body's Guest, The (MacLeod): 1958
Bodyguard, The (Mitchell): 1970
Book of Being, The (Watson): 1985
Book of Brian Aldiss, The (Aldiss): 1972
Book of Ian Watson, The (Watson): 1985
Book of John Brunner, The (Brunner): 1976
Book of the Beast, The (Lee): 1988
Book of the Damned, The (Lee): 1988
Book of the River, The (Watson): 1984
Book of the Stars, The (Watson): 1985
Books of the Black Current, The (Watson): 1986
Born in Space (Donson): 1968
Born Leader (McIntosh): 1954
Botanic Garden, The (Darwin): 1791

Bow Down to Nul (Aldiss): 1960
Boy Who Saw Tomorrow, The (Niall): 1952
Brain (Britton): 1930
Brain of Graphicon, The (Barrett): 1973
Brain, The (Harrison): 1953
Brainfix (Boyce): 1980
Brainrack (Pedler & Davis): 1974
Brass Bottle, The (Anstey): 1900
Brass Butterfly, The (Golding): 1958
Brave New World (Huxley): 1932
Brave New World Revisited (Huxley): 1958[E]
"Breakdown" (Bailey): 1963[FP]
Breakfast in the Ruins (Moorcock): 1972
Breaking of the Seals, The (Ashton): 1946
Breakthrough (Cowper): 1967
Brian Aldiss Omnibus (2), A (Aldiss): 1970
Brian Aldiss Omnibus, A (Aldiss): 1969
Bride from the Desert, A (Allen): 1896
Bride of Frankenstein, The (Harrison): 1936
Bridge, The (Banks): 1986
Briefing for a Descent Into Hell (Lessing): 1971
Bright Phoenix, The (Mead): 1955
Brink, The (Brunner): 1959
British Barbarians, The (Allen): 1895
British Fantasy Society: 1942[FAN]
British Interplanetary Society: 1933[FAN], 1946[FAN]
British Science Fiction Association: 1935[FAN], 1958[FAN], 1960[FAN]
British Science Fiction Magazine, see *Vargo Statten Science Fiction Magazine*
British Space Fiction Magazine, see *Vargo Statten Science Fiction Magazine*
Briton or Boer? ((Griffith): 1897
Broken Trident, The (Spanner): 1926
Brontomek! (Coney): 1976, 1977[W]
Brothel in Rosenstrasse, The (Moorcock): 1982
Brothers of the Head (Aldiss): 1977
Bruno Lipshitz (King): 1976
BSFA, see British Science Fiction Association
Bureau of Lost Souls, The (Fowler): 1989
Burning Ring, The (Burdekin): 1927
Burning World, The (Ballard): 1964
Bury My Heart at W. H. Smith's (Aldiss): 1990[E]
But Soft!--We Are Observed! (Belloc): 1928
Butterfly Planet (High): 1971
Button Brains (Clouston): 1933
By Aeroplane to the Sun (Horner): 1910
By and By (Maitland): 1873
Byzantium Endures (Moorcock): 1981

Cabal, The (Dunn): 1978
Cabinet Pudding (Young): 1967
Cain Factor, The (Lewis): 1975

Calculated Risk (Maine): 1960
Calends of Cairo, The (Mitchell): 1931
Call of Peter Gaskell, The (Wallis): 1948
Call of Utopia, The (Williams): 1971
Calling of Bara, The (Sullivan): *1975*
Caltraps of Time, The (Masson): 1968
Camberwell Miracle, The (Beresford): 1933
Camelot (White): 1958
Camford Visitation, The (Wells): 1937
Canal Dreams (Banks): 1989
Candle in the Sun (Wells): 1976
Candy Man (King): 1971
Canopy of Time, The (Aldiss): 1959
Capella's Golden Eye (Evans): 1980
Captain Ishmail (Griffith): 1901
Captain of the 'Mary Rose', The (Clowes): 1892
Captain of the Polestar, The (Doyle): 1890
Captains of Souls (Wallace): 1922
Carder's Paradise (Levene): 1968
Carpet People (Pratchett): 1971
Casablanca (Moorcock): 1989
Case of The Fox, The (Stanley): 1903
Castaway of Tanagar, The (Stableford): 1981
Castaway's World (Brunner): 1963
Castle of Otranto, The (*Walpole*): 1764
Cat Karina (Coney): 1982
Cataclysm, The (Sherriff): *1939*
Catacombs, The (Harrison): 1962
Catch a Falling Star (Brunner): *1959*
Catchworld (Boyce): 1975
Catharsis Central (Alban): 1968
Cave, The (Sisson): 1957
Cee Tee Man (Morgan): 1955
Celestial Steam Locomotive, The (Coney): 1983
Centauri Device, The (Harrison): 1974
Centenarians, The (Phelps): 1958
Ceres Solution, The (Shaw): 1981
Chain Reaction (Hodder-Williams): 1959
Chalk Giants, The (Roberts): 1974
Challenge of the Spaceship, The (Clarke): 1959[E]
Chaos (Desmond): 1938
Chaos Weapon, The (Kapp): 1977
Chariot of the Sun, The (Pocock): 1911
Charisma (Coney): 1975
Chase the Morning (Rohan): 1990
Cheetah-Girl, The (Blayre): 1923
Chekhov's Journey (Watson): 1983
Chemical Baby, The (Clouston): 1934
Chidermass, The (Lewis): 1928
Child Garden, The (Ryman): 1989, 1990[W]
Childe Roland (Lee): 1989
Childhood's End (Clarke): 1953
Children of Light, The (Lawrence): 1960
Children of the Morning (George): 1926
Children of the Night (Blackburn): 1966

Children of the Sphinx (Wallis): 1901
Children of the Thunder (Brunner): 1990
Children of the Void (Dexter): 1955
Chinese Agent, The (Moorcock): *1966*
Chocky (Wyndham): 1968
"Christmas Tree" (Christopher): 1949[FP]
Chromosome Game, The (Hodder-Williams): 1984
"Chronic Argonauts, The" (Wells): 1888
Chronicules (Compton): *1970*
Chronocules (Compton): 1970
Chronopolis (Ballard): 1971
Chrysalids, The (Wyndham): 1955
Chung Kuo: The Broken Wheel (Wingrove): 1990
Chung Kuo: The Middle Kingdom (Wingrove): 1989
Circuit-Breaker (MacLeod): 1978
City and the Stars, The (Clarke): *1953*, 1956
City Dwellers, The (Platt): 1970
City in the Autumn Stars, The (Moorcock): 1986
City in the Clouds, The (Thorne): 1921
City of the Beast, The (Moorcock): *1965*
City of the Sun, The (Stableford): 1978
City, The (Gaskell): 1966
Claret, Sandwiches and Sin (Duke): 1964
Cleft, The (Tabori): 1969
Clockwork Man, The (Odle): 1923
Clockwork Orange, A (Burgess): 1962
Clockwork Orange, A: A Play (Burgess): 1987
Clone (Cowper): 1972
Cloud on Silver (Christopher): 1964
Cloud Walker, The (Cooper): 1973
Cloudrock (Kilworth): 1988
Cold War in a Country Garden (Gutteridge): 1971
Collapse of Homo Sapiens, The (Graham): 1923
Collected Tales and Stories (Shelley): 1976
Collision Course (Bayley): 1973
Collision with Chronos (Bayley): *1973*
Colloghi Conspiracy, The (Hill): 1990
Colonists of Space (Carr): 1954
Colossus (Jones): 1966
Colossus and the Crab (Jones): 1977
Colour of Magic, The (Pratchett): 1983
"Combat's End" (Bayley): 1954[FP]
Come, Hunt an Earthman (High): 1973
Comet Chaos (Seymour): 1906
Comet Halley (Hoyle): 1985
Comic Inferno (Aldiss): *1972*
Coming Race, The (Bulwer-Lytton): 1871
Coming Self-Destruction of the U.S.A., The (Seymour): 1969
Commander-1 (George): 1965
Committed Men, The (Harrison): 1971
Common Enemy, A (Beresford): 1942
Complete Professor Challenger Stories, The (Doyle): 1952
Complete Short Stories of H. G. Wells, The (Wells): *1927*
Con: 1964[FAN]

Title Index

Concrete (Tillyard): 1930
Concrete Horizon, The (Morgan): 1976
Concrete Island (Ballard): 1974
Condition of Musak, The (Moorcock): 1977
Conditioned for Space (Ash): 1955
Congratulate the Devil (Marvell): 1939
Consider Her Ways (Wyndham): 1961
Consider Phlebas (Banks): 1987
Consolidator, The (Defoe): 1705
Contact Lost (Craig): 1970
Continuous Katherine Mortenhoe, The (Compton): 1974
Converts (Watson): 1984
Cornelius (Moorcock): *1977*
Cornelius Chronicles, The (Moorcock): 1977
Cosmic Carousel (Garnett): 1976
Cosmic Kaleidoscope (Shaw): 1976
Cosmic Spies, The (McIntosh): 1972
Count-Down (Maine): 1959
Countdown to Doomsday (Quest): 1966
Country Love and Poison Rain (Tate): 1973
Country of the Blind, The (Wells): 1911
"Country of the Blind, The" (Wells): 1904, 1927[FP]
Country of the Mind, The (Morgan): 1975
Coward's Paradise (Hodder-Williams): 1974
Crab Was Crushed, A (Graham): 1937
Crack of Doom, The (Cromie): 1895
Crack of Doom, The (Minto): 1886
Crack, The (Tennant): *1973*
Cracken at Critical (Aldiss): 1987
Cradle (Clarke & Lee): 1988
Cradle of the Sun (Stableford): 1969
Crash (Ballard): 1973
Criminal Croesus, A (Griffith): 1904
"Criminal Record" (Aldiss): 1954[FP]
Crisis 2000 (Maine): 1956
Crisis!-1992 (Herbert): 1936
Critical Threshold (Stableford): 1977
Croquet Player, The (Wells): 1936
Crucible of Time, The (Brunner): 1983
Crucified City, The (Van Greenaway): 1962
Cruise of the Crystal Boat, The (Stables): 1891
Cryptozoic! (Aldiss): *1967*
Crystal Age, A (Hudson): 1887
"Crystal Egg, The" (Wells): 1897, 1926[FP]
Crystal World, The (Ballard): 1966
Culmination (Furnill): 1932
Cure for Cancer, A (Moorcock): 1971
Cure for Death (Valentine): 1960
"Curfew Tolls, The" (McIntosh): 1950[FP]
Curse of Intellect, The (Constable): 1895
Curve of the Snowflake, The (Walter): 1956
Custodians, The (Cowper): 1976
Cypher: 1970[FAN]
Cyrion (Lee): 1982

Daedalus (Haldane): 1923[E]
Dagger of the Mind (Shaw): 1979
Damnation Game, The (Barker): 1985
"Dan Dare--Pilot of the Future": 1950[CX]
Dancers at the End of Time, The (Moorcock): 1983
Danger! (Doyle): 1918
Dargason (Cooper): 1976
Dark Andromeda (Merak): 1954
Dark Inferno (White): 1972
Dark Light Years, The (Aldiss): 1964
Dark Mind, The (Kapp): *1964*
Dark Night in Toyland (Shaw): 1989
Dark Side of the Sun, The (Pratchett): 1976
Dark Tides (Russell): 1962
Darkening Island (Priest): 1972
Darkest of Nights, The (Maine): 1962
Darkness and the Light (Stapledon): 1942
Dawn (Wright): 1929
Dawn in Andromeda (Large): 1956
Dawn of All, The (Benson): 1911
Dawn's Delay, The (Kingsmill): 1924
Day by Night (Lee): 1980
Day of Creation, The (Ballard): 1987
Day of Forever, The (Ballard): 1967
Day of Misjudgement, The (MacLaren): 1956
Day of the Star Cities (Brunner): 1965
Day of the Triffids, The (Wyndham): 1951
Day of the Women, The (Kettle): 1969
Day of Uniting, The (Wallace): 1926
Day of Wrath (O'Neill): 1936
Day of Wrath (Stableford): 1971
Day the Earth Caught Fire, The (Wells): 1961
Day the World Ended, The (Rohmer): 1930
Day They Put Humpty Together, The (Jones): 1968
Daybreak on a Different Mountain (Greenland): 1984
Days of Glory, The (Stableford): 1971
Days of Grass (Lee): 1985
Days of March, The (Brunner): 1988
Deadly Image (Cooper): 1958
Deadly Litter (White): 1964
Death Guard, The (Chadwick): 1939
Death Into Life (Stapledon): 1946
Death of a World (Farjeon): 1948
Death of Grass, The (Christopher): 1956
Death Ship, The (Edmonds): 1933
Death Star, The (Bridges): 1940
Death Watch (Compton): *1974*
Death's Master (Lee): 1979
Deathhunter (Watson): 1981
Deathworms of Kratos, The (*Cooper*): 1975
Deep Fix, The (Moorcock): 1966
Deep Range, The (Clarke): 1957
Deep Space (Russell): 1954
"Defense Mechanism" (King): 1966[FP]
Deluge (Doyle): 1976

Deluge (Wright): 1927
Delusion's Master (Lee): 1981
Demigods, The (Bennett): 1939
Denver Is Missing (Jones): 1971
Denver's Double (Griffith): 1901
Desire of the Eyes, The (Allen): 1895
Desolation Road (McDonald): 1988
"Desolator, The" (Williams): 1965[FP]
Despatches from...Female Mind (eds. Green & Lefanu): 1985[A]
Destined Maid, The (Griffith): 1898
Devil's Tor (Lindsay): 1932
Devil-Man from Mars (Corbett): 1935
Devil-Tree of El Dorado, The (Atkins): 1896
Diabols, The (Mackelworth): 1968
Dial of Ahaz, The (Vaughan): 1917
"Diamond Maker, The" (Wells): 1894
"Diary of a Translator" (Ryman): 1976[FP]
Diggers (Pratchett): 1990
Digital Dreams (ed. Barrett): 1990[A]
Dimension A (Davies): 1969
"Dimple" (Kippax): 1954[FP]
Dirk Gently's Holistic Detective Agency (Adams): 1987
Disappearing Future, The (ed. Hay): 1970[A]
Disaster Area, The (Ballard): 1967
Discovery of a World, The (Wilkins): 1638[E]
Discovery of the Future, The (Wells): 1902[E]
Disintegrator, The (Morgan & Brown): 1892
Distant Relations (Macey): 1975
Distant Suns, The (Moorcock & James): 1975
Disturbing Affair of Noel Blake, The (Southwold): 1932
Divine Endurance (Jones): 1984
Doings of Raffles Haw, The (Doyle): 1891
Doll Maker, The (Sarban): 1953
Dolphin Boy (Meyers): 1967
Dolphin Island (Clarke): 1963
Dolphin Rider, The (Meyers): *1967*
Dome, The (Jones): 1968
Domesday Story (Trevor): 1952
Domesday Village (Colvin): 1948
Domino (Cowper): 1971
Don or Devil? (Westall): 1901
Don't Bite the Sun (Lee): 1976
Don't Pick the Flowers (Jones): 1971
Doom of the Great City, The (Hay): 1880
Doomsday (Trevor): *1952*
Doomsday 1999 (MacTyre): 1962
Doomsday England (Cooney): 1967
Doomsday Men, The (Priestley): 1938
Doomsday Ultimatum, The (Follett): 1976
Door in the Wall, The (Wells): 1911
"Door in the Wall, The" (Wells): 1906
Doppelgangers (Heard): 1947
Double Emperor, The (Clowes): 1894
Double Illusion (High): *1966*
Double Phoenix (Cooper): 1971

Double Planet (Gribbin & Chown): 1988
Double, Double (Brunner): 1969
Down to Earth (Capon): 1954
Dr. Strangelove (George): *1958*
Dr. Faustus (Marlowe): 1604
Dr. Jekyll and Mr. Hyde, see *Strange Case of, The...*
Dr. Odin (Newton): 1933
Dracula (Stoker): 1897
Dragon Hoard, The (Lee): 1984
Dragon in the Sword, The (Moorcock): 1987
Dragon, The (Shiel): 1913
Dramaturges of Yan, The (Brunner): 1971
Dreadful Sanctuary (Russell): 1951
Dream (Wright): 1931
Dream Millennium, The (White): 1974
"Dream of Armageddon, A" (Wells): 1901
Dream of Kinship, A (Cowper): 1981
Dream of Wessex, A (Priest): 1977
Dream Wall, The (Martin): 1987
Dream, The (Wells): 1924
Dreamers, The (Manvell): 1958
Dreaming Earth, The (Brunner): 1963
"Dreams Are Sacred" (Phillips): 1948
Drinking Sapphire Wine (Lee): 1977
Drop In, The (Williams): 1977
Drought, The (Ballard): *1964*
Drowned World, The (Ballard): 1962
Dry Deluge, The (Nott): 1947
Dwellers, The (Wright): *1929*
Dying for Tomorrow (Moorcock): *1976*
Dynostar Menace, The (Pedler & Davis): 1975

Early H. G. Wells, The (Bergonzi): 1961[C]
Earth Cult (Hoyle): 1979
Earth Has Been Found (Jones): 1979
Earth Stopped (White): 1934
Earthdoom! (Langford & Grant): 1987
Earthjacket (Hartridge): 1970
Earthlight (Clarke): 1955
Earthwind (Holdstock): 1977
Earthworks (Aldiss): 1965
Eavesdropper, The (Payn): 1888
Echo in the Skull (Brunner): 1959
Echoing Worlds, The (Burke): 1954
Egg-Shaped Thing, The (Hodder-Williams): 1967
Eighth Seal, The (MacLeod): 1962
Eighty-Minute Hour, The (Aldiss): 1974
Einstein's Monsters (Amis): 1987
Electric Crocodile, The (Compton): 1970
Electric Forest (Lee): 1979
Electronic Lullaby Meat Market, The (Spencer): 1975
Element 79 (Hoyle): 1967
"Elephant in the Moon, The" (Butler): 1759

Elidor (Garner): 1965
Elixir of Life, The (Gubbins): 1914
Elnovia (Faber): 1925
Embedding, The (Watson): 1973
Emperor of the Air, The (Glendon): 1910
Emperor of the If (Dent): 1926
Emperor of the World (Hyne): *1910*
Empire Dreams (McDonald): 1988
Empire of Fear, The (Stableford): 1988
"Empire of the Ants, The" (Wells): 1905, 1926[FP]
Empire of the Sun (Ballard): 1984
Empire of the World (Hyne): 1910
Empire of Two Worlds (Bayley): 1972
Empty World, The (Stevenson): 1936
Enchantments of Flesh and Spirit, The (Constantine): 1987
Encyclopedia of Science Fiction (ed. Holdstock): 1978[C]
Encyclopedia of Science Fiction, The (ed. Nicholls): 1979[C]
End of All Songs, The (Moorcock): 1976
End of an Epoch, The (Green): 1901
End of the World News, The (Burgess): 1982
End of the World, The (Dennis): 1930[E]
End Product (Norman): 1975
Endless Shadow (Brunner): 1964
Enemies of England, The (Thorne): 1915
Enemies of the System (Aldiss): 1978
England 1940 (Slade): 1990
England Invaded (ed. Moorcock): 1977[A]
England Swings SF (ed. Merril): 1968[A]
England's Peril (Le Queux): 1899
English Assassin, The (Moorcock): 1972
English Utopia, The (Morton): 1952[C]
Enigma from Tantalus (Brunner): 1965
Entropy Exhibition, The (Greenland): 1983[C]
Entropy Tango, The (Moorcock): 1981
Entry to Elsewhen (Brunner): 1972
Episode of Flatland, An (Hinton): 1907
Equal Rites (Pratchett): 1987
Equator (Aldiss): 1958
Erewhon (Butler): 1872
Erewhon Revisited (Butler): 1901
Eric (Pratchett): 1990
Eric Brighteyes (Haggard): 1891
Erone (Kearney): 1943
Escape Orbit (White): 1965
Escape Plans (Jones): 1986
Escape to Venus (Lott): 1956
Escapement (Maine): 1956
"Escapement" (Ballard): 1956[FP]
"Escapism" (Roberts): 1964[FP]
Eva (Dickinson): 1988
Eva's Apple (Gerhardi): 1928
Evil That Men Do, The (Brunner): 1969
Evil Water (Watson): 1987
Evolution Man, The (Lewis): *1960*
Ex Minus (Conrad): 1974

Exchange of Souls, An (Pain): 1911
Excommunication (Aldiss): 1975
Exiles on Asperus (Wyndham): 1979
Exit Funtopia (Farren): 1989
Expedition to Earth (Clarke): 1953
Experiment with Time, An (Dunne): 1927[E]
Exploration of Space, The (Clarke): 1951[E], 1952[W]
Extinction Bomber (Gordon): 1956
"Extinction of Man, The" (Wells): 1894[E]
Extro Science Fiction: 1982[PUB]
Eye Among the Blind (Holdstock): 1976
Eye of Abu, The (Goodchild): 1927
Eye of Istar, The (Le Queux): 1897
Eye of the Lens, The (Jones): 1972
Eye of the Queen, The (Mann): 1982
Eyes Trilogy, The (Gordon): 1974

Fabulous Valley, The (Wheatley): 1934
Face & the Mask, The (Barr): 1895
Face of Heaven, The (Stableford): 1976
Faces in the Flames (Tate): 1976
Facial Justice (Hartley): 1960
Fade-Out (Tilley): 1975
Fall of Chronopolis, The (Bayley): 1974
Fall of Colossus, The (Jones): 1974
Fall of Moondust, A (Clarke): 1961
Fall of the Families, The (Mann): 1987
Fallen Sky, The (Crowcroft): 1954
Fancies and Goodnights (Collier): 1951, 1952[W]
Fancy Free (Phillpotts): 1901
Fantast, The: 1939[FAN]
Fantasy Review: 1947[FAN]
Fantasy: 1938[PUB], 1946[PUB]
Far Future Calling (Stapledon): 1980
Far Stars (Russell): 1961
Far Sunset, A (Cooper): 1967
Farewell, Earth's Bliss (Compton): 1966
Father of Lies (Brunner): 1968
Father to the Man (Gribbin): 1989
Fear Haunts the Roses (Edwards): 1936
Fear Rides the Air (Desmond): 1953
Fear: 1988[PUB]
Federation World (White): 1988
Feelies, The (Farren): 1978
Fellowship of the Ring, The (Tolkien): 1954
Fenris Device, The (Stableford): 1974
Fifth Child, The (Lessing): 1988
Fifth Planet (Hoyle & Hoyle): 1963
"Filmer" (Wells): 1901
Final Agenda, The (Hyams): 1973
Final Programme, The (Moorcock): 1968
Final War, The (Tracy): 1896
Fire in the Abyss (Gordon): 1983

Fire Past the Future (Maine): *1959*
Fire Pattern (Shaw): 1984
Fire Worm, The (Watson): 1988
Fireball (Davies): 1987
Fireclown, The (Moorcock): 1965
Firemantle (Mackelworth): 1968
Fireworks (Carter): 1974
First Men in the Moon, The (Wells): 1901, 1926[FP]
First on Mars (Gordon): *1956*
First One and Twenty (Gloag): 1946
First Through Time (Gordon): 1962
First to the Stars (Gordon): 1959
Fistful of Digits (Hodder-Williams): 1968
Fittest, The (McIntosh): 1955
Five to Twelve (Cooper): 1968
Fixed Period, The (Trollope): 1882
Flames, The (Stapledon): 1947
Flatland (Abbott): 1884
Fleshpots of Sansato, The (Temple): 1968
Flies of Memory, The (Watson): 1990
Flight from Rebirth (McIntosh): 1971
Flight of Dragons, The (Dickinson): 1979
Flight of the "Hesper" (Hay): 1952
Floating Gods, The (Harrison): *1982*
Floating Zombie, The (Jones): 1975
Flood, The (Creasey): 1956
Florians, The (Stableford): 1976
"*Flowering of the Strange Orchid, The*" (Wells): 1894
Flowers of February, The (Harker): 1970.
Flying Draper, The (Fraser): 1924
Flying Saucer, The (Newman): 1948
Food of the Gods, The (Wells): 1904
For England's Sake (Cromie): 1889
Foreign Bodies (Aldiss): 1981
Foreign Constellations (Brunner): 1980
Forests of the Night (Lee): 1989
Fortune from the Sky, A (Kuppord): 1902
Forty Years On (Wallace): 1958
Foundation: 1972[C]
Fountains of Paradise, The (Clarke): 1979, 1980[W]
Four Days' War (Wright): 1936
Four Encounters (Stapledon): 1976
Four Great SF Novels (Clarke): 1978
Four Hundred Billion Stars (McAuley): 1988, 1989[W]
Four-Dimensional Nightmare, The (Ballard): 1963
Four-Sided Triangle, The (Temple): 1949
Fourth Plague, The (Wallace): 1913
Fourth Programme, The (Adams): 1955
Frankenstein (Shelley): 1818
Frankenstein Unbound (Aldiss): 1973
Fratricide Is a Gas (Gutteridge): 1975
Fraxilly Fracas, The (Hill): 1989
Free Zone (Platt): 1988
Friendly Persuaders, The (Wheeler): 1968
Friends Come in Boxes (Coney): 1973

"From an Observatory" (Wells): 1894[E]
From the Ocean, from the Stars (Clarke): 1962
From This Day Forward (Brunner): 1972
Fugitive from Time (High): 1978
Fugitive Worlds, The (Shaw): 1989
Fugue for a Darkening Island (Priest): 1972
Fulfilments of Fate and Desire, The (Constantine): 1989
Full Circle (Collier): 1933
Full Moon at Sweatenham (Stanford): 1953
Furies, The (Roberts): 1966
Furious Masters, The (Bennett): 1968
Further Outlook (Walter): 1956
Future Imperfect (Chetwynd): 1946
Future Past (White): 1982
Futurian War Digest: 1938[FAN]
Futurian, The: 1938[FAN]
Futuristic Science Stories: 1950[PUB]

Galactic Storm (Brunner): 1951[FP]
Galactic Takeover Bid (McIntosh): 1973
Galactic Tours (Shaw): 1981
Galaxies Like Grains of Sand (Aldiss): *1959*
Gambles with Destiny (Griffith): 1899
Garbage World, The (Platt): 1967
Gardens 1,2,3,4,5 (Tate): 1971
Gardens of Delight, The (Watson): 1980
Gardens One to Five (Tate): 1971
Garments of Caean, The (Bayley): 1976
"Garth": 1943[CX]
Gas War of 1940, The (Southwold): 1931
Gates of Eden, The (Stableford): 1983
Gateway to the Stars (ed. Carnell): 1955[A]
Gateway to Tomorrow (ed. Carnell): 1954[A]
Gay Hunter (Mitchell): 1934
Gemini God (Kilworth): 1981
Gender Genocide (Cooper): 1972
Genesis Two (Davies): 1969
Ghost Pirates, The (Hodgson): 1909
Girl with a Symphony in Her Fingers, The (Coney): 1975
Girl with the X-Ray Eyes, The (O'Nair): 1935
"Girl" (Butterworth): 1966[FP]
Give Warning to the World (Brunner): *1959*
Glamour, The (Priest): 1984
Gland Stealers, The (Gayton): 1922
Gloriana (Dixie): 1890
Gloriana (Moorcock): 1978, 1979[W]
God's World (Watson): 1979
Gods of the Greataway (Coney): 1984
Gold-Finder, The (Griffith): 1898
Golden Barge, The (Moorcock): 1980
Golden Cat, The (Newton): 1930
Golden Star, The (Noel): 1935
Golden Witchbreed (Gentle): 1983

Gone to Ground (White): 1935
Gor Saga (Duffy): 1981
Gorgon, The (Lee): 1985
Gormenghast (peake): 1950
Goslings (Beresford): 1913
Governor Hardy (Blair): 1931
graffiti (Van Greenaway): 1983
Grain Kings, The (Roberts): 1976
Gráinne (Roberts): 1987, 1988[W]
Grand Canyon (Sackville-West): 1942
Grand Wheel, The (Bayley): 1977
Grasshoppers Come, The (Garnett): 1931
Gravitor (Darrington): 1971
Great Explosion, The (Russell): 1962
Great Fog, The (Heard): 1944
Great God Pan, The (Machen): 1894
Great Image, The (Beresford): 1921
Great Keinplatz Experiment, The (Doyle): 1894
Great Peril and How It Was Averted, The (Clowes): 1893
Great Pirate Syndicate, The (Griffith): 1899
Great Taboo, The (Allen): 1890
Great War in England in 1897, The (Le Queux): 1894
Great War of 189-, The (Colomb): 1893
Great Wash, The (Kersh): 1953
Great Weather Syndicate, The (Griffith): 1906
Great White Queen, The (Le Queux): 1898
Green Child, The (Read): 1935
Green Gene, The (Dickinson): 1973
Green Isle of the Great Deep, The (Gunn): 1944
Green Man of Graypec, The (Pragnell): *1936*
Green Man of Kilsona, The (Pragnell): 1936
Green Plantations, The (Marsh): 1955
Green Rain, The (Tabori): 1961
Green Rust, The (Wallace): 1919
Greencomber (Tate): 1979
Greybeard (Aldiss): 1964
Grimus (Rushdie): 1975
"Grisly Folk, The" (Wells): 1921
Ground Zero Man (Shaw): 1971
Groundstar Conspiracy, The (Davies): *1968*
Group Feast (Saxton): 1971
Guards! Guards! (Pratchett): 1989
Gulliver of Mars (Arnold): *1905*
Gulliver's Travels (Swift): 1726

H. G. Wells (Beresford): 1915[C]
Habitation One (Dunstan): 1983
"Hades Business, The" (Pratchett): 1963[FP]
Halcyon Drift, The (Stableford): 1972
Half a Glass of Moonshine (Martin): 1988
Half-Angels, The (Lovesay): 1975
Hampdenshire Wonder, The (Beresford): 1911
Harbottle (Hargrave): 1923

Hartmann the Anarchist (Fawcett): 1893
Haunted Woman, The (Lindsay): 1922
"Haunting, The" (Sellings): 1953[FP]
Hawksmoor (Ackroyd): 1985
He Owned the World (Maine): 1960
Heart Clock (Morland): 1973
Heart of the Moon (Grierson): 1928
Heart of the World (Haggard): 1895
Heavens for All (Spencer): 1955
Heels of Achilles, The (Groves): 1969
Helliconia Spring (Aldiss): 1982, 1983[W]
Helliconia Summer (Aldiss): 1983
Helliconia Winter (Aldiss): 1985, 1986[W]
Hello America (Ballard): 1981
Hello Summer, Goodbye (Coney): 1975
Hermes (ed. Russell): 1940[FAN]
Hermes Speaks (Jaeger): 1933
Hero of Downways, The (Coney): 1973
Hero's Walk (Crane): 1954
Heroes and Villains (Carter): 1969
Hesperides, The (Palmer): 1936
Heu-Heu (Haggard): 1924
Hidden Tribe, The (Wright): 1938
Hidden World, The (Gordon): 1988
Hieros Gamos of Sam and An Smith, The (Saxton): 1969
High Destiny, The (Morgan): 1973
High Spirits (Payn): 1879
High Vacuum (Maine): 1957
High-Rise (Ballard): 1975
Higher Things (Harrison): 1945
His Monkey-Wife (Collier): 1930
History of a Voyage to the Moon, A (Trueman): 1864
History of a World of Immortals (Barlow): 1891
History of the Science Fiction Magazine, The (ed. Ashley): 1974[C/A]
History of the World in 10 Chapters, A (Barnes): 1989
Hitch-Hiker's Guide to the Galaxy, The (Adams): 1979
Hitler Needs You (Story): 1971
Hobbit, The (Tolkien): 1937
"Holding Action" (Stephenson): 1971[FP]
Holding Your Eight Hands (ed. Lucie-Smith): 1969[A]
Hollow Lands, The (Moorcock): 1974
Holy Terror, The (Wells): 1939
Honeymoon in Space, A (Griffith): 1901
Hopkins Manuscript, The (Sherriff): 1939
Hospital Ship, The (Bax): 1976
Hospital Station (White): 1962
Hot Wireless Sets (Compton): *1970*
Hotel de Dream (Tennant): 1976
Hothouse (Aldiss): 1962, 1962[W]
Hour of the Thin Ox, The (Greenland): 1987
House of Sleep (Kavan): 1947
House on the Borderland, The (Hodgson): 1908
House Under the Sea, The (Pemberton): 1902
Hub, The (Beebee): 1987

Human Age, The (Lewis): 1955
"Human Seed, The" (Locke): 1957[FP]
Hundredth Millennium, The (Brunner): 1959
Hyphen: 1952[FAN]

I Am Lazarus (Kavan): 1945
I Speak for Earth (Brunner): 1961
I Warmed Both Hands (Dilnot): 1933
I'll Blackmail the World (Wood): 1935
Ice (Kavan): 1967
Ice Monkey, The (Harrison): 1983
Ice Schooner, The (Moorcock): 1969
Idler, The: 1892[PUB]
If (ed. Squire): 1931[A]
If It Had Happened Otherwise (ed. Squire): 1931[A]
"If Tomorrow Be Lost" (Ray): 1950[FP]
Illumination of Alice J. Cunningham, The (Webster): 1987
Imitation Man, The (Hargrave): 1931
Immortal Error, The (Trevor): 1946
Immortal Light, The (Mastin): 1907
Immortals' Great Quest, The (Barlow): *1891*
Imperial Earth (Clarke): 1975
Implosion (Jones): 1967
Impossible Man, The (Ballard): 1966
Impregnable City, The (Pemberton): 1895
Impregnable Women, The (Linklater): 1938
Impulse: 1966[PUB]
In Limbo (Evans): 1985
In Solitary (Kilworth): 1977
"In the Abyss" (Wells): 1896, 1926[FP]
"In the Avu Observatory" (Wells): 1894
In the Beginning (Douglas): 1927
In the Days of the Comet (Wells): 1906
In the Hollow of the Deep-Sea Wave (Kilworth): 1989
In the Kingdom of the Beasts (Stableford): 1971
In the Second Year (Jameson): 1936
In the Time of the Thetans (Johnson): 1961
In the Valley of the Statues (Holdstock): 1982
In the Wet (Shute): 1953
In the Wrong Paradise (Lang): 1886
In Viriconium (Harrison): 1982
Incandescent Ones, The (Hoyle & Hoyle): 1977
Incubated Girl, The (Jane): 1896
Indoctrinaire (Priest): 1970
Infernal Desire Machines of Dr Hoffmann, The (Carter): 1972
Inferno, The (Hoyle & Hoyle): 1973
Infinite Moment, The (Wyndham): 1961
Infinite Summer, An (Priest): 1979
Infinitive of Go, The (Brunner): 1980
Inheritors, The (Conrad & Hueffer): 1901
Inheritors, The (Golding): 1955
Inmost Light, The (Machen): 1894
Inner Circle (Peterkiewicz): 1966

Inner House, The (Besant): 1888
Inner Landscape, The (ed. *Moorcock*): 1969[A]
Inner Wheel, The (Roberts): 1970
Inside (Morgan): 1971
Inside Babel (Wilson): 1985
Insider, The (Evans): 1981
Intangibles, Inc. (Aldiss): 1969
"Intelligence Gigantic, The" (Fearn): 1933[FP]
"Intelligence on Mars" (Wells): 1896[E]
Interface (Adlard): 1971
Intermind (*Sellings*): 1967
Interpreter, The (Aldiss): *1960*
Interstellar Empire (Brunner): 1976
Interstellar Two-Five (Rankine): 1966
Interzone: 1982[PUB]
Interzone: The First Anthology (ed. Clute): 1985[A]
Interzone: The Fourth Anthology (ed. Clute): 1989[A]
Interzone: The Second Anthology (ed. Clute): 1988[A]
Interzone: The Third Anthology (ed. Clute): 1988[A]
Into Deepest Space (Hoyle & Hoyle): 1974
Into Other Worlds (Green): 1958[C]
Into the Slave Nebula (Brunner): *1960*
Into the Tenth Millennium (Capon): 1956
Introducing SF (ed. Aldiss): 1964[A]
Invader on My Back (High): 1968
Invaders, The (Tracy): 1901
Invasion from Space (MacKenzie): 1954
Invasion from the Air (McIlraith & Connolly): 1934
Invasion of 1910, The (Le Queux): 1906
Invasion of England, The (Bate): 1870
Inverted World (Priest): 1974, 1974[W]
Inverted World, The (Priest): 1974
Invisible Man, The (Wells): 1897, 1928[FP]
Invisible Voices, The (Shiel & Gawsworth): 1935
Ion War, The (Kapp): 1978
Iron Man, The (Hughes): 1968
Island (Huxley): 1962
Island Afloat, An (Stables): 1903
Island at the Top of the World, The (Cameron): 1961
Island Called Moreau, An (Aldiss): *1980*
Island of Captain Sparrow, The (Wright): 1928
Island of Doctor Moreau, The (Wells): 1896, 1926[FP]
Islands in the Sky (Clarke): 1952
Isle of Lies, The (Shiel): 1909
Isola (Dixie): 1903
Isotope Man, The (Maine): 1957
It's Bound to Happen (Low): 1950[E]
Iter Lunare (Russen): 1703
Ivan Greet's Masterpiece (Allen): 1893

Jade Man's Eyes, The (Moorcock): 1973
Jagged Orbit, The (Brunner): 1969, 1970[W]
Jane Saint and the Backlash (Saxton): 1989

Title Index

Jaws of Death, The (Allen): 1889
Jaws That Bite, The (Coney): 1975
Jazz and Jasper (Gerhardi): 1928
"Jeff Hawke": 1954[CX]
"Jimmy Goggles the God" (Wells): 1898
Jizzle (Wyndham): 1954
John Wyndham Omnibus, The (Wyndham): 1964
Jonah Kit, The (Watson): 1975, 1977[W]
Journal of the Plague Year, A (*Defoe*): 1722
Journey into Space (Chilton): 1954
Journey to the Center (Stableford): 1982
"Judge Dredd": 1983[CX]
Julia and the Bazooka (Kavan): 1970
Junk Day (Sellings): 1970
Jupiter Equilateral (Rackham): 1954
Jupiter in the Chair (Fraser): 1958
Justice of Revenge, The (Griffith): 1901
Justice, and the Rat (Wright): 1945

Kaeti and Company (Roberts): 1986
Kairos (Jones): 1988
Kalee's Shrine (Allen): 1886
Kark (Ryder): 1969
Karl Grier (Tracy): 1906
Kidnapped Into Space (Pearce): 1975
Kill the Dead (Lee): 1980
Killer Pine (Gutteridge): 1973
King and Joker (Dickinson): 1976
King of the Dead (Atkins): 1903
King Solomon's Mines (Haggard): 1885
King Who Was a King, The (Wells): 1929
King's Oak, The (Cromie): 1897
Kingdom of Content, The (*Beresford*): 1918
Kings of Infinite Space (Balchin): 1967
Kings of Space (Johns): 1954
Kiteworld (Roberts): 1985
Knights of the Limits, The (Bayley): 1978
Kontrol (Snell): 1928
Konyetz (Hussingtree): 1924
Koyama's Diamond (Berry): 1983
Kraken Wakes, The (Wyndham): 1953
Kronk (Cooper): *1970*
Krugg Syndrome, The (McAllister): 1988
Kuldesak (Cowper): 1972

Labyrinth of Lies (Berry): 1984
Labyrinth of Worlds (Cole): 1990
Ladder in the Sky (Brunner): 1962
Ladies from Hell (Roberts): 1979
Lake of Gold, The (Griffith): 1903
Lambda 1 (ed. Carnell): 1964[A]

Lampton Dreamers, The (Davies): 1966
Lanark (Gray): 1981
Land Beyond, The (Alderman): 1990
"Land Ironclads, The" (Wells): 1903
Land Leviathan, The (Moorcock): 1974
Land of Mist, The (Doyle): 1926
Land Under England (O'Neill): 1935
Landslide (Curtis): 1934
Last Adam, The (Duncan): 1952
Last and First Men (Stapledon): 1930
Last Continent, The (Cooper): 1969
Last Election, The (Davies): 1986
Last Galley, The (Doyle): 1911
Last Gasp, The (Hoyle): 1983
Last Generation, The (Flecker): 1908
"Last Generation, The" (Hill): 1964[FP]
Last Great Naval War, The (Seaforth): 1892
Last Man Alive, The (Neill): 1938
Last Man, The (Noyes): 1940
Last Man, The (Shelley): 1826
Last Men in London (Stapledon): 1932
Last Miracle, The (Shiel): 1906
Last of My Race, The (Tayler): 1924
Last of the Country House Murders, The (Tennant): 1974
Last Orders (Aldiss): 1977
Last Refuge, The (Petty): 1966
Last Revolution, The (Dunsany): 1951
Last Stand of the DNA Cowboys, The (Farren): 1989
Late Final (Gibbs): 1951
Laughter of Carthage, The (Moorcock): 1984
Lavondyss (Holdstock): 1988, 1989[W]
Leaky Establishment, The (Langford): 1984
Leftovers (Toynbee): 1966
Legends from the End of Time (Moorcock): 1976
Lemmus 1 (Savarin): 1972
Lepidus the Centurion (Arnold): 1901
Less Than Human (Platt): 1987
Lest Ye Die (Hamilton): *1922*
"Let's Go to Golgotha" (Kilworth): 1975[FP]
Lieut. Gullivar Jones (Arnold): 1905
Life and Adventures of Peter Wilkins, The (Paltock): 1751
Life Begins Tomorrow (Parkman): 1948
Life Comes to Seathorpe (Southwold): 1946
"Life Plan" (Kapp): 1958[FP]
Life, the Universe and Everything (Adams): 1982
Lifeboat (White): 1972
Light a Last Candle (King): 1969
Light Fantastic, The (Pratchett): 1986
"Light in the Sky, A" (Gordon): 1965[FP]
Like Nothing on Earth (Russell): 1975
Lilith (MacDonald): 1895
Lion of Comarre, The (Clarke): 1968
Lion, the Witch and the Wardrobe, The (Lewis): 1950
Listen! The Stars (Brunner): 1963
Literature and Science (Huxley): 1963[E]

Little Dog's Day (Story): 1971
Little Earnest Book, A (Wilson): 1851[C]
Little People, The (Christopher): 1967
Little Tours of Hell (Saxton): 1986
Lives and Times of Jerry Cornelius, The (Moorcock): 1976
"Living? Try Death!" (Bowen): 1957[FP]
London's Burning (Wootton): 1936
"Lone Voyager" (Malcolm): 1958[FP]
Long Afternoon of Earth, The (Aldiss): 1962
Long Dark Tea-Time of the Soul, The (Adams): 1988
Long Eureka, The (Sellings): 1968
Long Result, The (Brunner): 1965
Long Way Back, The (Bennett): 1954
Long Winter, The (Christopher): 1962
"Loophole" (Clarke): 1946[FP]
Lord Horror (Britton): 1989
Lord of Labour, The (Griffith): 1911
Lord of Life, The (Southwold): 1933
"Lord of the Dynamos, The" (Wells): 1894, 1929[FP]
Lord of the Flies (Golding): 1954
Lord of the Rings (Tolkien): 1957[W]
Lord of the Sea, The (Shiel): 1901
Lord of the Spiders (Moorcock): *1965*
Lord of the World (Benson): 1907
Lordly Ones, The (Roberts): 1986
Lost Cavern, The (Heard): 1948
Lost Continent, The (Hyne): 1900
Lost Horizon (Hilton): 1933
Lost Men in the Grass (Griff): 1940
Lost Ones, The (Cameron): 1961
Lost Provinces, The (Tracy): 1898
Lost Traveller, The (Todd): 1943
Lost Traveller, The (Wilson): 1976
Lost World of Cronus, The (Kapp): 1982
Lost World, The (Doyle): 1912
Lost Worlds of 2001, The (Clarke): 1972[E]
Love Among the Ruins (Waugh): 1953
Love and Napalm: Export USA (Ballard): *1970*
Love Eternal (Haggard): 1918
Low Notes on a High Level (Priestley): 1954
Low-Flying Aircraft (Ballard): 1976
Lucifer Experiment, The (Cole): 1981
Lud-in-the-Mist (Mirrlees): 1926
"Lunar Lilliput" (Temple): 1938[FP]
Lunatic Republic, The (Mackenzie): 1959

Machine in Shaft Ten, The (Harrison): 1975
Machine Stops, The (Smith): 1936
"Machine Stops, The" (Forster): 1909
Machines and Men (Roberts): 1973
Mad Metropolis, The (High): 1966
Made in His Image (Thorne): 1906
Madonna of the Music Halls, A (Le Queux): 1897

Magellan (Anderson): 1970
Maggot, A (Fowles): 1985
Magic of the Past, The (Aldiss): 1987
"Magic Shop, The" (Wells): 1903
Magic Toyshop, The (Carter): 1967
Magicians, The (Priestley): 1954
Mahatma and the Hare, The (Haggard): 1911
Main Event, The (Beebee): 1989
Main Experiment, The (Hodder-Williams): 1964
Major Operation (White): 1971
Making of the Representative, The (Lessing): 1982
Malacia Tapestry, The (Aldiss): 1976
Male Response, The (Aldiss): 1961
Man Alone (Horsnell): 1940
Man Divided, A (Stapledon): 1950
Man from Beyond, The (Wyndham): *1973*
Man in a Cage (Stableford): 1975
Man in His Time (Aldiss): *1988*
Man in Steel, The (Clouston): 1939
Man in the Moone, The (Godwin): 1638
"Man Must Die, A" (Clute): 1966[FP]
Man of Double Deed, A (Daventry): 1965
"Man of the Year Million, The" (Wells): 1893[E]
Man out of Nowhere (Davies): 1965
Man Who Could Work Miracles, The (Wells): 1936
"Man Who Could Work Miracles, The" (Wells): 1898, 1926[FP]
Man Who Couldn't Sleep, The (Maine): 1956
Man Who Held the Queen to Ransom, The (Van Greenaway): 1968
Man Who Mastered Time, The (Butler): 1986
Man Who Missed the War, The (Wheatley): 1945
Man Who Owned the World, The (Maine): *1960*
Man Who Stole the Earth, The (Holt-White): 1909
"Man Who Went Back, The" (Clark): 1949[FP]
Man with a Nose, The (Wells): 1984
Man with Only One Head, the (Barr): 1955
Man with Six Senses, The (Jaeger): 1927
Man with Two Memories, The (Haldane): 1976
Man's Mortality (Arlen): 1933
Man's Understanding (Hyne): 1933
Manalone (Kapp): 1977
Mandrake (Cooper): 1964
Manna (Gloag): 1940
Manrissa Man (Van Greenaway): 1982
Many Dimensions (Williams): 1931
Maracot Deep, The (Doyle): 1929
Marahuna (Watson): 1888
Mariners of Space (Collins): 1944
Marriages Between Zones, The (Lessing): 1980
Mars Breaks Through (Low): 1937
Martian Inca, The (Watson): 1977
Martian Sphinx, The (Brunner): 1965
Martian, The (Du Maurier): 1898
Mary's Country (Mead): 1957
Masks (Fleming): 1913
Masque of a Savage Mandarin (Robinson): 1969

Master of His Fate (Cobban): 1890
Master of Paxwax (Mann): 1986
Master of Space (Clarke): *1951*
Master of the Moon (Moore): 1952
Master Weed, The (Rackham): 1954
Masters of the Pit, The (Moorcock): *1965*
Mathematicall Magick (Wilkins): 1648[E]
Matter of Oaths, A (Wright): 1988
Maxwell's Demon (Sherwood): 1976
Maya: 1970[FAN]
Mayfair Magician, A (Griffith): 1905
Meat (Watson): 1988
Meccania (Gregory): 1918
Meda (Folingsby): 1891
Medusa (Visiak): 1929
Medusa Touch, The (Van Greenaway): 1973
Medusa's Children (Shaw): 1977
Meeting at Infinity (Brunner): 1961
Meeting Place, The (Beresford): 1929
"Meeting with Medusa, A" (Clarke): 1973[W]
Megiddo's Ridge (Wright): 1937
Meleager (Vaughan): 1916
Melmoth, the Wanderer (Maturin): 1820
Memoirs of a Spacewoman (Mitchison): 1962
Memoirs of a Survivor, The (Lessing): 1974
Memories of the Future (Knox): 1923
Memories of the Space Age (Ballard): 1988
Men Like Gods (Wells): 1923
Men, Martians and Machines (Russell): 1956
Menace from Mercury (Fanthorpe): 1954
Menace from the Moon (Lynch): 1925
Mercia, the Astronomer Royal (Mears): 1895
Merry Christmas, Ms Minerva (Cooper): 1978
Message Ends (Craig): 1969
Message from Mars, A (Lurgan): 1912
Messiah at the End of Time, A (Moorcock): *1977*
Meteor Flag of England, The (Stables): 1906
Midge (MacTyre): 1962
"Midget from Mars, A" (*Gillings*): 1938[FP]
Midwich Cuckoos, The (Wyndham): 1957
Million Cities, The (McIntosh): 1963
Mind at the End of Its Tether (Wells): 1945[E]
Mind of Max Divine, The (Trevor): 1960
Mind of Mr. Soames, The (Maine): 1961
Mind out of Time (Tonks): 1958
Mind Parasites, The (Wilson): 1967
Mind Readers, The (Allingham): 1965
Mind Riders, The (Stableford): 1976
Mind Warpers, The (Russell): *1964*
Miniature, The (Phillpotts): 1926
Minimum Man (Marvell): 1938
"Ministering Angels" (Lewis): 1958
Miracle Visitors (Watson): 1978
Mirror Image (Coney): 1972
Mirror in the Sky (Garnett): 1969

Missionaries, The (Compton): 1972
Mixed Pickles (Southwold): 1935
Modern Daedalus, A (Greer): 1885
Modern Utopia, A (Wells): 1905
Molecule Men, The (Hoyle & Hoyle): 1971
Molly Zero (Roberts): 1980
Moment of Eclipse, The (Aldiss): 1970, 1971[W]
Moment of Truth, The (Jameson): 1949
Monitor Found in Orbit (Coney): 1974
Monk, The (Lewis): 1795
Monkman Comes Down (Williams): 1969
Monster of Loch Ness, The (Hoyle & Hoyle): 1971
Monsters and Medics (White): 1977
Monstrous Regiment, The (Constantine): 1990
Moon of Gomrath, The (Garner): 1963
Moon on an Iron Meadow (Tate): 1974
Moon Raiders, The (Bounds): 1955
Moonlight Red (Morel): 1960
Moorcock's Book of Martyrs (Moorcock): 1976
Morag's Flying Fortress (Story): 1976
More Tales from the Forbidden Planet (ed. Kaveney): 1990[A]
More Things in Heaven (Brunner): *1963*
Moreau's Other Island (Aldiss): 1980
Morrow's Ants (Hyams): 1975
Mort (Pratchett): 1987
Morwyn (Powys): 1937
"Moth--Genus Novo, A" (Wells): 1895, 1928[FP]
Mother London (Moorcock): 1988
Mother of Storms (Cole): 1989
Moving Moosevan (Palmer): 1990
Moving Pictures (Pratchett): 1990
Mr. Blettsworthy on Rampole Island (Wells): 1928
Mr. Fortescue (Westall): 1888
Mr. J. Jay (Aldworth): 1933
"Mr. Skelmersdale in Fairyland" (Wells): 1901
Mr. Stranger's Sealed Packet (MacColl): 1889
Multiface (Adlard): 1975
Mummy and Miss Nitocris, The (Griffith): 1906
Mummy!, The (Loudon): 1827
"Muse, The" (Burgess): 1968
Mutant 59 (Pedler & Davis): 1971
My Experiences in the Third World War (Moorcock): 1980
My Friend the Murderer (Doyle): 1893
My Madness (Kavan): 1990
Mysteries and Adventures (Doyle): 1889
Mystery of Dr Fu-Manchu, The (Rohmer): 1913
Mystery of the Green Ray, The (Le Queux): 1915
Mythago Wood (Holdstock): 1984, 1985[W]
Myths of the Near Future (Ballard): 1982

Napoleon of Notting Hill, The (Chesterton): 1904
Narrative of the Life of...John Daniels, A (Morris): 1751
Natural History of the P. H., The (Roberts): 1989[E]

Title Index 215

Nature of the Catastrophe, The (eds. Moorcock & Jones): 1971[A]
Nature of the Universe, The (Hoyle): 1950[E]
Naviators, The (Spanner): 1926
Neanderthal Planet (Aldiss): 1969
Nebula Maker (Stapledon): 1976
Nebula Science Fiction: 1952[PUB]
Needle on Full, The (Forbes): 1985
Neptune's Cauldron (Coney): 1981
Neural Atrocity, The (Farren): 1977
Never Let Up (Maine): 1964
"New Accelerator, The" (Wells): 1901, 1926[FP]
New Arrivals, Old Encounters (Aldiss): 1979
New Atlantis (Bacon): 1627
New Eden, The (Hyne): 1892
New Futurian: *1938*[FAN]
New Gods Lead, The (Wright): 1932
New King, The (Shiel): 1980
New Maps of Hell (Amis): 1960[C]
New Messiah, A (Cromie): 1902
New Minds, The (Morgan): 1967
New Moon, The (Onions): 1918
New Ordeal, The (Chesney): 1879
New Pleasure, The (Gloag): 1933
New SF, The (ed. Jones): 1969[A]
"New Utopia, The" (Jerome): 1891
New Worlds: 1939[PUB], 1962[PUB], 1964[PUB], 1970[PUB], 1971[A], 1975[A], 1976[A], 1979[PUB]
New Worlds: An Anthology (ed. Moorcock): 1983[A]
New Writings in SF (ed. Bulmer): 1972[A]
New Writings in SF (ed. Carnell): 1964[A]
News from Elsewhere (Cooper): 1968
News from Nowhere (Morris): 1890
News from the Sun (Ballard): 1982
Next Crusade, The (Cromie): 1896
Next of Kin (Russell): *1958*
Nigel Fortescue (Westall): 1888
Night Callers, The (Crisp): 1960
Night Land, The (Hodgson): 1912
Night Mayor, The (Newman): 1989
Night of Kadar, The (Kilworth): 1978
Night of the Big Heat, The (Lymington): 1959
Night of the Trilobites (Leslie): 1968
Night's Master (Lee): 1978
Nightmares of Eminent Persons (Russell): 1954
Nights at the Circus (Carter): 1984
Nightshade and Damnation (Kersh): 1968
Nightwalk (Shaw): 1967
Nightwatch (Stephenson): 1977
Nine Billion Names of God, The (Clarke): 1967
Nineteen Eighty-Four (Orwell): 1949
Nineteen Impressions (Beresford): 1918
No Blade of Grass (Christopher): *1956*, 1957[PUB]
No Future in It (Brunner): 1962
No Highway (Shute): 1948

No Lack of Space (Martin): 1967
No Man Friday (Gordon): 1956
No Other Gods But Me (Brunner): 1966
No Other Man (Noyes): 1940
No Place Like Earth (ed. Carnell): 1952[A]
No Rates and Taxes (Pinkerton): 1902
No Refuge (Boland): 1956
"No Short Cuts" (Tubb): 1951[FP]
No Time Like Tomorrow (Aldiss): *1957*
No Traveller Returns (Collier): 1931
No Truce with Terra (High): 1964
Nomad of Time, The (Moorcock): 1984
Noman Way, The (McIntosh): 1964
Non-Stop (Aldiss): 1958
Nordenholt's Million (Connington): 1923
Norman Conquest 2066 (McIntosh): 1977
North Afire, The (Newton): 1914
Not Before Time (Brunner): 1968
Not by Bread Alone (Mitchison): 1983
Not in Our Stars (Hyams): 1949
Not in Our Stars (Maurice): 1923
Not Since Genesis (Clouston): 1938
Not with a Bang (Pincher): 1965
Novacon: 1971[FAN]
Novae Terrae: 1936[FAN], 1937[FAN]
"Novel Notes" (Jerome): 1893
Now Then! (Brunner): 1965
Nunquam (Durrell): 1970

October the First Is Too Late (Hoyle): 1966
Odd John (Stapledon): 1935
Of Demons and Darkness (Collier): *1951*
Of Earth and Fire (Barclay): 1974
Of Other Worlds (Lewis): 1966[E]
Of the Fall (McAuley): 1989
Of Time and Stars (Clarke): 1972
Offshore Island, The (Laski): 1955
Offtrail Magazine Publishers' Association: 1954[FAN]
Old Captivity, An (Shute): 1940
Old Man in New World (Stapledon): 1944
Old Men at the Zoo, The (Wilson): 1961
Olga Romanoff (Griffith): 1894
OMPA, see Offtrail Magazine Publishers' Association
On a Dark Night (West): 1949
On an Odd Note (Kersh): 1958
On the Beach (Shute): 1957
On the Last Day (Jones): 1958
Once and Future King, The (White): 1958
One by One (Gilliatt): 1965
One Came Back (*Southwold*): 1938
One Half of the World (Barlow): 1957
One in Three Hundred (McIntosh): 1954
One Last Mad Embrace (Story): 1970

One Million Tomorrows (Shaw): 1970
"One of Those Days" (Platt): 1964[FP]
One Sane Man, The (*Palmer & Saunders*): 1934
One-Eye (Gordon): 1973
Open Prison (White): 1965
Opening of the Eyes, The (Stapledon): 1954[E]
"Operation Exodus" (Wright): 1952[FP]
Operation Superman (Hawton): 1951
Opium General, The (Moorcock): 1984
Optiman (Stableford): 1980
Orbit Science Fiction Yearbook 1 (ed. Garnett): 1988[A]
Orbit Science Fiction Yearbook 2 (ed. Garnett): 1989[A]
Orbitsville (Shaw): 1975, 1975[W]
Orbitsville Departure (Shaw): 1983
Orbitsville Judgement (Shaw): 1990
Ordeal, The (Shute): 1939
Orgasmachine (Watson): 1976
Origin of Species, On the (Darwin): 1859[E]
Orlando (Woolf): 1928
Ossian's Ride (Hoyle): 1959
Other Days, Other Eyes (Shaw): 1972
Other Edens (eds. Evans & Holdstock): 1987[A]
Other Edens II (eds. Evans & Holdstock): 1988[A]
Other Edens III (eds. Evans & Holdstock): 1989[A]
Other Half of the Planet, The (Capon): 1952
Other Place, The (Priestley): 1953
Other Side of the Sky, The (Clarke): 1958
Other Side of the Sun, The (Capon): 1950
Other Times: 1975[PUB]
Other Voices (Greenland): 1988
Otranto: A Story, see *Castle of Otranto, The*
Our Man for Ganymede (Lauder): 1969
Our Stranger (Meredith): 1936
Out (Brooke-Rose): 1964
Out of Chaos (McIntosh): 1965
Out of My Mind (Brunner): 1967
Out of the Deeps (Wyndham): 1953
Out of the Silent Planet (Lewis): 1938
Out on Blue Six (McDonald): 1989
Out There Where the Big Ships Go (Cowper): 1980
Outcrop (Cooper): 1970
Outer Reaches, The (Vyse): 1980
Outlands: 1946[PUB]
Outlaw's Own: 1949[FAN]
Outlaws of the Air, The (Griffith): 1895
Outline of History, The (Wells): 1920[E]
Outward Urge, The (Wyndham): 1959
Over the Mountain (Todd): 1939
Overloaded Man, The (Ballard): 1967
Overman Culture, The (Cooper): 1971
Overmind (Wadsworth): 1967
Overworld (Vyse): 1980
Owl of Athene, The (Phillpotts): 1936
Oxford Mail: 1957[PUB]

Palace of Eternity, The (Shaw): 1969
Pale Ape, The (Shiel): 1911
Pale Shadow of Science, The (Aldiss): 1985[E]
Pall Mall Budget: 1868[PUB]
Pall Mall Magazine: 1893[PUB]
Panic O'Clock (Hodder-Williams): 1973
Paper Dolls, The (Davies): 1964
Papers of Andrew Melmoth, The (Davies): 1960
Paradise Game, The (Stableford): 1974
Paradise Is Not Enough (Elder): 1970
Paradise Lost (Milton): 1667
Paradox of Sets, The (Stableford): 1979
Parasaurians, The (Wells): 1969
Parasite, The (Doyle): 1894
Passing of the Dragons, The (Roberts): 1977
Passing Show, The: 1932[PUB]
Passion of New Eve, The (Carter): 1977
Passport to Eternity (Ballard): 1963
Pastel City, The (Harrison): 1971
Patterns of Chaos, The (Kapp): 1972
"Pauper's Plot" (Holdstock): 1968[FP]
Pavane (Roberts): 1968
Paw of God, The (Gordon): *1966*
Pawns in Ice (Gibbs): 1948
Peace Machine, The (Shaw): *1971*
Peacemaker, The (Forester): 1934
Pearson's Magazine: 1896[PUB]
Pearson's Weekly: 1890[PUB]
Pendulum (Christopher): 1968
Penguin Modern Poets (Thomas): 1968
Penguin Science Fiction (ed. Aldiss): 1961[A]
People of the Mist, The (Haggard): 1894
People of the Ruins, The (Shanks): 1920
Perelandra (Lewis): 1943
Perfect Lover, The (Priest): 1977
Perfect World, The (Scrymsour): 1922
Petron (Davies): 1935
Phantastes (MacDonald): 1858
Phantom City, The (Westall): 1886
Philosopher's Stone, The (Wilson): 1969
Phoenix (Cowper): 1968
Pictures at an Exhibition (ed. Watson): 1981[A]
Piece of Resistance, A (Egleton): 1970
Pig on a Lead (Ingrey): 1963
Pile (Aldiss): 1979
Pilgrimage of Strongsoul, The (Davidson): 1896
Pillars of Eternity (Bayley): 1982
Pillars of Midnight, The (Trevor): 1957
"Pioneer, The" (Ball): 1962[FP]
Pioneers (Mann): 1988
Pity About Earth (Hill): 1968
Plague 99 (Ure): 1989
Plague Over London (Craig): 1939
Plague Panic (Hedges): 1934
Planet Called Utopia, A (McIntosh): 1979

Planet Dweller, The (Palmer): 1985
Planet in Peril (Christopher): *1955*
Planet in the Eye of Time (Earnshaw): 1968
Planet of the Voles (Platt): 1971
Planet of Your Own, A (Brunner): 1966
Planet Plane (Wyndham): 1936
Planetfall (Tubb): 1951
Planetoid 127 (Wallace): 1929
Plasm (Platt): 1988
Plastic Magicians, The (Leslie): 1969
Plattner Story, The (Wells): 1897
"Plattner Story, The" (Wells): 1896, 1927[FP]
Player of Games, The (Banks): 1988
Players at the Game of People (Brunner): 1980
Plunge into Space, A (Cromie): 1890
Poison Belt, The (Doyle): 1913
Poison Oracle, The (Dickinson): 1974
Poison War, The (Black): 1933
"Pollock and the Porroh Man" (Wells): 1895, 1928[FP]
Polymath (Brunner): *1963*
Polyphemes, The (Hernaman-Johnson): 1906
Poor Artist, The (Horne): 1849
Possessors, The (Christopher): 1965
Possible Worlds (Haldane): 1927[E]
"Post-Mortem People, The" (Tate): 1966[FP]
Power (Wright): 1933
Power of Time, The (Saxton): 1985
Power of X, The (Sellings): 1968
Power, The (Watson): 1987
Prayer Machine, The (Hodder-Williams): 1976
Precious Porcelain (Southwold): 1931
Prelude in Prague (Wright): 1935
Prelude to Mars (Clarke): 1965
Prelude to Space (Clarke): 1951
"Prima Belladonna" (Ballard): 1956[FP]
Primal Urge, The (Aldiss): 1961
Prince of Abissinia, The, see *Rasselas*
Printer's Devil (Moorcock): 1966
Prisoner of Fire (Cooper): 1974
Private Selby (Wallace): 1912
Private Volcano, A (Sieveking): 1955
Prodigal Sun, The (High): 1964
Productions of Time, The (Brunner): 1967
Professor's Last Experiment, The (Edmonds): 1935
Profiles of the Future (Clarke): 1962[E]
Profundis (Cowper): 1979
Project Renaissance (Williams): 1973
Promise of Space, The (Clarke): 1968[E]
Promised Land (Stableford): 1974
Protectorate (Farren): 1984
Proud Man (Burdekin): 1934[E]
Providence Island (Hawkes): 1959
Psionic Menace, The (Brunner): 1963
Psychogeist (Davies): 1966
Public Faces (Nicolson): 1932

Pulsar 1 (ed. Hay): 1978[A]
Pulsar 2 (ed. Hay): 1979[A]
Purple Armchair, The (Hesky): 1961
Purple Cloud, The (Shiel): 1901
"Purple Pileus, The" (Wells): 1896
Purple Plague, The (Brockway): 1935
Purple Sapphire, The (Blayre): 1921
Purple Twilight, The (Groom): 1948
Purple-6 (Brinton): 1962
Putting Out (Ferguson): 1988
Pyramids (Pratchett): 1989, 1990[W]
Pzyche (Hemingway): 1982

Q: Seeking the Mythical Future (Hoyle): 1977
Q: The Gods Look Down (Hoyle): 1978
Q: Through the Eye of Time (Hoyle): 1977
Quality of Mercy, The (Compton): 1965
Quatermass (Kneale): 1979
Quatermass and the Pit (Kneale): 1960
Quatermass Experiment, The (Kneale): 1959
Quatermass II (Kneale): 1960
Queen of Atlantis, A (Atkins): 1899
Queen of Stones (Tennant): 1982
Queen of the States (Saxton): 1986
Queen of the World (Netterville): 1900
Queen Sheba's Ring (Haggard): 1910
Queen Victoria's Bomb (Clark): 1967
Queenmagic, Kingmagic (Watson): 1986
Queens of Deliria (Butterworth & Moorcock): 1977
Queer Race, A (Westall): 1887
Quest for the White Witch (Lee): 1978
Quest of the DNA Cowboys, The (Farren): 1976
Question Mark, The (Jaeger): 1926
Quicksand (Brunner): 1967
Quiet Woman, The (Priest): 1990
Quy Effect, The (Sellings): 1966

Radium Seekers, The (Atkins): 1905
Ragged Astronauts, The (Shaw): 1986, 1987[W]
Ragged Edge, The (Christopher): *1965*
Ragnarok (Desmond): 1926
Raid of 'Le Vengeur', The (Griffith): 1974
Raid of Dover, The (Ford): 1910
Rainbow and the Rose, The (Shute): 1958
Rama II (Clarke & Lee): 1989
Random Factor, The (Maine): 1971
Rasselas (Johnson): 1759
Rats and Gargoyles (Gentle): 1990
Rats, The (Herbert): 1974
Rax (Coney): 1975
Re-Birth (Wyndham): 1955

Reach for Tomorrow (Clarke): 1956
Real People (Beresford): 1929
Real-Time World (Priest): 1974
Reality Forbidden (High): 1967
Realms of Tartarus, The (Stableford): 1977
Rebel Passion, The (Burdekin): 1929
Recipe for Diamonds, The (Hyne): 1893
Red Alert (George): *1958*
Red as Blood (Lee): 1983
Red Dwarf (Naylor): 1989
Red Radio (Hadfield & Farncombe): 1927
"Red Room, The" (Wells): 1896
Red Shift (Garner): 1973
"Rediscovery of the Unique, The" (Wells): 1891[E]
Reflections in a Mirage (Daventry): 1969
Regenesis (Fullerton): 1983
Reign of George VI, The (Anon): 1763
Reign of the Saints, The (Trevena): 1911
"Remarkable Case of Davidson's Eyes, The" (Wells): 1895, 1927[FP]
Rendezvous with Rama (Clarke): 1973, 1974[W]
Repairmen of Cyclops, The (Brunner): 1965
Report on Planet Three (Clarke): 1972[E]
Report on Probability A (Aldiss): 1968
Restaurant at the End of the Universe, The (Adams): 1980
Retreat from Armageddon (Jaeger): 1936
Return of the King, The (Tolkien): 1955
Return of William Shakespeare, The (Kingsmill): 1929
Rev. Annabel Lee, The (Buchanan): 1898
Revolt of Aphrodite, The (Durrell): 1974
Revolt of Man, The (Besant): 1882
Revolution (Beresford): 1921
Rhapsody in Black (Stableford): 1973
Richest Corpse in Show Business, The (Morgan): 1966
Riddle of the Sands, The (Childers): 1903
Riddle of the Straits, The (Edmonds): 1931
Riddle of the Tower, The (Beresford & Wynne-Tyson): 1944
Riddley Walker (Hoban): 1980, 1982[W]
Ringstones (Sarban): 1951
Riot '71 (Peters): 1967
Rise of the Meritocracy, The (Young): 1958[E]
Rites of Ohe, The (Brunner): 1963
Rituals of Infinity, The (Moorcock): *1967*
Road to Corlay, The (Cowper): 1978
Robinson Crusoe (Defoe): 1719
Rockets in Ursa Major (Hoyle & Hoyle): 1969
Rod of Light, The (Bayley): 1985
Romance in Radium, A (Harris): 1906
Romance of Golden Star, The (Griffith): 1897
Romance of the Equator, A (Aldiss): 1989
Romance of Two Worlds, A (Corelli): 1886
"Roof Garden Under Saturn" (Watson): 1969[FP]
Roofworld (Fowler): 1988
Round the Fire Stories (Doyle): 1908
Ruins (Aldiss): 1987

Rule Britannia (Du Maurier): 1972
Rule of the Beasts, The (Murray): 1925
Rule of the Pagbeasts, The (McIntosh): *1955*
Ruled by Radio (Hadfield & Farncombe): 1925
Ruler of the World (McIntosh): 1976
Run to the Stars (Rohan): 1982
"Run, The" (Priest): 1966[FP]
Rune (Fowler): 1990
Running Wild (Ballard): 1988
Russian Hide-and-Seek (Amis): 1980
Russian Intelligence, The (Moorcock): *1966*

Sabella (Lee): 1980
Sacred Edifice (Gloag): 1937
Sacred Skull, The (Griffith): 1908
"Saga of Pelican West, The" (Russell): 1937[FP]
Salamander War (Carr): 1955
Salathiel (Croly): 1828
Saliva Tree, The (Aldiss): 1966
"Saliva Tree, The" (Aldiss): 1966[W]
Salvage Rites (Watson): 1989
Sanctuary in the Sky (Brunner): 1960
Sands of Mars, The (Clarke): 1951
Satan in the Suburbs (Russell): 1953
Satellite E One (Castle): 1954
Satellite in Space (Low): 1956
Saturday Evening Post: 1957[PUB]
Saturn Patrol (Tubb): 1951
Saurus (Phillpotts): 1938
Savoy Book, The (eds. Britton & Butterworth): 1978[A]
Savoy Dreams (eds. Britton & Butterworth): 1984[A]
Scent of New-Mown Hay, A (Blackburn): 1958
Scholars and Soldiers (Gentle): 1989
Science and Fiction (Moore): 1957[E]
Science Fantasy Society: 1948[FAN]
Science Fantasy: 1950[PUB], 1951[PUB]
Science Fiction Adventures: 1958[FAN]
Science Fiction Art (Aldiss): 1975[E]
Science Fiction as Science Fiction (Aldiss): 1978[C]
Science Fiction Association: 1937[FAN]
Science Fiction at Large (Nicholls): 1976[C]
Science Fiction Blues (Aldiss): 1988
Science Fiction Foundation: 1971[C]
Science Fiction Monthly: 1974[PUB]
Science Fiction Through the Ages (ed. Evans): 1966[A]
Scientific Romance in Britain (Stableford): 1985[C]
Scientific Romances (Hinton): 1886
Scientific Romances of H. G. Wells, The (Wells): 1933
Scientific Romances: Second Series (Hinton): 1896
Scientifiction: 1937[FAN]
Scoops: 1934[PUB]
Scorpion God, The (Golding): 1971
Scream from Outer Space (Wilding): 1955

Screaming Lake, The (Wright): 1939
Scudder's Game (Compton): 1985
Sea Lady, The (Wells): 1902
"Sea Raiders, The" (Wells): 1896
Seagulls Under Glass (Tate): 1975
Seahorse in the Sky (Cooper): 1969
Search for the Sun (Kapp): 1981
Seasons in Flight (Aldiss): 1984
Second Ending (White): 1962
Second Rising, The (Beresford): 1910
Secret Agent of Terra (Brunner): 1962
Secret Harmonies (McAuley): 1989
Secret of the Desert, The (Turner): 1923
Secret People, The (Wyndham): 1935
Secret Property, A (Noyes): 1985
Secret Sea-Plane, The (Thorne): 1915
Secret Visitors, The (White): 1957
Secret Voyage, The (Edmonds): *1935*
Secret War, The (Wheatley): 1937
Secret Weapon (Newman): 1942
Sector General (White): 1983
Seed of Evil, The (Bayley): *1972*
Seed of Light (Cooper): 1959
Seedbearers, The (Timlett): 1974
Seeds of Time, The (Wyndham): 1956
Sell England? (Balsdon): 1936
Send Him Victorious (Hurd & Osmond): 1968
Sentient Earth, The (Hoyle): 1979
Sentimental Agents, The (Lessing): 1983
Sentinels from Space (Russell): 1953
Serpent, The (Gaskell): 1963
Seven Days in New Crete (Graves): 1949
Seven Steps to the Sun (Hoyle & Hoyle): 1970
Seventh Bowl, The (Southwold): 1930
Sexmax (Cooper): 1970
SFA, see Science Fiction Association
SF Digest: 1976[PUB]
SF Horizons (eds. Aldiss & Harrison): 1964[C]
SF Impulse, see *Impulse*
SF Reprise (ed. Moorcock): 1966[A]
Shades of Darkness (Cowper): 1986
Shadow of Authority (Waller): 1956
Shadow of Heaven (Shaw): 1969
Shadow Over the Earth (Wilding): 1956
Shadowfire (Lee): *1978*
Shakehole (Mackelworth): 1981
Shape of Further Things, The (Aldiss): 1970[E]
Shape of Things to Come, The (Wells): 1933
Shapes in the Fire (Shiel): 1896
She (Haggard): 1886
She and Allan (Haggard): 1921
Sheep Look Up, The (Brunner): 1972
Shellbreak (Groves): 1968
Shift Key, The (Brunner): 1987
Shikasta (Lessing): 1979

Ship of Destiny (Slater): 1951
Ship of Strangers (Shaw): 1978
Shipwreck (Logan): 1975
Shockwave Rider, The (Brunner): 1975
"Shoddy Lands, The" (Lewis): 1956
Shoot at the Moon (Temple): 1966
Shoot, The (Trevor): 1966
Shores of Death, The (Moorcock): *1966*
Short History of the Future, A (Churchill): 1955
Short Stories of H. G. Wells, The (Wells): 1927
Sign of the Times, A (Kee): 1955
Signs and Wonders (Beresford): 1921
Silent Multitude, The (Compton): 1966
Silent Speakers, The (Sellings): *1962*
Silent Voice, The (Hodder-Williams): 1977
Silmarillion, The (Tolkien): 1977, 1978[W]
Silver Metal Lover, The (Lee): 1981
Simon Rack (James): 1974
Singing Citadel, The (Moorcock): 1970
Sinister Barrier (Russell): 1943
Sirian Experiments, The ((Lessing): 1981
Sirius (Stapledon): 1944
Six Gates from Limbo (McIntosh): 1968
Six Worlds Yonder (Russell): 1958
Sixth Day, The (Burley): 1978
Sixth Winter, The (Orgill & Gribbin): 1979
Sixty Days to Live (Wheatley): 1939
Sketches of the Future (Gorst): 1898
Skrine (Sully): 1960
Sky Lords, The (Brosnan): 1988
Sky-Raft (Clark): 1937
Skynappers, The (Brunner): 1960
Slant: 1948[FAN]
Slavers of Space (Brunner): 1960
Slaves of Heaven, The (Cooper): 1974
Sleep Has His House (Kavan): *1947*
Sleeper Awakes, The (Wells): *1899*
Sleepers of Mars (Wyndham): 1973
Slow Birds (Watson): 1985
Smallcreep's Day (Brown): 1965
Smashed World, The (Slater): 1952
Smile on the Void (Gordon): 1981
Snow White and the Giants (McIntosh): *1967*
Snow-White Soliloquies, The (MacLeod): 1970
So Long, and Thanks for All the Fish (Adams): 1984
"Sojan the Swordsman" (Moorcock): 1957[FP]
Sold for a Spaceship (High): 1973
Solution Three (Mitchison): 1975
Soma (Platt): 1990
Something Else: 1980[PUB]
"Something Strange" (Amis): 1960
Sometime, Never (ed. Anon): 1956[A]
Sometime-Never (Dahl): 1949
Somewhere a Voice (Russell): 1965
Somewhere in the Night (*Moorcock*): 1966

Son of Kronk (Cooper): 1970
Song of Phaid the Gambler, The (Farren): 1981
"Song of the Syren" (Wells): 1965[FP]
Songbirds of Pain, The (Kilworth): 1984
Songs of Distant Earth, The (Clarke): 1986
Soul of the Robot, The (Bayley): 1974
Soul-Stealer, The (Thorne): 1906
Sound Machine, The (Snell): 1932
Sound of His Horn, The (Sarban): 1952
Sourcery (Pratchett): 1988
Space Dreamers, The (Clarke): *1951*
Space Eater, The (Langford): 1982
Space Fact and Fiction: 1954[PUB]
Space Machine, The (Priest): 1976
Space Puppet (Rackham): 1954
Space Raiders, The (Beverley): 1936
Space Sorcerers, The (McIntosh): 1972
Space Time Juggler, The (Brunner): 1963
Space Treason (Bulmer & Clarke): 1952
Space Vampires, The (Wilson): 1976
Space Willies, The (Russell): 1958
Space, Time and Nathaniel (Aldiss): 1957
Space-Time Journal, The (ed. Merril): *1968*[A]
Spaceache (Wilson): 1984
Spaceflight--Venus (Wilding): 1954
Spaceways (Maine): 1953
Spaceways Satellite (Maine): *1953*
"Spaceways" (Maine): 1952[FP]
Speaking of Dinosaurs (High): 1974
Spectrum (eds. Amis & Conquest): 1961[A]
Speculation, see *Zenith Science Fiction*
"Sphere of Death, The" (Groves): 1931[FP]
Sphinx (Lindsay): 1923
Spider World: The Delta (Wilson): 1987
Spider World: The Tower (Wilson): 1987
Spider's War (Wright): 1954
Spiral Winds (Kilworth): 1987
Spirit of Bambatse, The (Haggard): 1906
Split Second (Kilworth): 1979
Split Worlds (Barr): 1959
"Spoor" (Passes): 1969[FP]
Spurious Sun (*Sava*): 1948
Squares of the City, The (Brunner): 1965
SS-GB (Deighton): 1978
Stained-Glass World, The (Bulmer): *1969*
Stampede (Sieveking): 1924
Stand on Zanzibar (Brunner): 1968, 1969[W], 1970[W]
Star Begotten (Wells): 1937
Star Called Wormwood, The (Bishop): 1941
Star Dust (Vivian): 1925
Star Healer (White): 1985
Star Maker (Stapledon): 1937
Star of Ill-Omen (Wheatley): 1952
Star Surgeon (White): 1963
Star Virus, The (Bayley): 1970

Star Winds (Bayley): 1978
"Star, The" (Clarke): 1956[W]
"Star, The" (Wells): 1897, 1926[FP]
Stardroppers, The (Brunner): *1963*
Starflight 3000 (Mackelworth): 1972
Staring at the Sun (Barnes): 1986
Stark (Elton): 1989
Stars of Albion (eds. Holdstock & Priest): 1979[A]
Starship (Aldiss): *1958*
Starswarm (Aldiss): *1963*
State of Mind, A (Lane): 1964
State of the Art, The (Banks): 1989
"Statics, The" (High): 1955[FP]
Station X (MacLeod): 1919
Stationary Orbit (Macey): 1974
"Statue, The" (Mackelworth): 1963[FP]
Steel Crocodile, The (Compton): 1970
Steel Grubs, The (Elmore): 1928
Steel Tsar, The (Moorcock): 1981
Steeleye Trilogy, The (Dunn): 1976
Stella Fregelius (Haggard): 1904
Stella, and an Unfinished Communication (Hinton): 1895
Stolen Bacillus, The (Wells): 1895
"Stolen Bacillus, The" (Wells): 1894
"Stolen Body, The" (Wells): 1898, 1928[FP]
Stolen Continent, The (Sibson): 1932
Stolen Planet, The (Mastin): 1905
Stolen Souls (Le Queux): 1895
Stolen Submarine, The (Griffith): 1904
Stone That Never Came Down, The (Brunner): 1973
Stopwatch (ed. Hay): 1974[A]
Storm Lord, The (Lee): 1976
Storm of Wings, A (Harrison): 1980
"Stormwater Tunnel" (Jones): 1964[FP]
Story of My Village, The (Stacpoole): 1947
"Story of the Days to Come, A" (Wells): 1897, 1928[FP]
"Story of the Inexperienced Ghost, The" (Wells): 1902
"Story of the Late Mr. Elvesham, The" (Wells): 1896, 1927[FP]
"Story of the Stone Age, A" (Wells): 1897, 1927[FP]
Story of Ulla, The (Arnold): 1895
Story Teller, The (Vansittart): 1968
Stowaway to Mars (Wyndham): *1936*
Strand Magazine: 1891[PUB]
Strange Case of Dr. Jekyll and Mr. Hyde, The (Stevenson): 1886
Strange Invaders, The (Llewellyn): 1934
Strange Papers of Dr. Blayre, The (Blayre): *1921*
Strange Stories (Allen): 1884
Strange World of Planet X, The (Ray): 1957
Strata (Pratchett): 1982
Struggle for Empire, The (Cole): 1900
Suaine and the Crow-God (Gordon): 1975
Subterfuge (Maine): 1959
Such (Brooke-Rose): 1966

Such Power Is Dangerous (Wheatley): 1933
Sugar in the Air (Large): 1937
Suiciders, The (McIntosh): *1972*
Summer Rising (Sullivan): 1975
Sundered Worlds, The (Moorcock): 1965
Sundog (Ball): 1965
Sung in Shadow (Lee): 1983
Sunset (Morison): 1932
Sunset People, The (Penny): 1975
Sunstroke (Watson): 1982
Super Barbarians, The (Brunner): 1962
Supernova 1 (ed. Anon): 1976[A]
Survival (Sherwood): 1975
Survival Game, The (Kapp): 1976
Survival Margin (Maine): *1962*
Survivors (Nation): 1976
Survivors, The (Griffiths): 1965
Survivors, The (Sibson): 1932
Swallowed by an Earthquake (Fawcett): 1894
Swan Song (Stableford): 1975
Swastika Night (Burdekin): 1937
Sweeney's Island (Christopher): 1964
Sweet Dreams (Frayn): 1973
Sweet Evil (Platt): 1977
Sweet, Sweet Summer, A (Gaskell): 1969
Sykaos Papers, The (Thompson): 1988
Sylvester (Hyams): 1951
"Symbiote" (Coney): 1969[FP]
Symmetrians, The (Harker): 1966
Synaptic Manhunt (Farren): 1976
Synthajoy (Compton): 1968
Syzygy (Coney): 1973

Take Back Plenty (Greenland): 1990
Tale of the Future (Clarke): 1961[C]
"Tale of the Twentieth Century, A" (Wells): 1887
Tales and Stories (Shelley): 1891
Tales from Planet Earth (Clarke): 1989
Tales from the Forbidden Planet (ed. Kaveney): 1987[A]
Tales from the White Hart (Clarke): 1957
Tales of Gooseflesh and Laughter (Wyndham): 1956
Tales of Space and Time (Wells): 1899
Tales of Ten Worlds (Clarke): 1962
Tales of Wonder: 1937[PUB]
Tamastara (Lee): 1984
Tapestry of Time, A (Cowper): 1982
Tarzan Adventures: 1957[FAN]
Telepath (Sellings): 1962
Telepathist (Brunner): *1964*
Tempest, The (Shakespeare): 1623
Temple of Fire, The (Atkins): 1905
Temple of Nature, The (Darwin): 1803
"Temptation of Harringay, The" (Wells): 1895

Ten Years to Oblivion (Cooney): 1968
Tenth Planet, The (Cooper): 1973
Terminal Beach, The (Ballard): 1964
Terminus (Daventry): 1971
Terminus (Edwards): 1976
Terrible Awakening (Desmond): 1949
Terror from Timorkal, The (Pragnell): 1946
Terror of the Air, The (Le Queux): 1920
Terror, The (Machen): 1917
Texts of Festival, The (Farren): 1973
That Hideous Strength (Lewis): 1945
Theatre of Timesmiths, A (Kilworth): 1984
Their Master's War (Farren): 1988
Their Winged Destiny (Horner): 1912
Then We Shall Hear Singing (Jameson): 1942
Theodore Savage (Hamilton): 1921
These Savage Futurians (High): 1967
They (Dick): 1977
They Found Atlantis (Wheatley): 1936
They Shall Not Die (Parkinson): 1939
Thief of Dreams (Cole): 1989
Things to Come (Wells): 1935
Thinking Seat, The (Tate): 1969
Thinktank That Leaked, The (Hodder-Williams): 1979
Third Millennium, The (Stableford & Langford): 1985
Third World War, The (Hackett): 1979
Third World War, The: The Untold Story (Hackett): 1982
Thirst (Maine): *1958*
Thirty Strange Stories (Wells): 1897
Thirty-First of June, The (Priestley): 1961
This Above All (Shiel): 1933
This Business of Bomfog (Duke): 1967
This Ever Diverse Pair (Barfield): 1950
This Is the Way the World Begins (McIntosh): 1977
This Knot of Life (Shiel): 1909
This Planet for Sale (Hay): 1951
This Was Ivor Trent (Houghton): 1935
This World and Nearer Ones (Aldiss): 1979[E]
Thousand Years Hence, A (Green): 1882
Three Came Unarmed (Robertson): 1929
Three Fantasies (Powys): 1985
Three Go Back (Mitchell): 1932
Three Hundred Years Hence (Hay): 1881
Three Men Make a World (Marvell): 1939
Three to Conquer (Russell): 1956
Threshold of Eternity (Brunner): 1959
Thrice-Born, The (Greenhough): 1976
Throne of Saturn, The (Wright): *1932*
Through the Looking Glass (Carroll): 1872
Through the Sun in an Airship (Mastin): 1909
Thunder and Lightning Man, The (Cooper): 1968
Thunder of Stars, A (Morgan & Kippax): 1968
Ticking Is in Your Head, The (Daventry): 1970
Tide Went Out, The (Maine): 1958
Tides of Time, The (Brunner): 1984

Title Index 229

Tiltangle (Mackelworth): 1970
Time and Timothy Grenville (Greenhough): 1975
Time Before This, The (Monsarrat): 1962
Time Factor, The (Gordon): *1962*
Time for a Change (McIntosh): 1967
Time for Survival, A (McCutchan): 1966
Time in Eclipse (Garnett): 1974
Time Injection, The (Williams): 1968
Time Jump (Brunner): 1973
Time Keepers (Gill): 1989
Time Machine, The (Wells): 1895, 1927[FP]
"Time Machine, The" (Wells): 1895
Time Mercenaries, The (High): 1968
Time Must Have a Stop (Huxley): 1944
Time of the Crack, The (Tennant): 1973
Time of the Hawklords, The (Moorcock & Butterworth): 1976
Time out of Mind (Cowper): 1973
Time Story (Gordon): 1972
Time Transfer (Sellings): 1956
Time-Dweller, The (Moorcock): 1969
Time-Lapsed Man, The (Brown): 1990
Time-Slip (Martin): 1986
Timeliner (Maine): 1955
Times Without Number (Brunner): 1962
Timescoop (Brunner): 1969
Timesnake and Superclown (King): 1976
Timewinders, The (Kapp): 1980
Tin Men, The (Frayn): 1965
"Tissue-Culture King, The" (Huxley): 1926
Tithonian Factor, The (Cowper): 1984
Titus Alone (Peake): 1959
Titus Groan (Peake): 1946
To Challenge Chaos (Stableford): 1972
To Conquer Chaos (Brunner): 1964
To End All Telescopes (Williams): 1969
To Mars Via the Moon (Wicks): 1911
To the End of Time (Stapledon): 1953
To Venus in Five Seconds (Jane): 1897
To-Morrow's Yesterday (Gloag): 1932
Tom's A-Cold (Collier): 1933
Tomato Cain (Kneale): 1949
Tomorrow Came (Cooper): 1963
Tomorrow Is Too Far (White): 1971
Tomorrow Laughs (Cooper): 1979
Tomorrow Lies in Ambush (Shaw): 1973
Tomorrow Revealed (Atkins): 1955
Tomorrow Sometimes Comes (Rayer): 1951
Tomorrow's Gift (Cooper): 1958
Total Eclipse (Brunner): 1974
Tourmalin's Time Cheques (Anstey): 1891
Transfinite Man, The (Kapp): 1964
Transformation of Miss Mavis Ming, The (Moorcock): 1977
Transit (Cooper): 1964
Transmigration (McIntosh): 1970
Transplant (Jones): 1968

Transplant (Weatherhead): 1969
Traps of Time, The (ed. Moorcock): 1968[A]
Travails of Jane Saint, The (Saxton): 1981
Traveller in Black, The (Brunner): 1971
"Traveller's Rest" (Masson): 1965[FP]
Travels in Nihilon (Sillitoe): 1971
Trillion Year Spree (Aldiss & Wingrove): *1973*[C], *1987*[W]
Trip to Mars, A (*Atkins*): 1909
Trip to the Moon, A (McDermot): 1728
Trip to Venus, A (Munro): 1897
Triuneverse, The (*Kennedy*): 1912
Trivana 1 (Abel & Barren): 1966
Trouble with Lichen (Wyndham): 1960
Trout's Testament (Fraser): 1960
"Truth About Pyecraft, The" (Wells): 1903
Tunc (Durrell): 1968
Turning Wheel, The (Creswick): 1928
Twelve Stories and a Dream (Wells): 1903
Twenty-Second Century, The (Christopher): 1954
Twilight Bar (Koestler): 1945
Twilight Journey (Davies): 1967
Twilight Man, The (Moorcock): 1966
Twilight of Briareus, The (Cowper): 1974
Twilight of the City, The (Platt): *1970*
Twilight of the Vilp (Ableman): 1969
Twin Planets (High): 1967
Two Film Stories (Wells): *1935*, *1936*
Two Hours to Doom (*George*): 1958
Two Towers, The (Tolkien): 1954
"Two's Company" (Rankine): 1964[FP]
Two's Two (Clouston): 1916
Two-Timers, The (Shaw): 1968
Tyrant of Hades, The (Kapp): 1982

Ulcer Culture, The (Bulmer): 1969
Ultimate Island, The (Sieveking): 1925
Ultimate Jungle, The (Coney): 1979
Ultimatum (MacClure): 1924
Unborn Tomorrow (Cooper): 1971
Unborn Tomorrow (Frankau): 1953
Unborn Tomorrow (Kendall): 1933
Uncensored Man, The (Sellings): 1964
Uncertain Midnight, The (Cooper): 1958
Uncharted Seas (Wheatley): 1938
Unconquered Country, The (Ryman): 1986
Under Heaven's Bridge (Watson & Bishop): 1981
Under Other Conditions (Lach-Szyrma): 1892
"Under the Knife" (Wells): 1896, 1927[FP]
Underkill (White): 1979
Unfortunate Princess, The (Haywood): *1736*
"Unicorn, The" (Cooper): 1951[FP]
Uninhibited, The (Morgan): 1961
Unknown To-Morrow, The (Le Queux): 1910

Title Index 231

Unlawful (Turner): 1927
Unlimited Dream Company, The (Ballard): 1979, 1980[W]
Unnatural Fathers (Storr): 1976
Unorthodox Engineers, The (Kapp): 1979
Unsleep, The (Gillon & Gillon): 1961
Unsleeping Eye, The (Compton): 1974
Untamed, The (Norwood): 1951
Unthinkable (Sibson): 1933
Up Above (Raphael): 1913
Up and Out (Powys): 1957
Up, Jenkins! (Hingley): 1956
Upsidonia (Marshall): 1915
Use of Weapons (Banks): 1990
Usual Lunacy, A (Compton): 1978
Utopia (More): 1516
Utopia 239 (Gordon): 1954
Utopia Minus X (Gordon): 1966
Utopian Fantasy (Gerber): 1955[C]

Valdar the Oft-Born (Griffith): 1895
Valiant Clay (Southwold): *1931*
Valley Beyond Time (Wilkins): 1955
Valley of Pretenders (Fearn): 1942
"Valley of Spiders, The" (Wells): 1903
Vandals of the Void (Walsh): 1931
Vanguard from Alpha (Aldiss): 1958
Vanguard to Venus (Castle): 1957
Vargo Statten Science Fiction Magazine: 1954[PUB]
Vazkor, Son of Vazkor (Lee): 1978
Vector for Seven (Saxton): 1970
Vector: 1958[FAN]
Vengeance of Gwa, The (Wright): 1935
Venus 13 (Hitchcock): 1972
"Venus Germ, The" (Pragnell): 1932[FP]
Venus Girl, The (Beresford): 1924
Venus Hunters, The (Ballard): 1980
Verbivore (Brooke-Rose): 1990
Vermilion Sands (Ballard): 1971
Vertigo (Shaw): 1978
Very Private Life, A (Frayn): 1968
Very Slow Time Machine, The (Watson): 1979
Vickers (Farren): 1988
Victims of the Nova (Brunner): 1989
Victorian Science Fiction (Suvin): 1983[C]
View from Serendip, The (Clarke): 1977[E]
View of the Island, A (Ross): 1965
Village of the Damned (Wyndham): *1957*
Violet Apple, The (Lindsay): 1976
Violet Flame, The (Jane): 1899
Viriconium Nights (Harrison): 1984
"Vision of Judgement, A" (Wells): 1899
"Vision of the Past, A" (Wells): 1887
Vision of Tomorrow: 1969[PUB]

Visit from Venus, A (Fraser): 1958
Visit of the Princess, The (Mottram): 1946
Voice from Another World, A (*Lach-Szyrma*): 1874
Voice from Mars, A (Broomhead): 1923
Voices from the Sky (Clarke): 1965[E]
Voices in the Dark (Cooper): 1960
Voices of Time, The (Ballard): 1962, *1963*
Voices Prophesying War (Clarke): 1966[C]
Volkhavaar (Lee): 1977
Volteface (Adlard): 1972
Vortex: 1977[PUB]
Voyage from Utopia, A (Bray): 1842
Voyage to Arcturus, A (Lindsay): 1920
Voyage to Cacklogallinia, A (Brunt): 1727
Voyage to the...Centre of the Earth, A (Anon): 1755
Voyage to Venus (Lewis): *1943*

Waking World (Stapledon): 1934[E]
Walking on Glass (Banks): 1985
Walking Shadow, The (Stableford): 1979
"*Wall of Time, The*" (*Davies*): 1960[FP]
Wall of Years, The (Stephenson): 1979
"*Wall, The*" (Saxton): 1965[FP]
Wanderers of Time (Wyndham): 1973
Wandering Worlds, The (Greenhough): 1976
Wanting Seed, The (Burgess): 1962
War Fever (Ballard): 1990
War Games (Stableford): *1980*
War in the Air, The (Wells): 1908
War of 1938, The (Wright): *1935*
War of Dreams, The (Carter): *1972*
War of the Sky Lords (Brosnan): 1989
War of the Worlds, The (Wells): 1898, 1927[FP]
War! (Newton): 1914
Wargods of Ludorbis (Cole): 1981
Warhound and the World's Pain, The (Moorcock): 1981
Warlord of Heaven (Cole): 1990
Warlord of the Air, The (Moorcock): 1971
Warrior Who Carried Life, the (Ryman): 1985
Warriors of Mars (*Moorcock*): 1965
Wasp (Russell): 1957
Wasp Factory, The (Banks): 1984
Watch Below, The (White): 1966
Watch the North Wind Rise (Graves): 1949
Watcher, The (Palmer): 1986
Watership Down (Adams): 1972
Way to Write Science Fiction, The (Stableford): 1989[E]
Weaveworld (Barker): 1987
Web (Wyndham): 1979
Web of Everywhere, The (Brunner): 1974
Web of the Magi, The (Cowper): 1980
Weirdstone of Brisingamen, The (Garner): 1960
Well at the World's End, The (Morris): 1896

Werewolves of London, The (Stableford): 1990
Westminster Disaster, The (Hoyle & Hoyle): 1978
What Did I Do Tomorrow? (Davies): 1972
What Dreams May Come... (Beresford): 1941
What Happened to the Corbetts (Shute): 1939
What Not (Macaulay): 1919
What We Did to Father (Lewis): 1960
What's the World Coming To? (Low): *1950*
When Darkness Comes (Swindells): 1973
When It Was Dark (Thorne): 1904
When the Moon Died (Savage): 1955
When the Sleeper Wakes (Wells): 1899
When the Whites Went (Bateman): 1963
When the Wind Blows (Briggs): 1982[CX]
When the World Reeled (Thorne): 1924
When the World Shook (Haggard): 1919
When William Came (Saki): 1914
Where No Stars Guide (Kippax): 1975
Where Time Winds Blow (Holdstock): 1982
White August (Boland): 1955
White Battalions, The (White): 1900
White Horse Tavern Circle: 1946[FAN]
White Hotel, The (Thomas): 1981
White Serpent, The (Lee): 1988
Who Can Replace a Man? (Aldiss): 1965
Who Goes Here? (Shaw): 1977
Who Is Lewis Pindar? (Davies): *1965*
Who Killed Enoch Powell? (Wise): 1970
Who Needs Men? (Cooper): 1972
Who Speaks of Conquest? (Wright): 1957
Whole Man, The (Brunner): 1964
Whores of Babylon (Watson): 1988
Why I Want to Fuck Ronald Reagan (Ballard): 1968
Wildeblood's Empire (Stableford): 1977
Wind from Nowhere, The (Ballard): 1962
Wind from the North (O'Neill): 1934
Wind from the Sun, The (Clarke): 1972
Wind in the Snottygobble Tree, The (Story): 1971
Windows (Compton): 1979
Winds of Limbo, The (Moorcock): *1965*
Wine of Death (Armstrong): 1925
Wings Across Time (Arnold): 1946
Wings of the Morning (Hyams): 1939
Wings Over Europe (Nichols): 1932
Winter's Children (Coney): 1974
Winter's Youth (Gloag): 1934
Winterwood (Roberts): 1989
Wisdom's Daughter (Haggard): 1923
Wishful Think, The (Newman): 1954
Wishing Well (Heard): 1953
Witchfinder, The (Wright): 1945
With a Strange Device (Russell): 1964
"With the Night Mail" (Kipling): 1905
Without Bloodshed (Gorst): 1897
Wizard of Anharitte, The (Kapp): 1975

Wizardry and Wild Romance (Moorcock): 1987[C]
Woman Clothed with the Sun, The (Lucas): 1937
Woman Dominant (Vivian): 1929
Women as Demons (Lee): 1989
Wonder, The (Beresford): *1911*
Wonderful Adventures of Phra, The (Arnold): 1890
Wonderful Visit, The (Wells): 1895
Wooden Spaceships, The (Shaw): 1988
Words of Wonder (Stapledon): 1949
Works of H. G. Wells, The (Wells): 1924
Works of M. P. Shiel, The: Vol. 1 (Shiel): 1979
"World at Bay, The" (Wallis): 1928[FP]
World Below, The (Wright): 1929
World Ends, The (*Jameson*): 1937
World in Eclipse (Dexter): 1954
World in Spell, A (Stevenson): *1936*
World in Winter, The (Christopher): 1962
World Masters, The (Griffith): 1903
World of Difference, A (Conquest): 1955
World of Difference, A (Cooper): 1980
World of Women, A (Beresford): 1913
World out of Mind (McIntosh): 1953
World Peril of 1910, The (Griffith): 1907
World Set Free, The (Wells): 1914
World Swappers, The (Brunner): 1959
World Well Lost (Paget): 1970
World Without Men (Maine): 1958
"World Without, The" (Herbert): 1931[FP]
World, the Flesh and the Devil, The (Bernal): 1929[E]
World-Birth (Desmond): 1938
Worldcon: 1957[FAN], 1965[FAN], 1979[FAN], 1987[FAN]
Worlds Apart (Cowper): 1974
Worlds Apart (ed. Locke): 1972[A]
Worlds Apart (McIntosh): *1954*
Worlds for the Grabbing (Pearce): 1977
Worlds of Eclos, The (Gordon): *1959*
Worlds of Sector P (Franklin): 1979
"Worlds to Barter" (*Wyndham*): 1931[FP]
"Worlds Without End" (Fanthorpe): 1952[FP]
Worm Ouroboros, The (Eddison): 1922
Wrath to Come, The (Oppenheim): 1925
Wreath of Stars, A (Shaw): 1976
Wreck of a World, The (Grove): 1889
Wrecks of Time, The (Moorcock): 1967
Wrinkle in the Skin, A (Christopher): 1965
Wrong End of Time, The (Brunner): 1971
Wrong Side of the Moon, The (Ashton & Ashton): 1951
Wulfsyarn (Mann): 1990
Wyrd Sisters (Pratchett): 1988

Xanthe and the Robots (MacLeod): 1977
Xeno (Jones): 1979
Xorandor (Brooke-Rose): 1986

Title Index   235

Year Before Yesterday, The (Aldiss): 1987
Year of Miracle, The (Hume): 1891
Year of the Comet, The (Christopher): 1955
Year of the Painted World (Mackelworth): 1975
Year of the Sex Olympics, The (Kneale): 1976
Year's Best SF, The (eds. Aldiss & Harrison): 1967[A]
Yellow Danger, The (Shiel): 1898
Yellow Fraction, The (Gordon): 1969
Yellow God, The (Haggard): 1908
Yellow Peril, The (Shiel): *1913*
Yellow Wave, The (Shiel): 1905
Young Diana, The (Corelli): 1918
Young Men Are Coming!, The (Shiel): 1937

'Z' Ray, The (Snell): 1932
Zalma (Ellis): 1895
Zardoz (Boorman & Stair): 1974
Zen Gun, The (Bayley): 1983
Zenith (ed. Garnett): 1989[A]
Zenith 2 (ed. Garnett): 1990[A]
Zenith Science Fiction: 1963[FAN]
Zenith Speculation, see *Zenith Science Fiction*
Zenith: 1941[FAN]
Zeppelin Destroyer, The (Le Queux): 1916
Zilov Bombs, The (Barron): 1962
Zit and Xoe (Curwen): 1887
Zoonomia (Darwin): 1794[E]

FTV Index

1984: 1955[F]
1984: 1984[F]
1990: 1977[TV]
2001: A Space Odyssey: 1968[F]

A for Andromeda: 1961[TV]
Adams, Douglas: 1983[TV]
Alien: 1979[F]
Ambor, Joe: 1958[F]
Amis, Martin: 1980[F]
Anderson, Gerry: 1969[F], 1969[TV], 1975[TV]
Anderson, Lindsay: 1973[F]
Anderson, Michael: 1955[F]
Anderson, Sylvia: 1969[F], 1969[TV], 1975[TV]
Andromeda Breakthrough: 1962[TV]
Animal Farm: 1954[F]
Antrobus, John: 1969[F]
At the Earth's Core: 1976[F]
Austin, Michael: 1984[F]
Austin, Ray: 1975[TV]
Avengers, The: 1962[TV]

Bachardy, Don: 1973[TVF]
Baker, Jane: 1967[F]
Baker, Pip: 1967[F]
Baker, Roy Ward: 1968[F], 1969[F]
Barron, Steve: 1984[F]
Barry, John: 1980[F]
Barwick, Tony: 1969[TV]
Batchelor, Joy: 1954[F]

Batt, Bert: 1971[F]
Bed-Sitting Room, The: 1969[F]
Bettinson, Ralph: 1955[F]
Biro, Lajos: 1936[F]
Black, Alfred: 1949[F]
Black, George: 1949[F]
Blake's Seven: 1977[TV]
Bogner, Norman: 1967[F]
Boorman, John: 1974[F]
Brazil: 1985[F]
Bridges, Alan: 1966[F]
Briley, Jack: 1963[F]
Bromly, Alan: 1965[TV]
Brook, Peter: 1963[F]
Brownlow, Kevin: 1963[F]
Budrys, Algis: 1974[F]
Burgess, Anthony: 1971[F]
Burroughs, Edgar Rice: 1975[F], 1976[F], 1977[F], 1984[F]

Campus, Michael: 1971[F]
Cardiff, Jack: 1973[F]
Carlton, Rex: 1963[F]
Carreras, Michael: 1966[F], 1968[F], 1969[F]
Cartier, Rudolph: 1953[TV], 1955[TV], 1956[TV], 1958[TV]
Cassie, Iain: 1982[F]
Cawthorn, James: 1975[F]
Chaffey, Don: 1966[F]
Children of the Damned: 1963[F]
Chilton, Charles: 1953[R]
Clarke, Arthur C.: 1968[F]
Clockwork Orange, A: 1971[F]
Coburn, Anthony: 1963[TV]
Connor, Kevin: 1975[F], 1976[F], 1977[F], 1978[F]
Cooke, Alan: 1969[F]
Cooper, Edmund: 1957[F]
Cooper, John C.: 1958[F]
Cosmic Monster, The: 1958[F]
Crabtree, Arthur: 1958[F]
Crawling Eye, The: 1958[F]
Creature, The: 1956[TV]
Creeping Unknown, The: 1955[F]
Cross, Henry: 1964[F]

Daleks--Invasion Earth 2150 AD: 1966[F]
Damned, The: 1961[F]
Dark Crystal, The: 1983[F]
Davenport, H. Bromley: 1982[F]
Davis, Gerry: 1970[TV]
Day of the Triffids, The: 1963[F]
Day the Earth Caught Fire, The: 1961[F]
Day, Robert: 1958[F]

Deathline: 1973[F]
DeFelitta, Frank: 1971[F]
Dicks, Terrance: 1973[TV]
Dighton, John: 1951[F]
Donen, Stanley: 1980[F]
Donner, Richard: 1978[F]
Doomwatch [TV]: 1970[TV], 1972[F]
Doomwatch [F]: 1972[F]
Doppelgangers: 1969[F]
Dr. Strangelove: 1963[F]
Dr. Who and the Daleks: 1965[F]
Dr. Who: 1963[TV], 1965[F], 1966[F]
Dudley, Terence: 1970[TV], 1975[TV]

Earth Dies Screaming, The: 1964[F]
Ehrlich, Max: 1971[F]
Electric Dreams: 1984[F]
Elliot, John: 1961[TV], 1962[TV]
Elvey, Maurice: 1935[F]
Enemy from Space: 1957[F]
Exton, Clive: 1972[F]

Falls, The: 1980[F]
Fiend Without a Face: 1958[F]
Final Programme, The: 1973[F]
First Man Into Space: 1958[F]
First Men in the Moon: 1964[F]
Fisher, Terence: 1953[F], 1964[F], 1967[F]
Fitzgerald, Prudence: 1977[TV]
Five Million Years to Earth: 1968[F]
Flash Gordon: 1980[F]
Flemyng, Gordon: 1965[F], 1966[F]
Four-Sided Triangle: 1953[F]
Francis, Freddie: 1963[F]
Frankenstein: The True Story: 1973[TVF]
Fuest, Robert: 1973[F]

Ganthony, Richard: 1913[F]
Geoffrey, Wallace: 1949[F]
George, Peter: 1963[F]
Gilliam, Terry: 1981[F], 1985[F]
Gladwell, David: 1981[F]
Gold, Jack: 1974[F]
Golding, William: 1963[F]
Gorgo: 1961[F]
Gould, John: 1974[F]
Grabbe, Kerry: 1981[F]
Graves, Robert: 1978[F]
Greatorex, Wilfred: 1977[TV]

Greenaway, Peter: 1980[F]
Greystoke: The Legend of Tarzan of the Apes: 1984[F]
Guest, Val: 1955[F], 1957[F], 1961[F], 1970[F]
Gunn, Gilbert: 1958[F]

Haggard, Piers: 1979[TVF]
Halas, John: 1954[F]
Hargreaves, Lance Z.: 1958[F]
Hayes, Michael: 1961[TV]
Hayles, Brian: 1978[F]
Henson, Jim: 1983[F]
Hessler, Gordon: 1969[F]
Hill, Reg: 1969[TV]
Hitch-Hiker's Guide to the Galaxy, The: 1983[TV]
Hodges, Michael: 1980[F], 1985[F]
Hoffman, Herman: 1957[F]
Holmes, Robert: 1966[F]
Hooper, Tobe: 1985[F]
Horror Planet: 1980[F]
Hoyle, Fred: 1961[TV], 1962[TV]
Hudson, Hugh: 1984[F]
Hughes, Ken: 1955[F]
Hume, Cyril: 1957[F]
Hyams, Peter: 1981[F]
Hyatt, Daniel: 1961[F]

Inseminoid: 1980[F]
Invasion of the Body Stealers: 1969[F]
Invasion: 1966[F]
Invisible Boy, The: 1957[F]
Isherwood, Christopher: 1973[TVF]
Island of Terror: 1967[F]
Island of the Burning Damned: 1967[F]
It Happened Here: 1963[F]

Jakoby, Don: 1985[F]
James, Donald: 1969[F]
Jones, Ceri: 1973[F]
Jones, Evan: 1961[F]
Jones, Griff Rhys: 1985[F]
Jones, Norman: 1961[TV]
Journey Into Space: 1953[R]
Journey to the Far Side of the Sun: 1969[F]
Juran, Nathan: 1964[F]

Kay, Peter: 1958[F]
Kellerman, Bernhard: 1935[F]

Kneale, Nigel: 1953[TV], 1954[TV], 1955[F], 1955[TV], 1956[TV], 1957[F], 1958[TV], 1964[F], 1968[F], 1968[TV], 1970[TV], 1979[TVF]
Knowles, Bernard: 1949[F]
Krish, John: 1963[F]
Krull: 1983[F]
Kubrick, Stanley: 1963[F], 1968[F], 1971[F]

Lambert, Verity: 1963[TV]
Land That Time Forgot, The: 1975[F]
Landau, Richard: 1953[F], 1955[F]
Last Days of Man on Earth, The: 1973[F]
Lawrence, Henry L.: 1961[F]
Lawrence, Quentin: 1958[F]
Leader, Anton M.: 1963[F]
Leder, Herbert J.: 1958[F]
Lemorade, Rusty: 1984[F]
Lessing, Doris: 1981[F]
Lester, Richard: 1969[F], 1980[F], 1983[F]
Letts, Barry: 1973[TV]
Levy, Gerry: 1969[F]
Life Force: 1985[F]
Liles, Ronald: 1967[F]
Long, Amelia Reynolds: 1958[F]
Lord of the Flies: 1963[F]
Loring, John: 1961[F]
Losey, Joseph: 1961[F]
Lost Continent, The: 1968[F]
Lourie, Eugene: 1961[F]
'Lurgan, Lester': 1913[F]
'Lymington, John': 1967[F]

MacDougall, Roger: 1951[F]
Mackendrick, Alexander: 1951[F]
'Maine, Charles Eric': 1953[F], 1955[F], 1969[F]
Maley, Gloria: 1980[F]
Maley, Nick: 1980[F]
Maloney, David: 1977[TV]
Man in the White Suit, The: 1951[F]
Man Who Could Work Miracles, The: 1936[F]
Man Who Fell to Earth, The: 1976[F]
Mankowitz, Wolf: 1961[F]
Mann, Edward Andrew: 1967[F], 1973[F]
Marcus, Peter: 1969[F]
Marshall, Roger: 1966[F]
Mayersky, Paul: 1976[F]
McGoohan, Patrick: 1967[TV]
McKeown, Charles: 1985[F]
Memoirs of a Survivor, The: 1981[F]
Mendes, Lothar: 1936[F]
Menzies, Wiliam Cameron: 1936[F]

Message from Mars, A: 1913[F]
Milligan, Spike: 1969[F]
Mind of Mr. Soames, The: 1969[F]
Mitchell, Basil: 1949[F]
Mollo, Andrew: 1963[F]
Moon Zero Two: 1969[F]
Moonbase 3: 1973[TV]
Moorcock, Michael: 1973[F], 1975[F], 1978[F]
Morons from Outer Space: 1985[F]
Mutations, The: 1973[F]

Nash, Michael: 1968[F]
Nation, Terry: 1975[TV], 1977[TV]
Newman, David: 1983[F]
Newman, Leslie: 1983[F]
Newman, Sydney: 1962[TV], 1963[TV]
Night of the Big Heat: 1967[F]
Nineteen Eighty-Four: 1954[TV]
Norman, Leslie: 1956[F]

O Lucky Man!: 1973[F]
O'Bannon, Dan: 1979[F], 1985[F]
Odell, David: 1983[F]
One Million Years B.C.: 1966[F]
Ordung, Wyott: 1958[F]
'Orwell, George': 1954[F], 1954[TV], 1955[F], 1984[F]
Out of the Unknown: 1965[TV]
Out of This World: 1962[TV]
Outland: 1981[F]
Oz, Frank: 1983[F]

Palin, Michael: 1981[F]
Parrish, Robert: 1969[F]
Pedler, Kit: 1970[TV]
Penfold, Christopher: 1975[TV]
People That Time Forgot, The: 1977[F]
Perfect Woman, The: 1949[F]
Prisoner, The: 1967[TV]
Privilege: 1967[F]
Pulman, Jack: 1965[TV]
Puzo, Mario: 1978[F], 1980[F]

Quatermass and the Pit [F]: 1968[F]
Quatermass and the Pit [TV]: 1958[TV], 1968[F]
Quatermass Conclusion, The: 1979[TVF]
Quatermass Experiment, The: 1953[TV]
Quatermass II [F]: 1957[F]

Quatermass II [TV]: 1955[TV], 1957[F]
Quatermass Xperiment, The: 1955[F]
Quest for Love: 1971[F]

Radford, Michael: 1984[F]
Ramsen, Alan: 1967[F]
Raw Meat: 1973[F]
Ray, René: 1958[F]
Read, Jan: 1964[F]
Rilla, Wolf: 1960[F]
Roach, Hal; 1966[F]
Roeg, Nicolas: 1976[F]
Rosenberg, Max: 1969[F]
Ryder, Paul: 1958[F]

Saady, Peter: 1972[F]
Sangster, Jimmy: 1956[F], 1958[F]
Saturn 3: 1980[F]
'Saxon, Peter': 1967
Scott, Ridley: 1979[F]
Scream and Scream Again: 1969[F]
Sekely, Steve: 1963[F]
Semple, Jr., Lorenzo: 1980[F]
Shelley, Mary: 1973[TVF]
Sherman, Gary: 1973[F]
Sherman, Stanford: 1983[F]
Sherwin, David: 1973[F]
Shout, The: 1978[F]
Shubik, Irene: 1962[TV]
Silliphant, Sterling: 1960[F]
Siodmak, Kurt: 1935[F]
Skolimowski, Jerzy: 1978[F]
Smight, Jack: 1973[TVF]
Smith, Mel: 1985[F]
Smith, Robert: 1982[F]
Southern, Terry: 1963[F]
Space 1999: 1975[TV]
Spaceways: 1953[F]
Spalding, Henry: 1964[F]
Speight, Johnny: 1967[F]
St. Clair, Mike: 1969[F]
Stoppard, Tom: 1985[F]
Strange World of Planet X, The: 1958[F]
Subotsky, Milton: 1965[F], 1966[F], 1969[F], 1976[F]
Superman II: 1980[F]
Superman III: 1983[F]
Superman--The Movie: 1978[F]
Survivors: 1975[TV]

Tabori, Paul: 1953[F]
Temple, William F.: 1953[F]
Templeton, William F.: 1955[F]
Tevis, Walter: 1976[F]
These Are the Damned: 1961[F]
Thin Air: 1969[F]
Things to Come: 1936[F]
Thomas, Ralph: 1971[F]
Tilley, Patrick: 1977[F]
Time Bandits, The: 1981[F]
Timeslip: 1955[F]
Tomblin, David: 1967[TV]
Towne, Robert: 1984[F]
Transatlantic Tunnel, The: 1935[F]
Trollenberg Terror, The: 1958[F]
Tunnel, The: 1935[F]

UFO: 1969[TV]
Unearthly Stranger: 1963[F]

Village of the Damned: 1960[F]

Waller, J. Wallett: 1913[F]
War Game, The: 1965[TVF]
Warlords of Atlantis: 1978[F]
Warren, Norman J.: 1980[F]
Watkins, Peter: 1965[TVF], 1967[F]
Weinbach, Robert: 1973[F]
'Wells, Barry': 1961[F]
Wells, H. G.: 1936[F], 1964[F]
Wheatley, Dennis: 1968[F]
When Dinosaurs Ruled the Earth: 1970[F]
White, Leonard: 1962[TV]
Who?: 1974[F]
Wicking, Christopher: 1969[F]
Wilson, Colin: 1985[F]
Wilson, Donald: 1963[TV]
Wine of India: 1970[TV]
Wolff, Lothar: 1954[F]
Wyndham, John: 1960[F], 1963[F], 1971[F]

X the Unknown: 1956[F]
Xtro: 1982[F]

Yates, Peter: 1983[F]

Year of the Sex Olympics, The: 1968[TV]
Yordan, Philip: 1963[F]

Z.P.G.: 1971[F]
Zardoz: 1974[F]
Zero Population Growth: 1971[F]

Works Consulted

It would be misleading to list all the works consulted to compile this chronology. Sometimes, for example, the function of one reference work was simply to cast doubt on another. However, some general reference works did prove valuable. As far as biographical information is concerned, the *Dictionary of National Biography*, *Who Was Who* (1897-1970), *Who Was Who Among English and European Authors 1931-1949*, the yearly issues of *Who's Who* and the various series of *Contemporary Authors* were all very useful. For bibliographic verification the many volumes of the *National Union Catalog*, the *English Catalogue of Books* (1837-1953), the *British Museum General Catalogue of Printed Books* (and supplement), and the *British National Bibliography* (1951-present) were used. Whenever possible, entries were verified by the texts themselves, especially those in the collection of the Science Fiction Foundation Library at the Polytechnic of East London, the scope of which offered a useful guide to the scope of this chronology. The books listed below were all of major importance, not simply in checking facts but also in the harder and more controversial problem of establishing the field.

Aldiss, Brian W., with David Wingrove. *Trillion Year Spree: The History of Science Fiction*. London: Gollancz, 1986.
Alpers, Hans Joachim, et al. *Lexicon der Science Fiction Literatur*. Munich: Heyne, 1987.
Ash, Brian, ed. *The Visual Encyclopedia of Science Fiction*. New York: Harmony, 1977.
Ashley, Mike. "Bob Shaw: A Bibliography." *Bob Shaw: British Science Fiction Writers Vol. 1*. Eds. Paul Kincaid & Geoff Rippington. London: British Science Fiction Association, 1981: 32-38.

Ashley, Mike. "Keith Roberts: Bibliography." *Keith Roberts: British Science Fiction Writers Volume Two*. Eds. Paul Kincaid & Geoff Rippington. London: British Science Fiction Association, 1983: 44-50.
---. *The Illustrated Book of Science Fiction Lists*. London: Virgin, 1982.
---. *Who's Who in Horror and Fantasy Fiction*. London: Elm Tree, 1977.
Barron, Neil, ed. *Anatomy of Wonder: A Critical Guide to Science Fiction*. 3rd. ed. New York: Bowker, 1987.
---. *Anatomy of Wonder: An Historical Survey and Critical Guide to the Best of Science Fiction*. 2nd. ed. New York: Bowker, 1981.
---. *Fantasy Literature: A Reader's Guide*. New York: Garland, 1990.
---. *Horror Literature: A Reader's Guide*. New York: Garland, 1990.
Bilyeu, Richard, comp. *The Tanelorn Archives: A Primary and Secondary Bibliography of the Works of Michael Moorcock 1949-1979*. Altona, Canada: Pandora, 1981.
Bishop, Gerald, comp. *New British Science Fiction and Fantasy Books Published During 1970 & 1971*. 1972. San Bernadino: Borgo, 1987.
---. *Science Fiction Books Published in Britain 1972 & 1973*. 1975. San Bernadino: Borgo, 1987.
---. *Science Fiction Books Published in Britain 1974-1978*. 1979. San Bernadino: Borgo, 1987.
Bleiler, E. F. *The Checklist of Science-Fiction and Supernatural Fiction*. Glen Rock: Firebell, 1979.
---. *The Guide to Supernatural Fiction*. Kent: Kent State UP, 1983.
---, ed. *Science Fiction Writers: Critical Studies of the Major Authors from the Early Nineteenth Century to the Present Day*. New York: Scribners, 1982.
Brosnan, John. *Future Tense: The Cinema of Science Fiction*. London: Macdonald & Jane's, 1978.
Brown, Charles N. & William G, Contento, comps. *Science Fiction in Print: 1985*. Oakland: Locus, 1986.
---. *Science Fiction, Fantasy and Horror: 1986-89*. 4 vols. Oakland: Locus, 1987-90.
Clarke, I. F. *The Pattern of Expectation 1644-2001*. London: Cape, 1979.
---. *Tale of the Future: From the Beginning to the Present Day*. 3rd. ed. London: Library Association, 1978.
Collins, Robert A. & Robert Latham, eds. *Science Fiction & Fantasy Book Review Annual 1988*. Westport: Meckler, 1988
---. *Science Fiction & Fantasy Book Review Annual 1989*. Westport: Meckler, 1990.
Contento, William G. *Index to Science Fiction Anthologies and Collections*. Boston: Hall, 1978.
---. *Index to Science Fiction Anthologies and Collections 1977-1983*. Boston: Hall, 1984.

Currey, L. W., comp. *Science Fiction and Fantasy Authors: A Bibliography of First Printings of Their Fiction and Selected Nonfiction*. Boston: Hall, 1979.
Day, Donald B., comp. *Index to the Science Fiction Magazines 1926-1950*. Revised ed. Boston: Hall, 1982.
De Bolt, Joe & Denise. "A John Brunner Bibliography." *The Happening Worlds of John Brunner*. Ed. Joe De Bolt. Port Washington: Kennikat, 1975: 195-209.
Enser, A. G. S. *Filmed Books and Plays*. Revised ed. Aldershot: Gower, 1986.
Gifford, Denis. *The British Film Catalogue 1895-1985: A Reference Guide*. New York: Facts on File, 1986.
---. *Encyclopedia of Comic Characters*. Harlow: Longman, 1987.
Greenland, Colin. *The Entropy Exhibition: Michael Moorcock and the British 'New Wave' in Science Fiction*. London: Routledge, 1983.
Hall, H. W., ed. *Science Fiction and Fantasy Reference Index: 1878-1985*. 2 vols. Detroit: Gale, 1987.
---, comp. *The Science Fiction Magazines: A Bibliographical Checklist of Titles and Issues Through 1982*. San Bernadino: Borgo, 1984.
Hammond, J. R. *Herbert George Wells: An Annotated Bibliography of His Works*. New York: Garland, 1977.
Hardy, Phil et al. *The Aurum Film Encyclopedia: Science Fiction*. London: Aurum, 1984.
Jakubowski, Maxim & Malcolm Edwards. *The SF Book of Lists*. New York: Berkley, 1983.
Justice, Keith L. *Science Fiction, Fantasy and Horror Reference: An Annotated Bibliography of Works About Literature and Film*. Jefferson: McFarland, 1989.
---, comp. *Science Fiction Master Index of Names*. Jefferson: McFarland, 1986.
Locke, George. *A Spectrum of Fantasy: The Bibliography and Biography of a Collection of Fantastic Literature*. London: Ferret Fantasy, 1980.
---. *Voyages in Space: A Bibliography of Interplanetary Fiction 1801-1914*. London: Ferret Fantasy, 1975.
Lofts, W. O. G. & D. J. Adley. *The Men Behind Boys' Fiction*. London: Baker, 1970.
Mackey, Douglas A. *The Work of Ian Watson: An Annotated Bibliography and Guide*. San Bernadino: Borgo, 1989.
Magill, Frank N., ed. *Survey of Science Fiction Literature*. 5 vols. Englewood Cliffs: Salem, 1979.
Moorcock, Michael, ed. *New Worlds: An Anthology*. London: Flamingo, 1983.
Nicholls, Peter, ed. *The Encyclopedia of Science Fiction: An Illustrated A to Z*. London: Granada, 1979.
Philmus, Robert M. *Into the Unknown: The Evolution of Science Fiction from Francis Godwin to H. G. Wells*. Berkeley: U of California P, 1970.
Pringle, David. *J. G. Ballard: A Primary and Secondary Bibliography*. Boston: Hall, 1984.
---. *The Ultimate Guide to Science Fiction: An A to Z of SF Books*. London: Grafton, 1990

Quinlan, David. *British Sound Films: The Studio Years 1928-1959*. London: Batsford, 1984.
Reginald, R. *Science Fiction and Fantasy Awards*. San Bernadino: Borgo, 1981.
---. *Science Fiction and Fantasy Literature: A Checklist, 1700-1974*, with *Contemporary Science Fiction Authors II*. 2 vols. Detroit: Gale, 1979.
Robinson, Roger. *Who's Hugh? An SF Reader's Guide to Pseudonyms*. Harold Wood, U.K.: Beccon, 1987.
Ruddick, Nicholas. "Annotated Bibliography." *Christopher Priest*. Mercer Island: Starmont, 1989. 82-98.
Samuelson, David N. *Arthur C. Clarke: A Primary and Secondary Bibliography*. Boston: Hall, 1984.
Satty, Harvey J. & Curtis C. Smith. *Olaf Stapledon: A Bibliography*. Westport: Greenwood, 1984.
Schlobin, Roger C. *Urania's Daughters: A Checklist of Women Science Fiction Writers, 1692-1982*. Mercer Island: Starmont, 1983.
Smith, Curtis C., ed. *Twentieth-Century Science-Fiction Writers*. 2nd ed. Chicago: St. James, 1986.
Stableford, Brian M. *Scientific Romance in Britain 1890-1950*. New York: St. Martins, 1985.
Stephenson-Payne, John. *Brian W. Aldiss: A Working Bibliography*. 2 vols. 2nd. revised ed. 1988 (self-published).
---. "A John Wyndham Checklist." *Science Fiction Collector* 8 (October 1978): 31-44.
Stone, Graham Brice, comp. *Index to British Science Fiction Magazines 1934-1953*. 3 vols. Sydney: Australian Science Fiction Association, 1977-80.
Suvin, Darko. *Victorian Science Fiction in the U.K.: The Discourses of Knowledge and of Power*. Boston: Hall, 1983.
Tuck, Donald H., comp. *The Encyclopedia of Science Fiction and Fantasy. Through 1968*. 3 vols. Chicago: Advent, 1974-82.
Tymn, Marshall B., ed. *The Science Fiction Reference Book*. Mercer Island: Starmont, 1981.
--- & Mike Ashley, eds. *Science Fiction, Fantasy and Weird Fiction Magazines*. Westport: Greenwood, 1985.
Wagar, W. Warren. *Terminal Visions: The Literature of Last Things*. Bloomington: Indiana UP, 1982.
Willis, Donald C. *Horror and Science Fiction Films: A Checklist*. Metuchen: Scarecrow, 1972.
---. *Horror and Science Fiction Films II*. Metuchen: Scarecrow, 1982.
Wingrove, David, ed. *The Science Fiction Film Sourcebook*. London: Longman, 1985.
Wright, Gene. *The Science Fiction Image: The Illustrated Encyclopedia of Science Fiction in Film, Television, Radio, and the Theatre*. London: Columbus, 1983.
Yntema, Sharon K. *More Than 100: Women Science Fiction Writers*. Freedom, CA: Crossing, 1988.

About the Author

NICHOLAS RUDDICK is associate professor of English, University of Regina. He is the editor of *State of the Fantastic*, a collection of essays (Greenwood, 1992), and the author of *Ultimate Island* (Greenwood, forthcoming).